Bathed in Blood

Bathed in Blood

Hunting and Mastery in the Old South

Nicolas W. Proctor

University Press of Virginia

Charlottesville and London

The University Press of Virginia
Printed in the United States of America on acid-free paper

First published 2002

9 8 7 6 5 4 3 2 1

Library of Congress Cataloging-in-Publication Data

Proctor, Nicolas W., 1969–
    Bathed in blood : hunting and mastery in the Old South / Nicolas W. Proctor
    p. cm.
    Includes bibliographical references (p.   ).
    ISBN 0-8139-2087-6 (cloth: alk. paper) — ISBN 0-8139-2091-4 (pbk.: alk. paper)
        1. Hunting — Philosophy — Southern States — History. 2. Hunting — Psychological
    aspects — Southern States — History. 3. Hunting — Social aspects — Southern States —
    History. I. Title.
    SK14 .P76 2002
    799.2975 — dc21

                                                              2001045354

For my grandparents

Contents

Illustrations

Acknowledgments

F IRST I would like to thank the earnest white-haired gentleman on the upstairs porch of Square Books in Oxford, Mississippi, who misheard me. He and I spent the better part of an afternoon discussing various kinds of hives and flowers, the dynamics of swarming, and the alleged health-giving powers of royal jelly. We drank many cups of coffee and I learned a good deal, but I would like to make it clear up front that this is not a book about honey in the Old South. This conversation did not shape the con-clusions of this book, but it does illustrate one of the great benefits of being a writer: you meet interesting people. This encounter marked one of the un-expected friendships that I struck up as a result of this project, and what-ever the merits of this work, I will always treasure the conversations and correspondences that grew out of the researching, writing, revisiting, and rewriting that produced this book.

Since I first became interested in antebellum hunting as a graduate student at Emory University I have depended upon the kindness of strangers. Sev-eral organizations provided me with generous financial support. The Andrew W. Mellon Foundation (through the Mellon Southern Studies Dis-sertation Fellowship), the National Society of the Colonial Dames (through the American History Scholarship Award), and Emory University gave me the funding I needed to complete the initial stages of the project.

This money would have been useless had it not been for the skill and good humor of librarians and archivists from a variety of institutions. The staffs of Duke University, Emory University, Historic New Orleans, the Li-brary of Congress, Louisiana State University, Tulane University, University of Georgia, University of North Carolina at Chapel Hill, University of South Carolina, University of Virginia, and the College of William and Mary all provided me with expert assistance. The interlibrary loan staffs of Emory University and Simpson College (Kristi Ellingson) deserve spe-cial thanks for all of their hard work on my behalf.

Archival work, interlibrary loan, and reel after reel of microfilm provided a mass of information. Making sense of it was the real challenge, and if there is anything interesting contained within these covers other than direct quotations it is doubtless due to the efforts of Christine Lambert. She read substantial portions of every draft, commented on everything, and undertook the labor of editing the penultimate draft. She is one smart cookie. James Roark also provided a great deal of guidance and feedback. After indulgently accepting my proposed dissertation topic, he provided patience, insight, and encouragement in equal and steady measure. He is a true gentleman scholar.

The foundation of this book was laid down in graduate school, and without the friendships that I forged at Emory the early stages of this project would have been hellish and unpleasant. Fortunately the EAYC crew (Andrew May, Daniel Aldridge III, Jonathan Heller, Steve Oatis, Dave Freeman, Kristian Blaich, and the lovely and enigmatic Meredith), Margaret Storey, Lara Smith, Jonathan Harris, Miche Baskett, Amy Rose Oatis, Belle and James Tuten, Mary Catherine Cain, and Christine Stolba made my years in Atlanta and Decatur pleasant ones. I would particularly like to thank Elizabeth Fox-Genovese and the other members of the Mellon Southern Studies Dissertation seminar for their feedback on my earliest, shabbiest attempts to make sense of the information that now appears (in greatly altered form) in chapters 2 and 3.

Other historians have graciously provided their comments, criticisms, and suggestions at every stage of this book's development. These luminaries include John Reiger, Michael Bellesîles, Mart Stewart, Patrick Allitt, Dan Carter, John Juricek, Eugene Genovese, and the two anonymous readers arranged by the University Press of Virginia. I have also profited from discussing the project with various Simpson College faculty, several of whom read or commented on the manuscript. Nancy St. Clair, Steve Rose, Bill Friedricks, Owen Duncan, John Pauley, and Brian Sandberg all shaped aspects of this work. The influence of my students — particularly those who braved the horrors of Historiography — also appears herein.

The academic world is not the pinnacle of myopia and fuzzy thinking that many condemn it as being, nevertheless I feel particularly fortunate to have had a number of insightful critics that usually steer clear of the world of caps and gowns. D. A. Brown, Linda L. Brown, Wiley Prewitt, David Criner Jr., Wister Cooke, Dan Kostopulos, Karl Serbousek, Devon Holder, Tom Ryan, Todd Mennotti, and Charles Portis helped me keep the text from wandering too far into the recondite world of theory and textual criticism. For that I thank them (and you should too).

The staff of the University Press of Virginia has done a good job shepherding me through the mysterious and convoluted publishing process. Dick Holway, Ellie Goodman, Ellen Satrom, and others have tolerated my inexperience with remarkable good cheer.

Show me a gentleman devoted to the chase and I will show you, with rare exception, "the noblest work of God, an honest man," respected for manly virtues, a good husband and father, a zealous friend, and an open enemy. "The rich man's equal, the poor man's benefactor" — richly adorning the pages of his life with the shining virtues of charity and benevolence — whose memory will be a green spot in the dreary waste of sordid worldliness.

Mississippi governor Alexander McNutt

Dey is one thing I would love fer folks to know an' dat is how de colored folks lak to take deir dogs at night an' go out in de swamps an' tree a possum. Dats' times wid de dogs a barkin' an' de moon a shinin' an a possum up a tree or in a stump hole. When de possum is kotched he will cull up, he is den put on de end ob a pole, he stays all culled up an' holds on tight. Yo' can throw day pole 'cross yo' shoulders an' go home an' bake dat possum on de hot coals in de fire place wid seet 'taters an coffee. Dat is a eatin'.

Mississippi slave Robert Laird

After the report, seeing nothing of the deer, I hurried forward, and there lay as fine a doe as I ever killed, with her brains blown out.

Maryland hunter Meshach Browning

Introduction

THE HUNT, like the church, courthouse, and family, played an integral role in the society and culture of the Old South. Regardless of color or class, southern men hunted; they shot, trapped, and ran their dogs after a great variety of animals. During the antebellum era most hunters favored black bear, deer, wild turkey, partridge, duck, and fox, but they also hunted opossum, raccoon, lynx, squirrel, rabbit, and an array of wildfowl. They also shot the occasional puma, wolf, and elk, although these species had become exceedingly rare by the antebellum era. Aspiring hunters who lacked their own guns and dogs could usually borrow them from neighbors, friends, or relatives. Many hunters also set snares and built traps, and if they knew where rabbits or opossums slept, particularly humble hunters needed nothing more than a big stick.

The resulting meat, hides, and furs reinforced hunters' claims to patriarchal authority as providers for their households. Hunters always recognized the symbolism that accompanied these utilitarian aspects of the hunt, but during the antebellum era, many white hunters began using the hunt as a venue for the display of increasingly complex ideas about gender, race, class, and community. As a definitively masculine pursuit, hunting made an effective stage for increasingly elaborate exhibitions of masculinity and power. In the woods and fields, in the company of other men, these hunters could demonstrate their masculinity with unparalleled clarity.

Race and class altered the form of these masculine displays. Members of the elite took great interest in emerging ideas of sportsmanship, which emphasized the act of hunting over the acquisition of meats and hides. Conversely, yeoman and poor white hunters focused on the utility of hunting because the products of the hunt helped confirm their patriarchal authority over their households. They rarely observed the elite rules of sport, but they did obey certain conventions when they hunted, which defined their position within their communities and families. Slaves hunted in a much more circumscribed world. Beholden to their owners and devoted to their families, they played multiple roles when they hunted. As loyal bondsmen, they sacrificed their personal safety for their owners' pleasure. As members of families, they used hunting as a tool for survival and an instrument of social cohesion.

Chapter 1 outlines the various historic developments that shaped hunting in the South from the colonial era to the outbreak of the Civil War. By chronologically examining the dynamics of hunting opportunity, method, and technology, this chapter sketches the context for the chapters that follow. This chapter considers the interactions between the environment, the supply of game, the development of hunting law, the rise of the sporting press, and the development of the various literary images of the hunter.

Subsequent chapters are more thematic. They examine different aspects of the social drama of the hunt during the period from 1800 to 1860. Chapters 2 through 5 focus on ruling-class whites because that is who the bulk of the material (books, letters, journals, and periodicals) discusses. Although the specifics about these conceptions of masculinity were the purview of the slaveholding elite, many of the broad conclusions regarding manhood and community can be applied to yeoman farmers, townspeople, and poor whites.

As a social construct, gender meant little unless verified by appreciative observers. Because the hunt contained manifold expressions of identity, hunters played to a variety of audiences in their search for recognition. The opinions and observations of white women and blacks were important to white hunters, but the primary audience for the exploits of white hunters was a select group of male peers. Hunters, particularly the young and inexperienced, relied upon the judgments of other hunters to validate their claims to manhood. The lessons of boyhood and the vagaries of these various audiences appear in chapter 2, which also describes the structure of hunting fraternities and details particular niche-oriented forms of display such as paternalism, gift giving, trophies, and storytelling.

Chapter 3 details the relationship between white manhood and the emergence of the hunter as a masculine ideal. Founded upon prowess, self-control, and mastery, this image of masculinity appeared in a variety of settings. This chapter focuses on the literary incarnations of the ideal, but it also draws upon a variety of related materials including correspondence, diaries, and periodicals.

Chapter 4 picks up on the idea of hunting fraternities and examines the various criteria of exclusion that hunters used to define exactly who their peers were. Some fraternities created exclusivity by snubbing urbanites and recognizably continental Europeans, while others used either conspicuous consumption or the emerging rules of sport to set them apart from the majority of white men. By creating the "other," fraternities simultaneously increased the exclusivity of their displays and clarified their identities. Despite the enthusiasm with which hunters advocated strict rules of sport and various criteria of exclusion in books and periodicals, few of these criteria were more than broad guidelines. Chapter 5 looks at the internal dynamic of hunting fraternities. Examining various sources makes it apparent that congeniality, group cohesiveness, and a sense of community tended to override churlish behavior once an individual was accepted as an equal. Despite the popularization of various criteria of exclusion and inclusion by the sporting press, the final assessment of other hunters depended upon firsthand experience. After being accepted into a community, the constraints popularized by the sporting press (including the rules of sport) became less important.

The peculiarities of southern hunting owed a great deal to the existence of slavery. Part of its popularity arose from the fact that hunting was a particularly effective venue for the demonstration of white supremacy. Chapter 6 focuses on the occasions when slaves hunted at their owners' behest and the times when they accompanied white hunters into the field where they performed a variety of duties. Slaves were brought into the field to perform menial labor, but they were also present so that whites could demonstrate the extent of their mastery. In some cases slaveholders felt so confident that they equipped particularly trusted slaves with firearms. Few scenes dramatized the paternalist ethos more pointedly than a slave and his master taking the field together.

Chapter 7 examines these interactions from the point of view of slaves who primarily considered the hunt as an opportunity to ameliorate their own condition. Game provided them with a supplementary food source, an item for trade, and a measure of autonomy. By sharing this valuable resource with their families and friends, enslaved hunters strengthened the bonds of community and kinship. Living in a society predicated upon constant degradation, a simple act of generosity could become a symbol of resistance. Likewise, property gained through illicit transactions with other slaves facilitated the stability of the slave family, which in turn buttressed the cohesion of the slave community. By reconceptualizing hunting as an activity that benefited the slave community, these hunters found ways to create their own meanings for the labor they performed at the behest of their owners.

Hunting stories appeared in various nineteenth-century magazines, including several, such as the *Spirit of Times,* that devoted themselves exclusively to the world of sport. Although rich, these sources do require a critical eye. Slaveholders' papers, diaries, and correspondence provide depth, while documents like the Works Progress Administration ex-slave interviews, court records, and travel accounts help provide a contrast to the planter vision. In these versions of the hunt, black and white participants occupied the same space, but the meanings they ascribed to their actions varied. These sources allow the white planter's oft-grandiloquent monologue to become a conversation among pseudo-aristocratic sporting poseurs, unapologetic market hunters, devoted outdoorsmen, naive thrill seekers, and pothunting pragmatists.

By exploring this conversation about hunting, I have tried to present a balanced description of an important and cherished southern institution. Indeed, for many white men hunting was a consuming passion. They hunted as avidly as they attended church. They wrote about their experiences in the field with the same care and detail that they devoted to their business dealings, and they selected their hunting companions as carefully as their political representatives. But hunting was more than the preserve of a few aficionados. It was an activity that all southerners, black and white, male and female, rich and poor, rural and urban, knew something about. It is this far-reaching familiarity that makes hunting a valuable window on antebellum society and culture as a whole.

1. Game, Landscape, and the Law

Oh shame, a burning shame, to every true sportsman—the farmer, the citizen, and legislator—who quietly and indifferently sanctions such a barbarous practice of wholesale destruction of the partridge, openly, as it were, under their very nose, and yet they will not enforce a word of rebuke to prevent and frown down, and punish by enactment of a proper game law, the rascally pot hunter, the poaching man hawk.

R. L. B., a South Carolina hunter, 1858

O NE OF THE central motifs of hunting in the South is the hunter's quest for plentiful game. Some of the earliest European settlers along the southeastern coast of North America worried that the supply of desirable game in the area was already diminishing. This concern, whether justified or not, meant that almost from the beginning of European settlement those hunters with political and social power tried to control the access of other, less powerful hunters to the best animals. This contest produced a series of laws, habits, narratives, and traditions that were rehearsed and refined throughout the eighteenth and nineteenth centuries. Unfortunately for later hunters, these efforts failed to maintain the supply of desirable game. However, this conflict did aid the articulation of a rich, varied, and abiding southern hunting culture.

Hunting played a critical role in the development of southern communities for thousands of years before the arrival of the first Europeans. Every major group of Indians in the southeastern portion of America relied upon hunting as an essential source of provisions, clothing, tools, and trade goods. Like the Europeans and Africans who began settling their territory in the early seventeenth century, these Indians associated hunting with masculinity and power. While Indian women took primary responsibility for agriculture and housekeeping, Indian men in this region generally consigned themselves to hunting and warfare. This Indian division of labor alarmed some Europeans observers who believed that Indian men should have spent more time working in the fields.[1]

This criticism reveals an important element of the dominant European understanding of hunting in the seventeenth century: it was a leisure activity reserved for members of the elite. Like many of the traditions, customs, and mores that Europeans brought to the New World, this idea became transformed by the conditions they discovered in North America. The abundance of land, the proliferation of property holding, an apparently bountiful supply of game, and the threat of hostile Indians transformed traditional European ideas about hunting during the colonial era. European laws and traditions customarily associated hunting with monarchs and aristocrats, but soon after their arrival in North America, many European settlers severed the link between hunting and class privilege. The democratizing influence of the New World accelerated this tendency, but necessity alone meant that hunting could no longer remain the preserve of the highborn or the wealthy. The ideal of the hunter-aristocrat quickly receded into dormancy.

Southerners hunted for a variety of reasons, but the prospect of fresh meat often provided reason enough. Few developed enough skill to support themselves on hunting alone, but the tenuousness and isolation of many colonial settlements meant that a diet diversified by hunting could be the difference between malnutrition and health. Indians initially supplied settlers with most of their game, but as Europeans and Africans adapted to life in North America, some of them became capable hunters and trappers as well.[2] Settlers, like Indians, valued wild animals both for their meat and for their hides and furs, which they could either trade or cure for use in their own households. In the South deer provided the most important source of hides, and by the mid-eighteenth century the deerskin trade had become a substantial component of the southern export economy. Meat and skin provided the most marketable commodities of the hunt, but many settlers found a variety of uses for the other parts of the animals they killed. Animal fat provided the raw material for a number of products, including shortening, candles, lye, and grease. Settlers also found uses for feathers, as pillow stuffing or writing quills; brains, as a tanning agent; and tripe, as food for hogs and dogs.[3]

While these prospects drew settlers into the field, others began hunting to protect their farming interests. The depredations of various predators (like wolves and pumas), which developed a taste for European livestock, and the constant raids of animals (like squirrels and crows), which ate produce and grain, encouraged coordinated eradication programs. Some communities managed these efforts themselves, but many colonies provided hunters with further incentive by passing bounty laws that offered rewards for the scalps and heads of various undesirable species.[4]

Because hunting played a more central role in the life and economies of the colonies than it had in the Old World, European settlers modified the common law to fit their situation. When Virginia passed the first southern game law in 1632, it swept away English restrictions regarding wealth and landownership by affirming the right of Virginians to hunt on common land. The House of Burgesses enumerated a number of reasons to justify this unprecedented step. "It is thought convenient," its members declared, "that any man be permitted to kill deare or other wild beasts or fowle in the common woods, forests, or rivers in regard that thereby the inhabitants may be trained in the use of theire armes, the Indians kept from our plantations, and the wolves and other vermine destroyed." Subsequent colonial laws attempted to impose some restrictions on this unfettered freedom by recognizing landowner sovereignty over posted land. The House of Burgesses, however, eventually opened the vast, uncultivated expanse of Virginia in 1643 by verifying the right of Virginians to hunt on any "land not planted or seated though taken up."[5]

Encouraged by fairly liberal hunting laws and the marketability of meat and skins, Indian, European, and African hunters quickly depleted game around most European settlements. By the early eighteenth century, a few observers became concerned about the depletion of various species of game, particularly deer. Some of them blamed the Indians, many of whom now carried guns. Increasingly dependent on European goods, Indians killed massive amounts of game to exchange with white settlers. Naturalist Mark Catesby observed Indian hunters firsthand when he traveled through Virginia and Carolina from 1712 to 1722. He believed that "the use of guns has enabled them to slaughter far greater number of deer and other animals than they did with their primitive bows and arrows. This destruction of deer and other animals being chiefly for the sake of their skins, a small part of the venison they kill suffices them; the remainder is left to rot, or becomes a prey to the wolves, panthers, and other voracious beasts."[6] Philadelphia naturalist William Bartram observed a similar dynamic when he traveled through the Deep South in the early 1770s. The Indians he encountered waged "eternal war against deer and bear, to procure food and clothing, and other necessaries and conveniences." Unlike Catesby, he saw the Indians in a sympathetic light and attributed their excesses to the pernicious influence of "the white people" who "dazzled their senses with foreign superfluities."[7]

Other observers blamed game depletion on poor white hunters living in sparsely settled game-rich areas along the margins of agricultural settlement. These "frontiersmen" were already being idealized by some inhabitants of more densely populated areas for their apparent toughness, familiarity with firearms, and knowledge of woodcraft, which made them an excellent vanguard for the expansion of settlement. Joseph Doddridge, an Episcopalian organizer who traveled throughout northwestern Virginia and the upper Ohio Valley from 1763 to 1783, applauded frontiersmen because they were "inured to hardihood, bravery and labor from their early youth." He gushed, "They sustained with manly fortitude, the fatigue of the chase, the campaign and scout, and with strong arms 'turned the wilderness into fruitful fields' and have left to their descendants the rich inheritance of an immense empire blessed with peace and wealth."[8]

Although most frontier settlers devoted themselves to agricultural pursuits and emigrated in family, ethnic, and religious groups, Doddridge's depiction of the hardy frontiersman as the tamer of the wilderness became a popular image of frontier development. Frontiersmen were commonly thought of as the first crucial step in an irreversible continuum of economic development, yet enthusiasm for the skills and lifestyle of the frontiersman quickly faded as soon as an area they occupied became more densely populated.[9] In an agricultural milieu frontiersmen became annoying, and potentially disruptive, anachronisms. Many farmers in newly settled areas considered hunting a possible source of supplementary provisions and an acceptable form of amusement and recreation, but at a certain point in the economic development of the area, farmers agreed, hunting became an unfit vocation. In doing so, they made an increasingly sharp distinction between farmers who occasionally hunted (themselves) and hunters who occasionally farmed (relict frontiersmen). The former increasingly equated the latter with banditry, theft, and disorder and occasionally described them as "little more than white Indians." Many frontiersmen inadvertently confirmed these fears by adopting Indian breechcloths, leggings, and moccasins.[10]

The portrait of frontiersmen that emerged from contemporary descriptions reaffirmed popular eighteenth-century notions about the corrupting influence of the "untamed" frontier environment. Some observers developed complex models that condemned the persistence of frontiersmen's way of life while celebrating their role as the vanguard of settlement. For example, essayist J. Hector St. John de Crèvecoeur described frontiersmen as a dangerous but necessary evil, a "kind of forlorn hope" that preceded a "respectable army" of yeoman farmers by ten or twelve years. Unlike his pleasantly gregarious "American Farmer," Crèvecoeur's hunters were "ferocious, gloomy, and unsociable." They often moved toward the frontier with good intentions, but whether enticed by the bountifulness of game or drawn into the field to protect their livestock, these would-be husbandmen "soon become professed hunters," and once hunters, Crèvecoeur lamented, they said "farewell to the plough." Spurning society, they eventually became "no better than carnivorous animals of a superior rank."[11]

Other critics of frontiersmen associated them with idleness, immorality, and bloodthirstiness. Wealthy Virginia planter William Byrd II associated these failings with their predilection for hunting. While accompanying a surveying expedition near the Great Dismal Swamp in 1712, he described the degraded character of the shiftless locals who subsisted off tiny plots of corn, free-range pigs, and game. Byrd believed that their idleness sprang from the bountifulness of the land. He postulated that "very little Labour is requir'd to fill their Bellies, especially where the Woods afford such Plenty of Game."[12]

Many observers believed that like the Indians who hunted for market, such hunters often killed more than they could easily carry. An initial orgy of killing around Boonesboro, Kentucky, in 1775 set a destructive tone for future settlement. After shooting all the bison they could find, a group of hunters gorged themselves on the choice hump and tongue and left the rest to rot. One pioneer remembered that because these were the first bison many of the settlers had seen, "many a man killed a buffalo just for the sake of saying so."[13]

During the early eighteenth century, concerns about the depredations of Indians, the character of frontiersmen, and the concomitant depletion of game encouraged a reassessment of the earliest colonial hunting statutes. In some ways this represented a return to a more European understanding of hunting and its place in civilized society. As a result of this reappraisal, several colonial legislatures passed laws restricting the most destructive hunting practices. Some of these laws penalized the owners of unkenneled dogs, which roamed the woods in search of deer and livestock; however, most of these statutes targeted two particularly destructive practices: ring-firehunting and night hunting by firelight (both of which were commonly referred to as firehunting).

Ring-firehunting involved numerous participants. The hunt began when hunters set a ring of fire around a large area of woods; the circumference of the ring could stretch up to five miles. The fire, combined with the sound of the hunters' advance, drove game of all kinds to another, smaller group of hunters stationed at the center of the ring who killed the panicked animals as they raced to escape the flames. Destructive of game, browse, and timber, dangerous (armed hunters occasionally shot one another in the confusion), and associated with Indians, who probably developed the technique, ring-firehunting had many critics. Maryland enacted the first prohibition on firehunting in 1730, and by 1790 every other southern legislature had passed some form of antifirehunting legislation. Ring-firehunting died out in the late eighteenth century, but the transformation of southern forests from parklike tracts (resulting from Indian burning practices) to mixed growth with a thick understory probably played a more important role in the demise of the practice than hunting laws.[14]

Night hunting by firelight was less destructive than ring-firehunting, but it also attracted a number of critics. The American version of English "jacklighting," this method resembled the twentieth-century practice of "spotlighting." Unlike ring-firehunting, it only required two hunters and darkness. One of the hunters (often a slave) carried a skillet full of glowing embers, while the other, walking in front of him, carried a gun. The firepan emitted a wash of light, which caught and illuminated animals' eyes. Once an animal looked at the light, it often remained transfixed, providing the shooter with an easy mark. This method received criticism because of its effectiveness and because firehunters occasionally mistook livestock for game, but it thrived despite various legislative efforts.[15]

Southern legislators also sought to alleviate the pressure on deer populations by prohibiting their pursuit during certain times of the year. Indians traditionally did most of their hunting during the winter because of the
lull in the agricultural cycle and because that season saw bears and deer at
their fattest, but the advent of coastal markets and the proliferation of
hunters turned hunting into a year-round activity.[16] Colonial legislatures
knew little (if anything) of Indian precedents, but many of them established legal hunting seasons that roughly coincided with the breeding cycle
of the white-tailed deer. By prohibiting hunting during the months when
does carried and cared for their young, these laws encouraged the survival
of future generations of deer. This idea spread relatively quickly. Maryland
established a deer season in 1730, and Virginia and North Carolina followed
in 1738 and 1745, respectively.[17]

Passed in the midst of furious denunciations of the depredation and dis-
ruption caused by frontiersmen, these laws all included an element of social control. Many of them included provisos that acknowledged the
importance of hunting for subsistence in frontier areas, but the prohibition of firehunting and the imposition of hunting seasons in more settled
parts of the colonies threatened anyone living in these areas who still depended upon hunting for a large part of their livelihood. By discouraging
the persistence of hunting as a viable form of year-round subsistence, these
laws encouraged hunters living in these areas either to relocate or to change
their way of life.[18]

At the same time they were restricting certain hunting practices, some
colonial legislatures extended special privileges to their wealthiest con-
stituents at the expense of other hunters. This aristocratic spirit was first
manifested in Virginia in 1705, when the House of Burgesses rolled back
the open range by prohibiting commoners from hunting on private land
without permission. Unlike earlier laws regulating trespass, the 1705 law included a rider that explicitly favored wealthier Virginians by exempting "any
person being owner of six slaves, at least." This meant that wealth alone
determined who could legally pursue game through "lands where he hath
not leave to hunt."[19] Similarly, North Carolina's act of 1745 to "prevent
killing Deer at Unseasonable Times" fiercely indicted "idle and disorderly
Persons, who have no settled Habitation, nor visible Method of supporting themselves, by Industry or honest Calling" as the cause of depletion.
In an effort to stem their depredations, the General Assembly insisted that

hunters carry an affidavit that they had planted at least 5,000 corn hills, therefore making the hunt the preserve of relatively substantial farmers.[20]

Because colonial governments usually lacked effective instruments of enforcement, most hunters freely flouted these restrictions. The House of Burgesses addressed this problem in 1748 by promising informers twenty shillings for every successfully prosecuted offense they reported. This incentive offered little improvement because, as historian Thomas Lund has pointed out, "of all techniques to enforce law, none could depend more for its effectiveness upon the very characteristic in which the American condition was most deficient: consensus that game law deserved to be enforced." Popular dissatisfaction with legal restrictions and the potential for backlash within their own communities meant that few informers came forward.[21]

Following the American Revolution, some white southerners continued hunting for utilitarian reasons, but many (especially members of the slave-holding elite) began placing more emphasis upon the recreational aspects of the hunt. Leisure hunting also became increasingly popular in the North, but by the 1830s some southerners began promoting it as an element of a distinctively southern way of life. During this period the pseudo-aristocratic sportsman, the rugged frontiersman, and the poor white backwoods hunter all became popular southern icons. These evolving images, emerging ideas about leisure hunting, and the growing sense of sectional identity influenced developments in hunting law and the sporting press. Together, these institutions played a critical role in shaping the cultural significance of the hunt and southern manhood.

Colonial hunting laws never enjoyed conspicuous success or popular acclaim, and in the wake of the American Revolution, they became increasingly irrelevant. In the decades that followed the end of the Revolution, southern courts and legislatures removed many of the restrictions that their predecessors had imposed during the first half of the eighteenth century. These changes made inclination and ability rather than wealth or landownership the determining factors in the exploitation of wildlife. State legislatures passed a variety of hunting laws in the late eighteenth and early nineteenth centuries, but they carefully avoided the aristocratic tinge of colonial law and the divisiveness of the harsh contemporary English "Black Laws."[22]

Even during the conservative retrenchment of the 1790s, southern legislatures limited themselves to laws that the vast majority of whites found unobjectionable. Few whites protested the passage of laws that advocated the abolition of firehunting, restricted the movements and actions of slaves and free blacks, encouraged the extermination of various undesirable species, and suspended hunting on the Sabbath. Because enforcement remained sporadic at best, hunters who objected to these measures frequently carried on as if they did not exist. The lack of meaningful enabling legislation and the absence of effective law enforcement ensured that hunting laws typically remained nothing more than feeble gestures.[23]

These critical weaknesses resulted in the effective nullification of almost every piece of hunting legislation in the antebellum South. This failure resembled most nineteenth-century efforts at regulation. As historian Lawrence Meir Friedman has explained, "Basically, the law left it to private persons, to enforce what regulation there was. If no one brought a lawsuit, or complained to the district attorney about some violation, nothing was done." This remained particularly true in the South.[24]

The most authoritative refutation of restrictive hunting laws came with *State v. Campbell,* an 1808 Georgia Superior Court decision that upheld the customary right of trespass on unimproved lands. Some states recognized this right in their statute law, but because Georgia lacked a clear statement on this subject, the court clarified the situation by observing that prohibiting trespass appeared ridiculous in "a country which was but one extended forest, in which the liberty of killing a deer, or cutting down a tree, was as unrestrained as the natural rights of the deer to rove, or the tree to grow." In an archly democratic conclusion, which verified the doctrine of free taking in no uncertain terms, the court asked, "Where was the aristocracy whose privilege [was] to be secured?"[25]

Some property holders continued to insist that they held a preemptive right to the use of their land, but they experienced little success when they sought to extend these rights over their uncultivated acreage. In 1818 South Carolina courts upheld the right of trespass on unimproved lands with *M'Conico v. Singleton.* This case forthrightly concluded that "the right to hunt on unenclosed and uncultivated lands has never been disputed, and it is well known that it has been universally exercised from the first settlement of the country up to the present time."[26]

By recognizing the right of trespass on unimproved land, southern courts removed an important, if generally ineffective, legal barrier between southern hunters and their quarry. Few hunters ever felt constrained by hunting law, but after these decisions they became confident that they could hunt on unimproved land whenever they pleased. Despite occasional efforts on the part of determined legislators or landowners, concerns about trespass fell into abeyance until the 1840s. Northern landowners faced a similar predicament and suffered through a comparable lack of law enforcement, but their courts rarely handed down such unequivocally democratic decisions.

As hunting law faded into temporary obscurity, the instrument of its eventual resurrection, the American sporting press, rose into prominence. In the colonial era knowledge of the hunt had come through personal channels like conversation and firsthand observation, but by the early nineteenth century, imported English books and periodicals, a handful of American books, and an intermittent column in a Baltimore-based periodical, the *American Farmer,* began providing literate southerners with "authoritative" information about effective hunting methods and "proper" technique. This trickle of information grew to a torrent, and by the early 1830s southerners could tap an ever-increasing stream of books and periodicals, which presented a variety of hunting accounts. These ranged from the unaffected and matter-of-fact to the mildly embellished to the grandiose and bombastic. Despite occasional flights of fancy, these narratives disseminated a great deal of practical information about hunting, horses, dogs, firearms, and the natural world. They also provided a sophisticated medium in which authors and readers could rehearse the connection between hunting and identity.[27]

During the 1830s hunting narratives began appearing in a variety of American periodicals (including the *Southern Literary Journal, Gentleman's Magazine,* the *Southern Literary Messenger,* and assorted local newspapers) as well as a considerable number of books and pamphlets. However, two periodicals, the *American Turf Register* (a monthly) and the *Spirit of the Times* (a weekly), assumed particularly central roles in the development, refinement, and popularization of the hunt in the antebellum South. The inaugural issue of the *American Turf Register* was published in Baltimore by Maryland native John Stuart Skinner in 1829 (he also served as the editor of the *American Farmer*). It provided the first national forum for the discussion of various "rural sports," which included horse racing, trotting matches, shooting, hunting, and fishing. Horse racing dominated the *Turf,* but Skinner, who was an enthusiastic hunter himself, included a number of hunting stories in almost every issue. His southern sympathies ensured that many of these came from southern contributors.[28]

The success of the *Turf* helped encourage William Porter of New York City to publish "a paper, devoted . . . to the pleasures, amusements, fashions and divertissements of life." The resulting *Spirit of the Times* first appeared in 1831. It soon became the keystone of the American sporting press. Consciously modeling his project on the English sporting periodical *Bell's Life in London,* Porter filled the pages of the *Spirit* with a dazzling variety of text ranging from police reports and clippings from the English sporting press to jokes, theater reviews, racing news, and hunting stories. Porter's fascination with the South, his friendship with his southern contributors, his brothers' travels in the South, and his rigorously apolitical stance ensured a consistent and strong southern presence in the columns of the *Spirit* despite the location of its offices and the vagaries of sectional tension.[29]

These periodicals and their audiences quickly developed a reciprocal relationship. Both the *Turf* and the *Spirit* depended upon their readers for most of their material on hunting in the United States. Almost every issue included a few pseudonymous pieces. Some of these writers only published a single piece, but some became regular contributors. Many mimicked the structure and sentiment of romantic fiction, and although genre conventions occasionally obscured elements of the hunt in these accounts, these narratives provided a wealth of information. Many of the narratives took the form of tall tales or adventure stories, but many short pieces were merely reports from the field. Generally presented as instructions rather than fiction, these pieces remained fairly down-to-earth. Tone and editorial comment distinguished the occasional tall tale or flight of fancy from the regular fare of burnished nonfiction. The editors of the sporting press played a role in selecting the images of the southern hunt that appeared in their pages, but because their periodicals relied upon the submissions of readers, they came to serve as a public arena where literate southerners could refine their ideas of the hunt. These writers blended a wealth of everyday details with idealized images of southern society and manhood. These characteristics make these sources an invaluable tool for charting the development of hunting in the South.[30]

The sporting press expanded in volume and influence throughout the antebellum era, but hunting never received universal acclaim. Historian Michael Bellesîles has argued that as hunting became more popular, it attracted the attention of critics who held it up to "ever increasing ridicule." Some portrayed hunters as tedious bores while others criticized hunting as a waste of money. Although a few southerners picked up on these themes (usually for purposes of humorous self-deprecation), the vast majority of the pieces expressing outright hostility originated in the North. With very few exceptions, white southerners who found a voice in print embraced the practice of leisure hunting with uncritical enthusiasm.[31]

These enthusiasts depended upon the sporting press as a source of reliable information. By appealing to tyros and old hands alike, this growing stream of popular literature effectively transformed the way many southerners thought about hunting. By confirming the distinction between recreational hunters and semisubsistence hunters who hunted for meat and hides, the sporting press helped elevate hunting into the realm of sophisticated amusement and elaborate display. When hunters put what they read in the sporting press into action, the affectations of genre could come stumbling into life.

When combined with the rise of romanticism and the growing distance between the settled areas of the eastern seaboard and much of the frontier, the rise of leisure hunting also contributed to the rehabilitation of frontiersmen (at least in the pages of books and periodicals). The first important departure from the "retrogression school" came in 1786, when John Filson presented an adventurous biography of Daniel Boone as an appendix to his book *The Discovery, Settlement, and Present State of Kentucke.* Filson, a Delaware schoolmaster turned surveyor and land speculator, intended his work as a promotional brochure, so he offered an optimistic portrait of a frontier filled with adventure and promise, which he assured his readers would eventually become a paradise built on crops and livestock. His embellished biography of Boone illustrated how determined settlers could wring wealth and happiness from the "dark and bloody ground" of Kentucky. In Filson's eyes Boone's capacity for hunting and Indian fighting revealed his connection with colonial frontiersmen, but unlike those reprobates, he remained a husbandman at heart. Rather than obstructing progress, he capably and responsibly fulfilled his ascribed role as a vanguard of future settlement.[32]

In subsequent years a variety of writers refined this heroic image. Drawing upon romantic conceptions of nature as the wellspring of truth and beauty, they recast the frontiersman as a sort of "noble savage," well versed in woodcraft but childishly innocent of the sullied ways of civilized man. New York novelist James Fenimore Cooper became the most important of these writers. When he published *The Pioneers,* the first of his enormously successful Leather-Stocking Tales, in 1823, he enshrined the romanticized frontiersman as a mythic pillar of American literature. The similarities between Cooper's Nathaniel Bumppo and Filson's Daniel Boone began with suspiciously similar names but went much deeper. Boone and Bumppo both acted as somewhat reluctant vanguards for white settlement, but each performed this service with efficiency and effectiveness. Each also appeared ready to move onward once settlement reached a certain level of development. Bumppo's lack of a family made him doubly appealing, ensuring that he remained as conveniently doomed and outmoded as his Indian companion, Chingachgook. Isolated and childless, they would not propagate their kind. These characters fixed the romantic vision of frontiersmen in American literature, but while rehabilitated frontiersmen remained admirable in a frontier context, Filson, Cooper, and their imitators made it clear that they still had no place in the midst of farms and plantations. They would die out or move on.[33]

Romantic frontiersmen gained a cadre of urban admirers, but for most southerners who lived near actual semisubsistence hunters, familiarity still bred contempt. Similarly, most writers who spent time with frontier hunters remained convinced of their depravity. Naturalist John James Audubon appreciated their knowledge and abilities more than most, but he agreed with the majority of southern farmers and slaveholders when he made it clear that hunting should remain nothing more than a "pleasant recreation." He frequently relied upon poor white hunters for information, but he always denounced hunting as "a very unprofitable trade" which could lead to "idleness, intemperance, and poverty." The development of the staple crop economy left little room for those who pursued alternate paths. Whether frontiersmen were characterized as a noble vanguard or degenerate scum, their way of life clashed with the requirements and expectations of agricultural society.[34]

Like their colonial counterparts, nineteenth-century frontiersmen remained admirable only as long as they either became farmers or left their homes in search of game-rich areas. Some, however, discovered niches within agricultural society. Various geographical features that discouraged the development of market agriculture allowed some southerners to preserve something resembling a frontier way of life in the heart of the South. Often referred to as the "backwoods," these areas included the highlands of the Appalachians and the Ozarks, swamps like the Everglades, the Okefenokee, the Great Dismal, and the Atchafalaya, and various pieces of marginal land like sandhills, pine barrens, and wiregrass. Because these "backwoodsmen" and their families usually lived in comparative isolation, other white southerners often tolerated them despite their unpolished and wasteful ways because they were at once white, dangerous, and useful.[35]

Slaveholders railed against backwoodsmen in their letters, essays, and books, but few openly challenged backwoodsmen in the field or the courts. In some cases slaveholders even modified their behavior to maintain good relations with their backwoodsmen neighbors. While traveling through Alabama in 1854, Frederick Law Olmsted described the manipulative relationship between a "vagabond" named John Brown, who eked out a marginal existence as a hunter, and a local planter who occasionally loaned him his pack of hounds in exchange for half of Brown's venison. Brown and his family supplemented game with whatever corn and hogs they could lay their hands on. Olmsted estimated that they "killed about as many shoats and yearlings as deer and turkeys." Despite his reliance upon hunting and theft, Brown remained at least a marginal member of the white community. The planter tolerated the Browns because he could do little about them without disturbing the secure picture of white supremacy. Fear probably also played a role in the planter's stoicism. A move against Brown might endanger himself, his family, or his property.[36] Some members of the elite even inveigled backwoodsmen with their hospitality in an effort to keep their goodwill. Novelist John Esten Cooke's father detested backwoodsmen, but when they crossed onto his land near Martinsburg, Virginia (now West Virginia), he sent them trays loaded with ham, bread, and wine.[37] These fears were not misplaced. When a less solicitous party of planters set out on a hunt in Covington County, Alabama, they unintentionally drew the wrath of a local hunter, who sniped at their camp during the night and wounded a prize mare. Eager to avoid a turf war, the party withdrew and escaped the "Arabs of the wilds of Covington."[38]

"The Death-Blow." Backwoodsman Henry Herbel kills a bear. From Porte Crayon [David Hunter Strother], *Virginia Illustrated: Containing a Visit to the Virginian Canaan, and the Adventures of Porte Crayon and His Cousins* (New York, 1871), 285.

Some southern elites valued backwoodsmen because they were useful. Many felt that they could serve as effective auxiliaries of plantation society. Whenever he hunted in a "frontier" area, Kentuckian Charles Webber sought out local backwoodsmen because he felt that they remained better acquainted with the outdoors "than many fops are with the contents of their pockets." The hunters he encountered usually obliged him, and in exchange for a share of the kill, they shepherded him through whatever passed as the local wilderness.[39]

Backwoodsmen could make effective guides, but slaveholders also tolerated them because the presence of the large, growing population of potentially rebellious slaves created a bond of racial solidarity among whites that usually overrode concerns about character or game depletion. Slaveholders might regret the wastefulness of backwoodsmen or their proclivity for trespassing and petty theft, but they never overlooked the roles that they could play in the militia and the slave patrol.[40] Class conflict among whites was always circumscribed in the South because of issues of race and slavery. Just as surely as the slaveholding elite used these issues to prevent the formation of a common cause between blacks and poor whites, clever poor whites could use them as a shelter from the wrath of the gentry. An important result was the respect that white elites extended to the patriarchs of poor white families in their role as masters of their households and property; they were, as historian Stephanie McCurry has put it, "masters of small worlds."[41] By recognizing backwoodsmen's claims to the open range, liminal membership in the broader white community, and a subsistence-oriented way of life, slaveholders transformed these potential class enemies into useful allies.

Elites ignored the depredations of backwoodsmen and used egalitarian rhetoric to their advantage in business and politics, yet they still sought to distinguish themselves from their less fortunate white neighbors. Many of the writers who propagated images of the romanticized frontiersman and the rude (but useful) backwoodsman also advanced a third, more refined image of the white hunter. This image promoted a resurgence of the quiescent association between hunting and the gentry. It was in many ways part of an attempt to overcome the egalitarian tenor that flowed from the leveling effect of universal white patriarchy and Jacksonian democracy. Drawn from the ranks of the elite, "sportsmen" deliberately shared few of the characteristics of their poor white counterparts. Defined by their adherence to the rules of sport (as dictated by the sporting press), sportsmen transformed the hunt from a convenient source of meat and hides into a rarefied form of recreation and public display. In time, the sportsman evolved into a paragon of a particularly southern vision of white manhood.[42]

Most of the southerners who embraced this image developed their ideas of sport from the sporting press. The *Spirit of the Times* and the *American Turf Register* never sought the codification of the principles of sport, but the narratives and anecdotes that they published often suggested rules and guiding principles. By providing a forum for debate, the sporting press helped create a measure of uniformity, but the regional variations and determined individualism of the antebellum South led most self-professed sportsmen to interpret these lessons to suit the particulars of their social and geographic milieus. This ensured that sport remained an evolving collection of ideas that varied from community to community rather than a set code.

Whatever their sources and variations, one principle remained fairly constant: sport created situations to challenge a sportsman's hunting abilities. This appealed to leisure hunters because by making killing more difficult, sport elevated the recreational act of hunting over the actual results. In the pursuit of this end, self-proclaimed sportsmen created challenges for themselves in any number of ways. For example, instead of shooting waterfowl whenever possible, they began shooting them only when they were "on the wing." Explaining this distinction in the *Spirit of the Times* in 1832, a hunter from Nashville proudly wrote, "With us it is hardly accounted sport, to shoot any thing sitting or stationary on the water, but there can be no finer amusement than duck shooting, as they pass, 'on the wing.'"[43] Given the opportunity, he intimated, anyone could shoot a bushel of "sitting ducks," but only a sportsman possessed sufficient prowess, self-control, and economic independence to risk waiting to shoot them on the wing. This distinction imposed a definite class boundary because it favored those who hunted for amusement over those who hunted for food. It also drew a line between the gentry who usually hunted with shotguns (like the English gentlemen who appeared in the sporting press) and poor whites who favored the otherwise versatile rifle, which required less powder and shot. Rifle-wielding poor whites rarely shot on the wing, because although shooting a flying bird with a shotgun was difficult, shooting one with a rifle was all but impossible.

Because most self-professed sportsmen relied on farming and slave labor for their livelihood, they primarily hunted for amusement rather than profit or provisions. This endowed the hunt with a new bundle of meanings. A hunter's ability to provide his family with meat always signified his ability and masculinity, but by obeying the rules of sport, hunters displayed a more refined image of white masculinity that drew upon class as well as patriarchy. It divorced sportsmen from the base concerns of frontiersmen and backwoodsmen and provided southern elites with an acceptable way to distance themselves from other white hunters without explicitly invoking the specter of aristocracy. This was particularly important in the South because of the necessity to present a united front of white manhood in the face of slavery.

Mississippi governor Alexander McNutt rhapsodized about the panoply of virtues that characterized the sportsman in a piece that appeared in the

PARTRIDGE SHOOTING.

"Partridge Shooting." Shooting on the wing with the assistance of dogs. From *The Sportsman's Portfolio of American Field Sports* (1855; rept. New York, n.d.), 27.

Spirit of the Times in 1845. "Show me a gentleman devoted to the chase, and I will show you, with rare exception, 'the noblest work of God, an honest man,' respected for manly virtues, a good husband and father, a zealous friend, and an open enemy. 'The rich man's equal, the poor man's bene-factor'—richly adorning the pages of his life with the shining virtues of charity and benevolence—whose memory will be a green spot in the dreary waste of sordid worldliness." McNutt's paean summarized the appeal of the image of the sportsman for southern hunters: if a "gentleman" fol-lowed the rules of sport, he could define himself as a paragon of southern manhood without directly invoking the potentially divisive and rather base category of wealth.[44]

In their effort to distinguish themselves as sportsmen, many members of the southern elite began redefining previously acceptable hunting methods, such as baiting ground, setting out salt licks, and shooting sit-ting ducks, as the unsporting work of slaves and poor whites. Hunters who wrote detailed descriptions of these methods usually explained that al-though desperate hunters might find them very effective, no true sports-man could tolerate them because they transformed the "manly and legitimate" contest between a hunter and his quarry into unsportsmanlike slaughter.[45]

As the sporting press expanded in size and influence and hunting law faded into insignificance, deer and other desirable game became increasingly scarce in many parts of the South. Specific populations are difficult to track, but it is clear that some species became depleted in certain areas as early as the seventeenth century. By the early nineteenth century, even the once abundant bear and prolific and adaptable deer were becoming rare in many parts of the South. As the phenomenal herds and flocks that crowded the landscape during the colonial era became thinner, some hunters, particularly those who considered themselves sportsmen, began casting about for the culprits.[46]

Some of these hunters recognized the role of technology in the accel-eration of game depletion in the early nineteenth century. Advances in firearms, particularly the invention of the percussion cap, proved signifi-cant because they greatly increased the effectiveness of hunters in the field. Before the advent of the percussion cap, gun-hunters used flintlocks, which were fairly effective against stationary targets at relatively short ranges but had a number of weaknesses. Many hunters expressed frustration at the delay between the snap of the flint and the discharge of shot because it gave their targets a critical moment of reaction time. Others complained about the delicacy of the firing mechanism, which depended on the ignition of loose priming powder that lay in an open pan beside the breech. This made double-barreled guns impossible; it also meant that dampness or jostling could result in a misfire. The percussion-cap system eliminated these problems because it replaced a firing pan filled with priming powder with a water-resistant copper-encased cap of fulminate of mercury. This eliminated the delay between snap and discharge, made guns easier to handle, and greatly reduced the problem of damp powder. It also allowed for double barrels, which could be fired in quick succession. Many hunters kept their flintlocks because of poverty, sentimentality, or habit, but after 1820 or so, enthusiastic hunters began buying new guns or had their flintlocks retrofitted.[47]

Other technological advances like the steamboat and railroad also played key roles in the depletion of game because they collapsed the distance between game-rich rural areas and cities. Steam-powered transport greatly increased the range of many wealthy hunters who possessed sufficient resources for pleasure travel. The 1851 "expedition" into a remote valley of the Alleghenies that novelist John Pendleton Kennedy described in *The Blackwater Chronicle* became possible because the extension of the railroad across what is now northern West Virginia opened a large area to excursionists from the coast. Once "remote and inaccessible," these areas became an easy day's travel from the seaboard.[48] The growth of the railroads also facilitated short hauls from coastal cities into the hinterland. By 1860 a group of hunters from Charleston, South Carolina, thought little about setting out from home in the morning to enjoy a delightful "change of air and recreation." By evening of their second day in the country, "the endeared attachments of such dear homes, and the calls of business, urged and required their return to city duties," so they rode the rails back into town where their display of freshly killed game excited "surprise and admiration of many sportsmen and friends."[49]

Because steam-powered transport provided rapid delivery, it also greatly extended the range of poor white hunters who supplied hotels, restaurants, and city markets along the seaboard with game from the interior. As Henry

William Herbert, the dean of the sporting press, wrote in 1848, "The rail-roads by which the country is everywhere intersected, enable the city pot-hunter to move about with his dogs, and to transmit the subject of his butchery to the market, easily, cheaply, speedily." The increase in market hunting that followed the growth of the railroads alarmed many recreational hunters who wanted to preserve the declining population of game.[50]

Several factors contributed to the depletion of game, but like Herbert, most conservation-minded hunters in the South placed the blame on hunters who ignored the rules of sport. These reformers recognized the utility of hunting, but they argued that the lack of hunting laws and the deceptive abundance of American wildlife encouraged profligate wastefulness. Their complaints spawned the "pothunter," a popular villain who became the fourth image of the white hunter and the true antithesis of the sportsman. Pothunters lacked the admirable qualities of frontiersmen and the potential usefulness of backwoodsmen, but they retained and magnified all of their defects. Contributors to the sporting press lamented pot-hunters' complete disregard for property rights and decried the wretched squalor of their homes, but nothing aggravated them more than their reckless prodigality when it came to game.[51]

Pothunter proved a remarkably versatile term. Most writers reserved the designation for poor hunters who literally "hunted for the pot," but they also used it when referring to market hunters who supplied urban markets with wild game. South Carolina planter-politician William Elliott blamed these professional hunters for much of the depletion of desirable game in his section of South Carolina. He complained that after "settling themselves wherever the game is abundant, and cultivating merely corn enough to sustain themselves, their horses and a couple of hounds," these hunters devoted "their days and nights to hunting." As a result, they eventually killed most of the game in the neighborhood. After a few years, when the game ran out, these hunters would simply move on and recommence their "career of destruction" somewhere else.[52] The southern gentry customarily associated pothunting with poor whites, but a few particularly combative writers used the term when attacking wealthy whites who showed equally wanton disregard for other hunters and their property.[53]

Most of the writers who complained about pothunters grounded their critiques in fact. Whether hunting for their families or for the market, some

"The Hunters." An ominous-looking group of backwoods pothunters. From Porte Crayon [David Hunter Strother], *Virginia Illustrated: Containing a Visit to the Virginian Canaan, and the Adventures of Porte Crayon and His Cousins* (New York, 1871), 173.

of the poor whites who hunted killed a prodigious amount of game. Meshach Browning, a poor white hunter who lived in western Maryland, estimated that during the course of his career, which stretched from 1795 to 1839, he had killed 1,800 to 2,000 deer, 300 to 400 bears, 50 "panthers and catamounts," and scores of wolves and lynx. Although few sportsmen killed more than a small fraction of this amount, they certainly remained capable of wanton killing. Even an accomplished hunter and a leading proponent of sport like William Elliott occasionally crowed over the volume of his killing. At the conclusion of a successful deer hunt, he exclaimed: "Three deer were started—they were all at our feet—and without the aid of a dog! It was the work of five minutes!"[54]

In many cases the difference between the sportsman and the pothunter remained subjective. In general, whenever professed sportsmen killed large numbers of animals, they considered it a sporting triumph, but when criticizing others, they recast it as pothunting slaughter. Whatever the local supply of game or the claims of hunters to the contrary, most hunters simply blazed away at any targets that presented themselves, just as they routinely slaughtered more game than they could carry or use.[55] There was no mistaking the ability of a hunter who stood beside a few dead bears, a pile of deer, or a heap of birds. Some contributors to the sporting press expressed dismay at such destruction, but because most hunters remained fixated upon counting the number of their kills, the slaughter continued.

Most contemporaries recognized that technological innovation and the actions of hunters had deleterious consequences for wildlife, but only a few noted the third factor that affected the population of game: the environmental impact of settlement upon game habitat.[56] This is hardly surprising, for commercial logging, turpentine tapping, girdling, firewood gathering, brush clearing, cultivation, and the introduction of free-range livestock all affected different animals in different ways. The complexity of the interaction between hunting, predation, and environmental change ensured that the pattern of game depletion varied greatly. In some areas certain species became hunted out fairly rapidly, but the variety of southern landscapes and the vast stretches of uncultivated land that lay throughout the South (as much as 87 percent of the South remained unimproved as late as 1850) ensured that many areas retained sizable populations of certain species of game throughout the antebellum era.[57]

A few species even benefited from the mixed forest cover created by clearing, girdling, and old-field succession. As historian Gordon Whitney has explained, "If the disappearance of the forest resulted in the loss of forest dwellers, it also favored the multiplication of a number of other species. . . . Edge species like the cottontail, the skunk, the woodchuck, the opossum, the quail (bob-white), the woodcock, and the mourning dove prospered in the newly formed landscape."[58] These species, together with the elusive wild turkey and the enormous flocks of migratory waterfowl that came down the Atlantic or Mississippi flyways, interested many hunters, but the most popular barometer of game depletion was the white-tailed deer. Because they combined fine meat with valuable skins and ex-citing hunts, deer were very popular targets. They attracted the interest of market hunter, subsistence hunter, and sportsman alike. This resulted in tremendous hunting pressure, and despite the whitetail's compatibility with edge habitats, most hunters perceived the downward trajectory of deer populations in settled areas by the early eighteenth century. Various con-servation efforts failed to stem their overall decline, but their resilience and the relative abundance of undisturbed habitat ensured their survival in many areas.[59]

Other species presented a more complex dynamic. Wolves, pumas, foxes, and lynx all suffered declines because of the determined eradication efforts of settlers. On the other hand, predators also benefited from the presence of settlements because farm animals provided them with a new source of food. This supply helped healthy populations of foxes and lynx survive (as did the reluctance of some foxhunters to kill fox pups), but the determined efforts of farmers and bounty hunters all but eliminated wolves and pumas from the eastern United States by the early nineteenth century. Unlike edge species and small predators, large quadrupeds like elk and bison proved particularly vulnerable to the changes wrought by settlement. They disap-peared from the eastern slopes of the Appalachians before the Revolu-tionary War. Bear proved somewhat more resilient, but hunting and the elimination of unbroken forest cover greatly reduced their numbers and range as well. By the end of the antebellum era, they had become a rare prize in most parts of the South.[60]

Technological change, overhunting, and the expansion of settlement all contributed to the acceleration of game depletion in the early nineteenth century. This presented hunters with several immediate options. They could adopt new species as their principal targets, protect their favorite species in an effort to increase their numbers, or pursue their favorite game in other, less heavily exploited areas. Although the shift often took generations, the first option proved the most popular. Most colonial era whites seemed to prefer hunting bear and deer, but as the number of these animals gradually declined, later hunters appear to have made a slow, unconscious shift to various species of wildfowl, fox, and the occasional lynx or raccoon. In time, some of these species also became depleted. By the 1850s many small predators still thrived, but even the once seemingly inexhaustible supply of wildfowl appeared imperiled by development and overhunting.

A few landowners sought the preservation of game by treating portions of their holdings as private game reserves. First attempted in the late eighteenth century, these efforts met with limited success because of the porousness of the boundaries they placed around their preserves. Long, unprotected overland boundaries made the exclusion of other hunters almost impossible. In some cases large bodies of water proved fairly effective barriers, but even game preserves on the relatively isolated "hunting islands" along the coasts of Georgia and South Carolina suffered from frequent raids by poachers.[61] William Elliott noted that "several gentlemen of my acquaintance have been proprietors of islands; which were a source of perpetual annoyance to them." He reported that "no sooner were they stocked with game, than the amateurs, if not the professed poachers, would find their way to them; and if a bailiff was employed to keep them off, he often proved, as in other countries, the principal poacher." When Elliott set some of his own land aside as a game preserve, he even forbade his overseers from hunting; his frequent absences ensured that they became the enforcers of his edict. As a result, the "unrestricted in the neighborhood . . . took a malicious pleasure in destroying the game which the proprietor had presumed to keep for himself."[62]

Traveling to game-rich areas was the last resort of the committed hunter. The development of steam-powered transport made this an increasingly attractive option for wealthy hunters who lived in overhunted districts. By traveling into less heavily exploited areas, they could hunt the bear, deer, and (for those who traveled farther west) bison pursued by some of their fathers and grandfathers. Less wealthy hunters adopted this tactic out of necessity. When game became scarce around their homes, they either went on extended "long hunts" in game-rich areas or simply relocated their entire households. Most elites endorsed this strategy because it fit the accepted image of the frontiersman as a constantly advancing vanguard. As the most widely recognized representative of frontier life, Daniel Boone helped define incremental westward migration as the normative model of development.[63]

These three strategies for dealing with game depletion sidestepped the root causes of overhunting or environmental change, but as the influence of the sporting press expanded and game became increasingly scarce, some hunters began agitating for a fourth option: hunting legislation that would actually alter behavior in the field. Most of these reformers advocated familiar restrictions like hunting seasons and the protection of does, but as the idea of sport became more influential, some of them began advocating the passage of new laws prohibiting various pothunter methods. These efforts were a continuation of the rather feeble post-Revolution legislation, but the existence of a vital and popular sporting press endowed them with new urgency and a renewed sense of feasibility.[64]

The most ambitious drive for effective antebellum conservation legislation centered around the Chesapeake Bay. It began in the 1830s, when locals and the Virginia legislature tried to halt the depredations of market hunters by prohibiting some of their preferred methods. By discriminating against market hunters (who formed a disorganized minority), the legislators who crafted these laws avoided some of the snares that had resulted in the nullification of earlier conservation efforts. By respecting the right of small landowners to hunt on their own land, they deftly avoided the brand of aristocratic privilege. Because every white landholder in the tidewater could still hunt for household consumption or amusement, yeoman farmers had little cause for complaint. Market hunters did not complain much about these restrictions either, because without an effective policing force, enforcement remained quite lax.[65]

While the Virginia legislature tightened restrictions on hunting in the tidewater, a second set of defenders of Chesapeake wildfowl emerged. Encouraged by the reports of plentiful game that appeared in the sporting press, hunters from Philadelphia, Baltimore, Washington, and Annapolis began expanding their areas of operation. Drawn by the promise of good shooting but lacking political influence in Virginia, and perhaps even targeted by certain residency laws, these hunters developed a capital-intensive strategy of game conservation. In an effort to preserve good hunting for themselves, they began organizing hunting clubs, which identified and purchased particularly game-rich areas. After securing title, the clubs quickly created their own private game reserves by posting "No trespassing" signs. When local hunters ignored these warnings, many of these clubs attempted to defuse the situation with cash—they simply hired the trespassers as guards.[66]

For the most part, however, these conservation efforts proved disappointing, and the depletion of game continued apace; indeed, the sheer magnitude of killing on the Chesapeake continued to astound observers. A correspondent of the *New York Journal of Commerce* who visited the area in 1856 marveled at the slaughter and attributed it to the presence of professional hunters who had reduced hunting "to a science."[67] Some conservation-minded hunters, frustrated by this conspicuous lack of success, lashed out at the democratic ethos of southern society. Infuriated by the intransigence of the Maryland legislature and the obstinacy of pothunters, a professed sportsman from western Maryland named Campbell asked his protégé, Frederick Gustavus Skinner (publisher J. S. Skinner's grandson), "Why enact game laws for a people who have less regard for the rights of the land-holder than any civilized nation on the face of the globe?" Even though he was a vociferous advocate of hunting laws and a proponent of game conservation, he felt that game laws would remain a dead letter because most white southerners still looked upon them as "an aristocratic usurpation of their rights as free-born American citizens."[68]

Many contributors to the sporting press predicted that the depletion of game would continue, but few could match the apocalyptic vision sketched by William Elliott in his collection of sporting anecdotes, *Carolina Sports*. Elliott prophesied that "in another generation, this manly pastime will no longer be within our reach." He blamed the inevitability of this decline on the doctrine of free taking. As a landowner and a devoted sportsman, it greatly distressed him that "the right to hunt wild animals is held by the great body of the people, whether landholders or otherwise, as one of their franchises, which they will indulge in at discretion; and to all limitations on which, they submit with the worst possible grace!" "The 'feræ naturæ,'" he concluded, "are, in their code, the property of him who can take them — irrespective of any conflicting right in the owner of the soil."[69]

Like Campbell, Elliott considered the private ownership of game a legitimate aspect of landowning, but he realized that the legal recognition of landholder sovereignty remained impossible given the democratic climate of southern politics.[70] Elliott bitterly illustrated the supremacy of the hunter's prerogative with a piece of courtroom drama. Drawn from the testimony for an action for trespass that came before South Carolina's southeastern circuit court, the dialogue showed the distance between Elliott's pseudo-aristocratic position and the prevailing beliefs of most South Carolina hunters. The dramatic moment came when one of the defendants took the stand.

> He was himself a landholder, and a man of some property, and the question was put by the counsel:
>
> "Would you pursue a deer if he entered your neighbor's inclosure?"
>
> *Witness*—"Certainly."
>
> *Counsel*—"What if his fields were planted, and his cotton growing, or his grain ripe?"
>
> *Witness*—"It would make no difference; I should follow my dogs, go where they might!"
>
> *Judge*—"And pull down your neighbor's fence, and trample on his fields?"
>
> *Witness*—"I should do it—though I might regret to injure him!"
>
> *Judge*—"You would commit a trespass; you would be mulcted in damages. There is no law for such an act!"
>
> *Witness*—"It is hunter's law, however!"

Elliott understood this distinction, and it disgusted him, but he recognized that "the hunter's law, is likely somewhat longer to be the governing law of the case in this section of country; for the prejudices of the people are strong against any exclusive property in game, as every one feels who attempts to keep it to himself." Even if a jury convicted a trespassing hunter, the threat of punishment rarely provided much of a deterrent because "the fine or imprisonment of a freeman for so trifling and venial an offence, as shooting a wild animal, would be deemed a measure of odd-

est severity!" The popularity of this sentiment ensured that hunting law remained untenable in South Carolina until ideas about property and the role
of the state began changing in the late nineteenth century.[71]

Faced with intransigent hunters, a hesitant legislature, and hostile juries,
Elliott came to a bleak conclusion. He predicted that reform would come
only when there was no longer any game to kill. Once that day arrived, he
felt confident that "the juries will have no interest in construing away the
law. So that we may yet hope to see the time when men may, under the sanction of the law, and without offense, or imputation of aristocracy, preserve
the game from extermination—and perpetuate, in so doing, the healthful,
generous, and noble diversion of hunting."[72] Lest some consider him an
eccentric opponent of progress, Elliott inserted a whiggish caveat: "Sportsman that I am, I am not one of those who regret the destruction of the
forests, when the subsistence of man is the purpose. It is in the order of
events that the hunter should give place to the husbandman; and I do not
complain of it. It is the wanton, the uncalled-for destruction of forests and
of game, that I reprehend."[73] Like Crèvecoeur before him, Elliott placed
hunting in a continuum of progress.

Frustrated by experience but spurred on by the continuing depletion of
game, southern sportsmen searched for inspiration. Many found it in the
pages of the *Spirit of the Times,* which devoted a great deal of attention to
the innovative steps taken by conservation-minded hunters in New York
during the 1840s and 1850s. They faced familiar problems, and like their
counterparts in the Chesapeake, they began organizing. In 1844 eighty influential New Yorkers created the New York Sportsmen's Club. Greatly influenced by William Henry Herbert, the club drafted a law providing for
restricted seasons for their preferred quarry (deer, woodcock, ruffled
grouse, and quail). By criminalizing the possession of out-of-season game,
this law shifted the locus of enforcement to cities where market hunters
(or their intermediaries) plied their wares. Hunters could evade the law with
ease as long as they remained in the field, where they possessed considerable advantages, such as easy avenues of escape and possible recourse to
violence; poachers also benefited from sympathetic local juries that were
usually quick to acquit. But the hotels, markets, and restaurants that bought
their game were vulnerable to surveillance and legal action. Pressured by

the influential members of the club, the Board of Supervisors of the County of New York adopted a similar ordinance in 1846. Familiar with the shortcomings of earlier hunting laws, club members then took matters into their own hands and began pursuing convictions without the assistance of the government. The efforts of the New York Sportsmen's Club set off a little revolution in American hunting law. Prohibiting the possession of out-of-season game was not a new idea (it appeared in several southern colonial statutes), but an active citizenry was.[74]

Buoyed by the apparent success of the New York Sportsmen's Club, conservation-minded hunters in the South lobbied for new legislation in the closing years of the antebellum era. Despite a long list of failures, they had some reason to be optimistic. Thanks to the perseverance of their predecessors and the influence of the sporting press, they possessed a number of formidable weapons, including a considerable array of legal precedent, a few pieces of model legislation, and a popular scapegoat: the pothunter. These elements, when combined with the continuing depletion of game, set off a protracted struggle for hunting legislation in several southern states. The rhetoric of the proponents was sharpest in South Carolina.

South Carolina reformers began agitating for a new round of hunting legislation in the summer of 1857 when an anonymous Charleston subscriber sent a letter to William Porter, the editor of the *Spirit of the Times*. Despite earlier setbacks he optimistically predicted "that a large proportion of the residents of the State will advocate such a Bill and its passage." He focused his commentary on the trapping of quail, which he considered "obnoxious to many sportsmen, and a public nuisance, in its wanton destruction." He recognized the deleterious effects of recent harsh winters on their numbers, but he placed the bulk of the blame for their disappearance on "the avaricious plunder of the poaching pot-hunters." With a note of alarm, he predicted that "in a very few seasons the delightful note of 'Bob White' will not resound to cheer up the heart of the true sportsman, and assure him that a golden season, in the way of sport, awaits his dog and gun." Without a hint of irony, he concluded with a short description of a recent outing during which he bagged fifty-eight woodcock only twenty miles outside of Charleston. He felt that had it not been for his pointer's excitedness, he could have bagged a hundred.[75]

A letter appearing in the *Charleston Courier* in 1857 made several specific suggestions for South Carolina game law, including a statewide hunting season for partridges, doves, songbirds, wild turkey, and deer. In accordance with the New York model, the proposed law targeted Charleston's city markets where hunters customarily dispensed their wares.[76] The following spring a piece in the *Spirit of the Times* sorrowfully noted the failure of a conservation bill during the preceding session of the South Carolina legislature. However, the author felt sure that the "true sportsmen" of the state would "not quietly submit to some half dozen or more old fogy legislators, who preconceive absurd prejudicial notions about game laws being aristocratic and restrictive of every man's right or rights to kill or shoot game birds, turkies, and deer, at any and all times, in disregard of any prohibition or penalty." He blamed the failure of the 1857 effort on intractable upcountry legislators, but he also blamed "every class of pot-hunters."[77] But South Carolina's sportsmen abandoned the fight for meaningful legislation. Try as they might, they could not overcome the taint of aristocratic privilege. This defeat ensured that South Carolina hunting law would remain moribund until Reconstruction.

Statutory hunting law failed in South Carolina, but the struggle for game conservation continued. Rather than advocating the renewal of the struggle in the state house, the anonymous author of an omnibus article entitled "Dogs — Rabies — Game in South Carolina" appearing in the *Spirit of the Times* in the fall of 1858 endorsed the extralegal authority of the rules of sport. Thrilled with the prospect of a delightful fall of hunting, he hoped that "no true sportsman" would "violate a principle so proper as to attempt to hunt until at least the middle or latter end of September, at which period the birds are grown and vigorous in flight." He worried, however, that "some of our most restless and impatient sportsmen" might endorse killing the quail as early as the beginning of September. Because the laws of South Carolina could not restrain these overeager sportsmen or the greedy "gunners," he pinned his hopes on the coercive power of the newly formed Charleston sportsman's club. He promised that the group would "frown down and suppress, as far as lies in our power, all illegal trapping and pot hunting of game within the precincts of our city and the surrounding parishes."[78] Unfortunately for this eager sportsman, the influence of his group appears to have been rather limited. The utility and popularity of hunting, commitment to white male democracy, the indispensability of white unity, and the near nonexistence of law enforcement meant that southern elites could do little more than shake their heads in disapproval.

By the end of the antebellum era, a host of laws moldered on the books; they had proved both unpopular and unenforceable. Even in Virginia, which possessed a two-hundred-year legacy of hunting legislation, the efforts of sportsmen and legislators came to naught. Elisha J. Lewis recognized this critical weakness in his 1851 study, *The American Sportsman,* in which he lamented that "the game-laws of most of our States are a mere bagatelle that no one regards. In other words, they are all a dead letter, and there are few if any persons willing to take upon themselves the trouble and responsibility of enforcing them, or calling willful offenders to account for their many misdeeds." The ideals of sport offered some hope to conservation-minded hunters, but few could actually restrain themselves when presented with the opportunity to make an impressive kill. Indeed, antebellum hunting laws remained so obscure that the writer Alexander Hunter claimed he helped pass Virginia's first hunting laws while serving as a member of the state legislature in 1878.[79]

2. Hunters at Home and in the Field

I love it for the hunting, I love it for the fatigue, I love it for the rest promised,
and never taken, the story telling, the boasting, the freedom from conventional
restraint, and lastly, the promise of the morrow's sport.

"Diving Bell," a Georgia hunter, 1854

IN THE EARLY eighteenth century, most of those who hunted did so out
of necessity. Shooting and trapping game for provisions and exchange
helped men fulfill their role as providers, but as settlement expanded, technology improved, and the number of hunters multiplied, most kinds of
game began dwindling. This decline and the expansion of market agriculture meant that fewer and fewer southerners hunted with purely economic motives. By the early nineteenth century, the vast majority of white
men in the South provided for their families by directing slave labor, spec-
ulating in real estate, mastering a craft, practicing a profession, operating
a business, or tilling the earth. Hunting still provided many yeomen and
poor whites with a source of food, but men of the upper classes increasingly defined hunting as a leisure activity.

Because eighteenth-century writers like William Byrd II and J. Hector
St. John de Crèvecoeur had often associated hunting with idleness, indo-
lence, and sloth, these upper-class antebellum hunters drew a careful distinction between idleness (wasted time) and recreation (a time of rest and
relaxation). Predicated upon the virtue of labor, this distinction distanced
them from the images of the forlorn frontiersman and the dissipated
backwoodsman by drawing upon the bourgeois rationale that a reasonable
measure of amusement yielded a renewed sense of health and vigor. Such
advocates insisted that the hunt was more than a simple diversion. They
maintained that if pursued with moderation, it could actually ensure future productivity. R. L. R. of Charleston, South Carolina, maintained that
hunting "tends to develope the muscles of the body, and gives vigor and
strength to the constitution, enabling the invalid to withstand a greater

degree of labor and endurance."[1] G. T. N. of Danville, Virginia (an inveterate hunter), endorsed a similar position in 1836 when he insisted that his fondness for hunting never "had any injurious effect upon my success in the affairs of life, either in a pecuniary or professional point of view." "For, although it may occasionally have taken an hour from professional duties," he contended, "I am sure it has enabled me to bring to their discharge, afterwards, a clearer head and a healthier body." He recognized that some deemed "all kinds of amusement highly improper—in fact, sinful," but he considered hunting an enjoyable form of exercise and wished he could persuade other men who led sedentary lives to follow his example.[2]

Eagerly promoting their favorite diversion, some hunting advocates took the offensive against their perceived detractors. In the conclusion of his book *Carolina Sports,* South Carolina planter-politician William Elliott launched a vitriolic attack against anyone who denounced hunting as wasteful extravagance. He insisted that "the history of man, in every phase of his existence—in every stage of his progress, from the grossest barbarism to the highest pitch of refinement—shows that *amusement,* under some shape or other is indispensable to him. And if this be so, it is a point of wisdom, and it is even promotive of virtue, to provide him such as are innocent. Field sports are both innocent and manly."[3] A contributor to Charleston's *Southern Quarterly Review* supported Elliott's assertion that hunting provided an "innocent and rational" amusement, but he considered Elliott's defensiveness a bit excessive because he himself had never encountered a "denouncer" of the hunt.[4]

Whether southern hunters took the field for food, entertainment, health, or some combination of the three, they also sought a fourth goal—the affirmation of their masculinity. Sex and skin color endowed white men with a nascent form of masculinity, but most southern men looked for opportunities to demonstrate their masculinity in the context of their communities. Politics, law, planting, business, brawling, and dueling each provided an arena for the demonstration of masculinity, but none of these venues possessed the hunt's combination of excitement, convenience, utility, and drama. As an important part of daily life that took place in a rarefied and almost exclusively homosocial space, hunting provided an important venue for the display of a man's character before a variety of audiences.

This interest in displays of masculinity echoed the southern preoccupation with honor. As intensely social concepts, each required an appreciative audience. Historian Elliott Gorn has explained that southern honor rested upon "reputation, community standing, and the esteem of kin and compatriots." Historian Bertram Wyatt-Brown has developed a similar model; he argued that self-perception depended upon the judgments of the members of the community. This meant "neighbors, not the individual himself, decided when he was a fool, a hero, a useful ornament, or a creature unworthy of comment." Masculinity required an identical form of verification; the type of audience required for validation depended upon the concerns of individual hunters and their standing in their community.[5]

Although women were an important audience for some hunters, more often other hunters became the final arbiters of masculinity. Unlike peripheral audiences (women, slaves, and white men who did not hunt) who assessed the tangible products of the hunt (meat and hides), only fellow hunters could observe the action in the field. Meat and hides helped establish a man's credibility as a provider, but as more and more hunters took the field for recreation, many of them began promoting the act of hunting as an effective barometer of masculinity in itself. Subsistence and market hunting remained important because they helped many hunters maintain their cherished economic independence, but for others, these concerns became increasingly subsidiary to a more intricate conception of masculinity based upon the display of prowess, self-control, and the multifaceted concept of mastery. The hunt provided them with a dramatic stage upon which they could both learn and articulate the qualities of white masculinity with clarity and power.[6]

Masculinity was never a finished product; it required an ongoing process of instruction and self-reflection. Participation in the hunt usually began in boyhood. As they matured, boys learned their first lessons about social expectations and the implications of their nascent membership in a society predicated upon patriarchy and white supremacy. Unlike young girls, most boys began leaving the house at an early age. As they explored the outdoors, they began experimenting with the simplest, most convenient, and least expensive aspects of the hunt—setting traps and training dogs.

Boys and dogs chase after a rabbit. From Charles Wilkins Webber, *The Hunter-Naturalist: Romance of Sporting; or, Wild Scenes and Wild Hunters* (Philadelphia, 1851), 34.

These efforts yielded a succession of snared birds and small animals that were customarily presented to the white women in their households.[7] Although these gifts reassured many mothers that their boys were becoming men, they could not blunt the feeling of loss. Writing to her cousin Josephine Favrot in 1818, Caroline de Clouet Benoist, a Louisiana Creole, seemed saddened by the newfound independence of her young relative Declouet, who accompanied his uncle on his frequent outings to shoot bobolinks. She became frustrated because she "could not prevent them from going out" or from tracking mud through the house when they returned. After one outing Declouet came in with "his shoes in one hand and a box of birds in the other." "His big feet were bleeding from the ice which had cut them," she reported anxiously. "He tried to tell me that it was the blood from the birds which had dripped on his feet (he was wild with delight that he felt nothing) so that I would not forbid him to go out again." Bloody, laden with dead birds, and numb with cold, Declouet seemed to relish his budding masculine power. Benoist, on the other hand, could feel her young charge slipping from her influence into the masculine space of the out-of-doors. "My dear," she sighed, "there is an emptiness here."[8]

Like Declouet, many southern males learned the skills of hunting alongside an experienced hunter who acted as mentor. Some boys, like Nathan Boone, learned from true masters. Finishing his formal schooling at thirteen, he accompanied his father, Daniel Boone, on a hunting trip on the north shore of the Ohio River. After Nathan proved himself by killing his first buck, his father began his schooling in earnest and "took him into the woods and began to teach him the tricks of his woodcraft." Fathers often instructed their sons on the specifics of the hunt, but some left the role of mentor to other male relatives, friends, neighbors, overseers, or trusted slaves. Others apparently followed a third option and emphasized self-reliance. Virginia planter Peter Jefferson simply gave his ten-year-old son Thomas a gun and sent him into the woods. Several hours later the inexperienced boy found a turkey trapped in a pen; he promptly shot it. The intrepid younger Jefferson returned home in triumph. Whether by design or oversight, many young hunters dispensed with tutorials and simply educated themselves through trial and error. Boredom, curiosity, peer approbation, and the opportunity to make some quick cash (from the sale of meat, skins, and feathers) all drove boys into the outdoors.[9]

When men reflected upon the days of their youth, those with mentors often remembered them with fond affection. Locksley, a white hunter from Fort Jesup, Louisiana, used the *American Turf Register* as a venue to reminisce about the "growth of a long life of mutual kindness" between himself and his mentor, a wealthy friend of his parents and a colonel of "true sporting blood." He recalled fondly that he had never seen "greater coolness and command of nerve, when in the field, in any one. Indeed, it was his possessing this faculty in so eminent a degree that rendered him so excellent a hunter, and, under all circumstances, so sure a marksman." Unlike the relationships between slave mentors and their students, which usually ended when the boy reached adulthood, Locksley continued hunting with his mentor as an adult. The durability of this relationship provided him with a final triumph when he was finally able to best his aging tutor. The besting of a white mentor rarely appeared in hunting narratives, but accounts that featured slave mentors invariably included such an eclipse.[10]

The slaves who served as hunting mentors for the sons of their white owners typically were older, trusted members of the households. When these slaves taught their owners' sons the essentials of woodcraft, they often drew upon years of firsthand experience. Their knowledge and station endowed them with a special measure of trust that gave them a favored place in the household hierarchy. Yet while the abilities of slaves in the field might be valued by whites, white hunters never competed with, or felt threatened by, the expertise of their slave auxiliaries. Slaves might provide quality instruction in the essentials of tracking and marksmanship, but white hunters insisted that the loftier qualities of self-control and mastery remained an exclusively white domain.

South Carolina rice planter D. E. Huger Smith learned how to shoot from his father's slave Old Bunc, but he eventually reached a point when he believed that he had surpassed Bunc's knowledge. Afterward, he taught himself through trial and error. Slaves still accompanied him on his hunts, but he described them as nothing more than "small darkey boys."[11] Whatever their disdain for the limits of slave knowledge and perception, some adult white hunters remembered their slave tutors with warm sentimentality. When the wealthy young George Mercer returned to Savannah while on holiday from Princeton, he was touched when his mentor, Pompey, shook his hand "with the warmth of an old friend."[12] Still, Mercer remained the exception; most whites simply discarded these relationships without a second thought once they became confident in their own abilities.

The apprenticeship of young hunters varied in intensity, but it often lasted for several seasons. After the young Baltimorian Frederick Gustavus Skinner killed his first buck in the hills of Frederick County in western Maryland, he confessed his nervousness to his mentor, who he called the "Chief." "Ah, my dear boy!" came the reply. "You cannot expect to become a Nimrod in a day or even many days, so you had better come up here and live for a year or two."[13] Delighted at this invitation, Skinner consulted with his family in Baltimore and ended up spending the rest of the year absorbing his mentor's lessons of quiet praise and silent reproach as well as his occasional expositions on technique and ethics. With fond remembrance Skinner described himself as "a sort of Paul at the feet of this Gamaliel of field sports."[14]

Some writers invoked the authority of aristocratic English precedents when they promoted hunting as a component of a young gentleman's education, but skill in the field never became the monopoly of the wealthy. The sons of yeomen and poor whites often contented themselves with the inexpensive delights of traps and dogs, but those who acquired guns often became expert in their use. Regardless of their social position, white southerners universally agreed that hunting provided white boys with invaluable lessons and experiences, which laid a solid foundation for their future identities as men.[15]

These identities were bound up with white male supremacy. Few white hunters described the entwined development of masculinity and a sense of racial superiority as aptly as Kentucky sportsman Charles Webber. He began his autobiography, *The Hunter-Naturalist,* with an account of a boyhood hunt for squirrel and chipmunk with his dog, Milo, and a young slave, Pompey.[16] Webber's story begins on a winter morning as he and Pompey check their box traps, which they had set around the Kentucky plantation of Webber's father. Marching through the snow, they pull up short when they both spot a sprung trap in the distance. For a moment Webber struggles between boyish excitement and mature self-control. "My heart jumps! I long sorely to run!—Pompey starts off, I call him back! It is necessary I should be dignified—should prove to him and all the world, by my unhurried calmness." As Pompey runs forward, the box trap shakes, and each boy hears "the heavy beat of struggling wings." This proves too much for Webber, and he springs forward. They meet at the box. Disgusted, they find only "a common thieving jay!"[17]

The two boys react in different ways. Webber reels with boyish shame: "I almost stagger with the revulsion of my soaring aspirations." Pompey directs his anger outwards. He unleashes a torrent of "sundry abusive epithets and gabbed threats of neck-wringing" upon the unlucky bird; slipping into a superstitious rage, he yells: "Yah! yah! old feller!—cotch at last! Carry sticks to de debbil, to make fire, burn dis child wid, will you! Da! now you carry sticks to debbil!" With that, Pompey beheads the jay— "and away flutters the obnoxious jay's headless body over the bloodied snow." Endowed with the powers of retrospection, Webber used these struggles with his passions to show himself as a young incipient member of the slaveholding elite, while Pompey's behavior reinforced the dominant white stereotype of African Americans as cowardly and potentially violent savages who remained capable of moments of furious passion despite their ordinarily childlike simplicity.[18]

These early experiences with dogs and traps taught valuable lessons to young white hunters, but whatever the merits of these methods, many boys desired access to what had become a decisive symbol of white masculinity: a gun. Possession of a gun signified more than a step up in equipment. Because state laws prevented slaves from legally owning guns and tradition restricted their use to men, guns acted as talismans of white manhood. They represented the dominion of white men over slaves, animals, and the natural world, as well as their responsibilities toward white women and children as protectors and providers. When combined with the constitutional consecration of the right to bear arms, gun ownership resonated with martial valor and the fraternity of white male democracy.[19]

As the firearms industry became increasingly industrialized, the national rate of gun ownership increased. In the antebellum era these industries developed primarily in the North, yet the rate of gun ownership in the South remained higher than in any other part of the nation.[20] If boys could get them, they began carrying guns as soon as they were physically able. Reflecting on his youth, Savannah lawyer George Mercer happily remembered: "Never, never shall I forget the day when first a gun was mine. It stands out bright among the brightest scenes of my boyhood. I could not compute my happiness. My gun was a treasure without price." Properly equipped, he "became a hunter, a lover of Nature."[21]

Boys often received their first gun as a gift from their fathers or older male relatives. Charles Webber recalled how he pleaded with his father for a rifle and "by one tremendous effort, learned to say my multiplication table backwards, to win it as a reward, and then grasping the bright new weapon, in truculent rage, slew, with my first shot, the audacious intruder [a songbird], as it fluttered in triumph above the house it had usurped." Killing a bird might seem of little consequence, but for Webber it marked another stage in his ascent into manhood. Armed with a gun, he imagined himself defending his father's household, albeit from a rather feeble threat.[22] The death of his first victim and the sight of blood on his hands brought an epiphany; Webber philosophically reflected that "blood, warm, dropping blood, maddens our race, and makes fiends of us." But rather than losing his self-control at the sight of blood, he proved himself worthy of the gift by calmly embracing the "fiercer impulse of the hunter."

Killing could potentially change him into a "fiend," but in his eyes self-control made him "the champion of weakness and the oppressed." He believed that his cool acceptance of the blood distinguished him from his mercurial subordinates — women and slaves. Equipped with a gun, washed in the blood of a songbird, and replete with self-confidence, Webber became a man.[23]

Women occasionally acted as the intermediaries in the gift of guns, but they never presented or received the guns themselves. They could not bestow manhood. Women could interpret and transmit the desires of their kinsmen, but the act of gift giving remained in male hands. Corresponding with her Aunt Lucinda, Octavia Wyche of Meridianville, Alabama, relayed her cousin Fletcher's desire for a percussion-cap gun. Wyche hoped her aunt would pass the information on to her Uncle John, so that he would purchase the gun. Under extraordinary circumstances women might even occasionally use guns, but this was as close as they came to this important exchange.[24]

Once armed, boys sallied forth into the fields and forests around their homes in search of game. Despite their dreams of noble elk and fierce panthers, they usually contented themselves with a variety of small animals. During one long weekend on a plantation outside Savannah, young George Mercer shot "16 black birds, 3 doves, 3 larks, 2 partridges, 2 jack daws, 2 night hawks, 1 snipe, 1 squirrel, 4 blue cranes or herons, 1 scow, (a kind of bittern or heron) 2 blue peters and a large water turkey." For good measure, he also killed several snakes and shot an alligator.[25]

For some boys the promise of earning pocket money provided further encouragement. Trading with local shopkeepers or their parents, boys often exchanged their kills for cash. Low-country North Carolina planter Armand DeRossett Young's childhood diary succinctly described a successful outing as "the good fortune of making a quarter of a dollar by killing a large hawk." Even without guns, boys engaged the market. North Carolina landowner Henry Beasley Ansell remembered that the boys living near the Currituck inlet in tidewater North Carolina employed a variety of hunting equipment, including "birding-clubs," crossbows, rabbit springs, and bird traps. "By this measure," he wrote, "hundreds of strings of dead birds, even sparrows, were shipped to market by the boys, whence were obtained ginger-cakes, tops and other trinkets." Teaching themselves through trial and error, these budding hunters usually pursued small game and birds, which adult whites often considered beneath their notice. The destruction of songbirds frustrated some adults, but most tolerated it as part and parcel of healthy boyhood.[26]

Hunting was an important part of a southern white boy's daily life, but some observers, like aspiring English naturalist Philip Henry Gosse believed that boys spent far too much of their time in the field. Working as a schoolteacher in Dallas County in the Black Belt of central Alabama in 1838, he criticized his students' fixation on hunting because it distracted them from their studies. Hunting inverted Gosse's cerebral world of scholarship and replaced it with the hierarchy of the field, which privileged woodcraft over "book-learning." He lamented that his students remained "incomparably more at home in 'twisting a rabbit,' or treeing a 'possum,' than in conjugating a verb."[27] Rather than judging one another by the standards favored by their foreign teacher, the boys relied upon their own criteria. In their community hunting remained much more important (and exciting) than schoolwork.

As an outsider Gosse characterized rural Alabama as an oddly ordered world. He complained that in the field "the stupid one is expert at all games and exercises; is acquainted with every bird by sight; knows the colour, size, shape, and number of the eggs of each; can lay his paw upon all the nests in the neighbourhood; can ride, swim, trap a mole, shoot a hawk, hook a trout [black bass], like a professed adept." His frustration grew because in this setting "the genius is become a mope; he sees no pleasure in all this; can't learn it when he tries."[28] Despite this frustration and disapproval, Gosse eventually came to believe that the character of the country, a need for self-defense, and the "natural craving for excitement" compelled the boys to hunt. So, despite his reservations as a teacher, Gosse recognized the influence of the natural and cultural environment on his students' priorities. In a final assessment he explained that hunting seemed "the appropriate occupation of a new, grand, luxuriant, wild country like this." Because the inhabitants hunted with "eagerness and zest" at every opportunity, he concluded that a predilection for the hunt must be a desirable trait.[29]

In many communities the youthful friendships between boys eventually evaporated. Farmers' sons and slave boys grew old enough for the fields, while young members of the elite became active in business, pursued their fortunes, began managing family holdings, or went off for schooling. Sometimes boyhood friends made the transition into adulthood together, but more often differences of class, color, and circumstance intervened and pulled them apart.[30]

As they aged, young men began aligning themselves with the expectations of the adult world. They grew from boys into bachelors. Bachelorhood might last for anything from a few months to an entire lifetime (hunting narratives contain a full complement of resolutely unmarried uncles), but regardless of its duration, it composed an important part of a young man's life. Poised on the cusp of manhood but lacking definitive evidence of their masculinity — a wife, legitimate children, or worldly success — many bachelors adopted hunting as a convenient and entertaining instrument for the expression of their emerging manhood.[31] While boys primarily sought the approval of their families and mentors, bachelors turned their aspirations beyond the family circle. As they moved into the broader community, they desired the attention of a wider audience.

The drama of the hunt, the presence of their companions, and the acquisition of fresh meat addressed a variety of audiences, ranging from hunters' peers to their families and slaves, but accomplishments in the field quickly faded, necessitating the pursuit of new triumphs. Bachelors might revel in their freedom from domestic constraint, but they never escaped the burden of repeatedly demonstrating their masculinity. If their performance lagged, their status might slip, depositing them back in the frustrating crèche of boyhood.[32]

From a historical perspective white society may appear static, but from the point of view of the historical actors, especially these bachelors, it remained an arena of unstable flux. Perceptions of an individual's masculinity, in particular, required constant tending. Thus hunting could remain an important vehicle to prove one's manhood well into middle age. This imperative to affirm one's identity in the field subsided in many older hunters, but like those who desired public expression of their wealth or piety, they also often craved an audience.

For most white hunters the most important audience was composed of other men. Unlike the surly frontiersmen described by eighteenth-century writers like Crèvecoeur or the solitary backwoodsmen described by nineteenth-century writers like novelist John Pendleton Kennedy, most nineteenth-century hunters sought the company of other men whenever they went hunting. Hunters who lived in settled districts quickly collected a circle of friends and acquaintances.[33] These fraternities played an important role in the structure of southern society. By bringing white men together in a common endeavor, these groups created an instrument for peer socialization and the authentication of individual masculinity. Because other hunters provided a discerning and reasonably appreciative audience, hunting in groups gave individuals numerous opportunities for display. Perhaps more importantly, these hunts created bonds between white men on a par with those created by church and family.

Loosely organized and infinitely malleable, these fraternities revealed the relative ease with which white men could band together for a common purpose in the antebellum South. White hunters acknowledged certain barriers of class and origin, but in the field they regularly fell into quick and easy camaraderie. In a society based upon patriarchy and white supremacy, commonalities of race and gender usually proved sufficient to create a sense of community. Tensions between sportsman and pothunter might provide grist for the mill of genre writing, but once white hunters took the field together, such differences usually gave way to the overriding qualities of whiteness and maleness.

Some fraternities collected around the influence of a single individual. In these cases an array of friends, neighbors, kin, and visitors orbited around his central presence. Neighborhood hunts usually centered on his home where he played host. When hunters took the field, he usually assumed a position of leadership. He would choose the site of the hunt and arrange and direct other white hunters, the slave huntsmen, and the pack.[34] Neither published narratives nor manuscript sources precisely define the process by which these captains of the hunt assumed their posts, but they usually distinguished themselves with their experience, charisma, and prowess in the field. They also established their position through the mastery of dogs, horses, equipment, slaves, and liquor. Many hosts fortified their standing through generosity. They shared their knowledge and equipment, opened their homes, and even provided other members of the hunt with food and board. As historian Elliott Gorn has observed, "Conviviality became a vehicle for rivalry and emulation."[35]

A fraternity could also form around a stable core of several dedicated hunters. Sharing the duties of host, each contributed a few dogs, horses, or slaves. Such groups usually orbited around two or three avid hunters, but members occasionally brought various friends, relatives, and acquaintances along on their hunts. This flexibility ensured that a wide variety of guests and visitors drifted through, but the core usually remained fairly stable. South Carolina rice planter Keating Simons Ball usually hunted with his kinsman N. Harleston, but he also hunted with other members of the local hunting club (the Wallet Club) and a constellation of neighbors and relatives. On special occasions small groups of relatives and friends made the trip out from Charleston for a visit and a hunt. Just as these hunts strengthened the ties between members of his extended family, Ball's hunts with the other members of the Wallet Club strengthened the bonds between himself and the other plantation owners in his neighborhood. Ball's relationship with Harleston crossed all of these lines: he was a neighbor, a relative, and the president of the Wallet Club. These events formed the core of Ball's social life. A thirty-one-year-old bachelor, Ball lived in what could be a lonely masculine world. The slaves that surrounded him offered no succor (at least none that he acknowledged), but by hunting with his peers from three to six times each month, he made and retained his primary social contacts.[36]

The lines of class and family that defined Ball's pool of possible companions varied in other parts of the South, but the sense that neighbors and relatives made the best companions remained true everywhere. When poor white hunters in the Ozarks went hunting, they too customarily took the field with their blood kin, in-laws, and neighbors. When Taylor Frazier went bear hunting in Marion County, Arkansas, his companions were "Berry Wood, a brother-in-law of mine, and Ozz D. Dearman, one of my half-brothers, and a Mr. Paxton." When they arrived at their campsite on nearby Music Creek, they met up with one of their neighbors, Sam Howard. Because he was also hunting bear, they camped and hunted together for the duration of the outing.[37]

Similar connections functioned for urban professionals. Soon after making his first call as a doctor in the neighborhood around Port Jackson, Florida, novelist Caroline Lee Hentz's son Charles A. Hentz began hunting birds with two other physicians, Dr. Isaac A. Caldwell and Dr. Mitchell. As the young bachelor settled in, he hunted for birds and squirrels with a variety of old and new acquaintances including his father, brother, and his landlord, Hugh Rusk. As time passed, hunting became one of his regular amusements. He and his gradually changing circle of companions rambled around and shot a variety of birds, partly out of scientific curiosity (Hentz made a hobby out of rearticulating their skeletons), but none of them distinguished themselves "by any great deed of sportsmanship."[38]

Informal and amorphous, hunting fraternities sprang up wherever hunters clustered together. Institutionalized fraternities remained something of a rarity, but a handful of hunting clubs cropped up along the eastern seaboard. These clubs were the product of stable and homogeneous communities, and their boundaries usually followed class lines. Individuals could join these clubs fairly easily, but only if they knew an existing member and subsequently proved themselves congenial to the membership as a whole. After a few visits these guests could become members in good standing with a simple majority vote.[39]

Exclusive clubs survived in a few cities and in some areas of the low country because a relatively large number of wealthy candidates lived in the neighborhood. In less intensively developed sections of the South, few official clubs existed. Not many of the communities in other parts of the South could sustain the set-piece exclusivity of the low-country clubs. Because most areas lacked the wealth and stability of the low country, hunters in these areas relied upon less-organized instruments of exclusivity like preexisting friendships, letters of introduction, and invitations.

Hunters desired companions, but fraternities balanced their inclusiveness with exclusivity. By limiting the pool of possible initiates and imposing various social barriers, a hunting fraternity became a bastion of social power. No one mistook the hunt for a neighborhood barbecue, polling station, or church. When a hunter drew up a list of the friends, neighbors, and relatives he considered worth inviting, he constructed a peer group. Unlike such broadly democratic institutions, the hunt drew much of its appeal from its exclusiveness. The first cut proved the easiest—women rarely accompanied these outings. When South Carolina rice planter Thomas Chaplin took the field with his male neighbors and kinsmen, he "emphatically left his wife behind." The absence of women created a homosocial space, which allowed a certain ease while reinforcing hunters' insistence that they were engaged in a rigorously masculine activity.[40] Rather than expressing genuine misogyny, these writers usually presented the exclusion of women as evidence of their affinity for the hunt. One confirmed bachelor extolled the pleasures of masculine companionship in the field. "Speak of love — the charms of a wedded life, — a cheerful fire-side — with the usual incumbrance of a half dozen of squalling children — as the acme of happiness," he remarked, "why, to such who prefer that state I would say, 'Marry, in God's name, and fulfil the scriptural injunction, — 'increase and multiply.'" "But as for me!" he concluded, "give me my dog and gun, a clear October morning, and place me on the 'Blue Ridge,' and I will envy the life of no poor demented creature, who has been silly enough to prefer a *wife* to his *gun!*"[41]

Despite such vehement outbursts, in a handful of communities white hunters actually sought the presence of white women in the field. This only occurred under certain special circumstances, and in all but a few situations, men made it quite clear that when women participated in the hunt, they did so as spectators rather than as actual competitors. Fox-hunting was the form of hunt most accommodating of women because while it insulated most of the participants from the dirty work of the kill, it made the pageantry and excitement of the hunt accessible to all. Customarily the whippers-in (usually slaves) and master of the hunt (an experienced white hunter) directed the pack (which did most of the actual work) with shouts and blasts of their horns. The rest of the hunters simply followed the sound of the pack; this gave them plenty of opportunities for socialization and display. Eager young men often rode wildly after the pack in a thrilling display of horsemanship, but many experienced hunters would hang back, monitoring the progress of the dogs with trained ears and their knowledge of the terrain. Because each hunter determined the intensity of his or her own involvement, women and less enthusiastic men could ride along at whatever speed suited them. Protected from danger, they also had ample opportunities for socialization with the other hunters.[42]

A foxhunt could conclude in one of three ways. Oftentimes the pack lost the scent of the fox. If this happened early in the day, it could cause disappointment (unless the pack quickly located another trail), but if the fox escaped after an hours-long chase, most considered it a satisfactory day out. The second conclusion occurred when a fox "went to earth" — that is, ran into a burrow or den. Again, this could cause frustration among the hunters. Many foxhunters remedied the situation by requisitioning a slave with a shovel. After he dug the fox out, the chase could continue, or they could pop the fox in a sack and save it for the next day. Each of these conclusions possessed certain merits, but nothing proved as satisfying as catching the fox after a good run. In this scenario the pack pulled up to within a few feet of the flagging fox, which usually turned and fought in exhausted and futile desperation. With ferocity and sheer numbers, the pack often killed the fox rather quickly. Before the hounds could tear apart the body, either the master of the hunt or one of the whippers-in waded into the roiling dogs and extracted whatever remained of the fox. After cutting off the tail—or "brush"—he tossed the fox back to the dogs and presented the trophy to the most remarkable rider who was "in at the death."

All three of these scenarios allowed for the participation of women. When women took the field, men showered them with praise and trophies. This effusiveness drained women's accomplishments of any meaning that might put them on a par with the male participants. Women could never compete because the complicity and collusion of their hosts ensured that women participants always "won." Victory meant nothing because it was assured. In the Washington Hunt this combination of influence and powerlessness manifested itself in the promise of a bag fox whenever women took the field. Captured ahead of time and considered unchallenging quarry by many hunters, frightened and disoriented bag foxes ensured an easy chase, usually at a slow, manageable pace. This apparently helped entice women hunters into the field, but their presence and the lack of real challenge made the competition for the kill a secondary concern. If a woman was present at the death of a bag fox, she received the brush. But because the fox had not been able to give the pack a hard run, this prize held no real meaning. The patronizing, saccharine attitude of the men confirmed their dominance.[43]

Only a handful of southerners openly advocated hunting as an acceptable activity for women. The sporting press never encouraged it. Yet on the occasions when women appeared in the field, no one openly denounced their presence. A few even delighted in it. Part of this apparent indifference arose from the type of woman who took the field. Young and unmarried, they stood at the dawn of mature sexuality. Thus they did not seriously threaten the dominant paradigm of gender duality. Poised on the brink of womanhood, these young hunters slipped through the tightly policed boundaries of acceptable female behavior because in the eyes of most white observers (men and women alike), they were not yet fully women.[44]

The correspondence and diaries of Octavia Wyche of Meridianville, Alabama, illustrate the enthusiasm with which some young women hunted. They also dramatize the decisive role that marriage played in circumscribing women's participation in the hunt. The first documentation of Octavia's awareness of women's direct participation in the hunt appears in her correspondence with another young woman, her cousin Olivia. Returning a letter to her cousin "Reel" (Octavia), Olivia praised field sports, not for their social opportunities, but because they were fun. In a glowing description of her hunting exploits, her youthful enthusiasm was unbridled. "Oh Reel," she sighed, "I wish you could see me ride after a fox or cat. I lay right flat on rosy's neck and I just lope through briers and thorn thickets that you could not see anything 3 feet from you in. I come home *minus* a dress skirt." She admitted that "sometimes . . . it is a right *skeary* sight to see a *catamount* as large as a dog standing on his hind feet right *strait* his tusks *shining* an the foam flying from his mouth an I tell you the way he fights is *curious* whip 8 or 10 dogs with ease." She concluded, "If it was not for hunting, I would die with *ennui*." Surprisingly, despite Olivia's loss of clothing and composure, her mother was complacent about her energetic pursuits. "Your Cousin Olivia," she wrote to Octavia, "has improved more than you can well imagine in her personal appearance & is really becoming fat, weighs now 125 & thinks nothing by way of exercise & amusement to Gallop 10 or 15 miles over the hills in a fox chase."[45]

Although Octavia never indicated that she shared her cousin's passion for the hunt, other relatives encouraged her interest. H. C. Wyche, a male cousin and bachelor schoolteacher, advocated hunting as a healthy and exciting diversion. In a letter he posted from Arkansas in 1847, he wrote Octavia: "I wish I had you out here to ramble in the woods, and hunt with me, as I know you would be delighted. How would you like to go a wolf hunting, and see them whip the dogs a fair fight." The following year he again encouraged a trip to Arkansas and promised her abundant deer and turkey. Perhaps his years as a bachelor and his memories of his young cousin gnawed at him, for he concluded his letter by declaring, "I want you to come out here, with Uncle John, and live with us."[46]

Octavia's association with hunting ended once she married William Madison Otey, a merchant and cotton planter, in 1849. Marriage transformed Octavia from a potentially active participant in the hunt to a spectator—a silent judge of her new husband's efforts in the field. After their wedding her only engagement in the outdoor world appears to have consisted of tending her garden and commenting upon her husband's successes and failures in the field.[47] Whatever their interest in hunting before marriage, women retired from the field after they were wed. Sexual maturity closed women's access to the field forever.

Because the action of the hunt took place in the vast reaches of uncultivated land surrounding the farms, plantations, and towns that dotted the South, the vast majority of adult white women could only observe a few select moments of the hunt: expectant departure and triumphant (or crestfallen) return. Sometimes their only knowledge of events in the field came through casual references in their correspondence or snippets of occasional conversation.[48] Women apparently paid the greatest attention to the hunting exploits of boys, whose gender identities had not yet firmed to meet the rigid expectations of adulthood. Their immaturity kept their accomplishments within the purview of mothers and sisters. Writing his mother in January 1820, John T. Barraud of Fluvanna County, in piedmont Virginia, described an unsuccessful hunting outing recently taken by his younger brother Byrd Barraud. "I endeavor to get him to hunt & exercise himself," he complained, "but he is so poor a hand with the gun, that it affords him little pleasure. He went with John & Wilson Cary thro' the snow to the low grounds, to hunt Hares and they came back the most leg wearied party I ever beheld. What made it worse they brought in nothing, not even a snow bird."[49]

Other correspondents enclosed reports of hunters who flooded their families with game. Writing to Ella Noland in March 1849, C. R. Cochran of Middleburg, Virginia, reported, "Your brother William is a monomaniac just now on the subject of wild pigeons—he has a net & is up before light every morning takes a cup of coffee & is off till dinner—yesterday they brought in a hundred & thirty five." Cochran did not view this success with unbridled delight, adding, "I expect we shall eat them till we loathe them as the Israelites did the quails."[50]

Because most of the activity in the field remained hidden from women's view, many hunters believed that women were more interested in the products of the hunt than in the display of masculinity in the field. Tethered to their homes and charged with the maintenance of the household, women were affected by the hunt in fairly mundane ways. As cooks and household managers, they usually focused their assessments of hunters on their contributions to the household economy.[51] Many hunters felt the weight of their expectations. Wealthy as he was, South Carolina planter Thomas Chaplin considered "putting venison on the table in winter" as important as the prospect of associating with his friends in the field.[52]

Limited to judging a hunter's success solely by his ability to provide for his family, women played only a simplified role as arbiters of masculinity. They became mere recipients of a hunter's largesse.[53] This ensured that if men aspired to a more exalted form of masculine identity, they needed to turn to other hunters—preferably other members of a hunting fraternity. In the world of the hunt, the final arbiters of a hunter's masculinity were his male peers. Like politics, law, duels, military service, and business, hunting created a sex-segregated arena for the development and display of masculinity. It was important that women realized men were engaged in a masculine activity when they hunted, but the specifics rarely mattered as long as the hunt was a leisure activity. Indeed, men who provided for their families by other means needed little more than an occasional success in the field. Simply taking the field displayed a measure of masculinity and protected some young men from the "reproach of effeminacy."[54]

Even among other men, however, the provider role was a simple and effective way of conveying a host of meanings, and many hunters dispensed their kills as gifts. Writing in 1829, a low-country sportsman found that while "hunting is a fine and manly amusement," many preferred the gift of venison "to all the exhilaration of the chase." His gift of a choice haunch moved one of his neighbors to express himself in verse: "Thanks, good sir, for your venison, for finer or fatter, Ne'er ranged in a forest, or smoked in a platter." William Elliott enthusiastically touted the pleasures of dispensing game as gifts: "How pleasant to eat! Shall I say it—how much pleasanter to give away! Ah, how such things do win their way to *hearts*—men's, and *women's* too! My young sporting friends, a word in your ear: the worst use you can make of your game, is to eat it yourselves!" These dispensations reinforced the bonds of community (when exchanged among equals) and hegemony (when dispensed to subordinates). No component of the hunt reached audiences of women, nonhunting white men, and slaves as effectively as the gift of game. Regardless of a hunter's method or motive, game provided welcome variety in a monotonous diet that too often consisted of little besides "hogmeat and hoecake."[55]

Although only one hunter could claim credit for the kill, hunters who took the field together regularly divided the meat at the conclusion of a hunt. They could all take some home to distribute it among their family, friends, and neighbors. Different groups of hunters employed various methods when dividing the party's meat, but most awarded a roughly equal share for each white participant.[56] This egalitarian division of meat recognized the cooperative nature of most hunts, bound hunters together as a fraternity, confirmed a certain shared identity as white men, and assured them of a certain measure of prestige when they returned home. Scenes of men bickering over the rightful ownership of a felled deer hardly contributed to the maintenance of an image of benevolent white patriarchy. By containing competition within the action of the hunt itself, this ritual of division reinforced the bonds of the master class and (not incidentally) defused the potential for fratricidal violence.

The social utility of gift giving provided many hunters with an excuse to put aside the requirements of sport. When he hunted in western Maryland as a boy, Frederick Gustavus Skinner's network of gift giving extended as far as Baltimore, where he dispatched game for his friends and family via stagecoach. The prospect of gift giving raised Skinner's "youthful ardor" because it meant he could "go forth and slay without sparing and with a clear conscience, as it would be no violation of my hosts' cynegetic moral code." He excitedly explained, "I might now kill without stint, as there would be no danger of waste."[57] By dispensing their kills as gifts, hunters could transform slaughter into a noble gesture and, in addition, a symbol of their power. Because their game remained divorced from the market, giving it as gifts also aided hunters who defined themselves as sportsmen. By ostentatiously displaying their generosity through gifts, they showed that they did not depend upon their kills for their livelihood. By not taking their rightful share of meat if they hunted with poor white neighbors or guides, some hunters implied that they had surpassed the prosaic motives of their poorer counterparts.[58]

Women's receptiveness to the gift of game meant that some hunters used it to facilitate their entrée into family groups. The most frequent gift giving was that from a bachelor to an unmarried woman. By presenting the gift of game, a suitor illustrated an easily recognizable aspect of white masculinity, his ability as a hunter. Sometimes married hunters continued this practice by presenting game to their in-laws.[59] The second most frequent recipients of hunters' gifts were the bedridden, another segment of southern society that depended on the benevolence of healthy white men. When young Mississippi planter Armand DeRossett Young left his kills to his mother's disposition, "she sent some of them to M John Cawan who is sick of consumption, and is not expected to live more than a month longer." Florida physician Charles Hentz ordinarily shot birds and squirrels with friends as recreation, but when his daughter Molly took ill, he shot doves expressly for her; he noted in his diary, "I carry my gun now all the time for her sake."[60]

Hunters realized that meat satisfied their presumed subordinates, but when they sought to impress their peers, they often relied upon the display of trophies. Because other hunters usually possessed a desire for display, they shared an appreciation for the less prosaic aspects of other hunter's accomplishments. Unlike meat, which can be eaten, trophies were free of any entanglements with practical concerns; they existed only as proof of their owners' abilities.[61] To most audiences, a hunter who emerged from the forest after a rollicking hour-long chase filled with adventure and irrefutably masculine acts carried the same cut of venison as an amateur who might receive a share of the meat from a successful group hunt even if he never fired his gun. But to another hunter a trophy (be it a rack of antlers or a bearskin rug) preserved the transcendent moment of the kill and provided a physical representation of hunting acumen. It was more than meat.

Once they brought their trophies home, many hunters placed them around their houses as a permanent display. When Major Hazzard, a low-country planter, showed the visiting poet William J. Grayson his immense double-barreled gun and assured him that "it was fatal to every buck or doe that came within its range," he supported his claim with the antlers of his numerous victims, which were nailed to a large live oak near the front door of his home. This desire for display cut across class lines. While traveling through the Ozarks in 1818, inexperienced adventurer Henry Rowe

Schoolcraft encountered an Arkansas backwoodsman who had covered his mountain cabin with an "innumerable quantity of deer, bear, and other skins, which had been from time to time stretched out, and hung up to dry on poles and trees around the house." This display retained some functionality, but he also festooned the interior of his home with "horns of deer and buffaloe, rifles, shot-pouches, leather-coats, dried meat, and other articles." Not everyone required such grand displays. A wealthy hunter in low-country South Carolina discreetly commemorated his accomplishments with rows of small ivory pegs that embellished the stock of his prized Wesley Richards shotgun. Each represented a deer that he had killed.[62]

Because most white hunters placed a premium upon impressive trophies, they often ignored smaller game. In an article that appeared in the *Spirit of the Times* in 1839, a Mississippi hunter explained that in his neighborhood few hunted partridge and squirrels, "for why disturb the proud covey and the nut-loving family when on every side you may bleed the fallow deer and stop the invading and destroying march of that fatter, bigger and sweeter Doge of the forest, called the bear?"[63] Some southerners, like Virginia agricultural reformer Edmund Ruffin, considered all hunting except trophy hunting uninteresting. Writing in his diary, Ruffin confided that although he had "no fancy for pursuing small game of any sort," he never lost his desire for hunting large, toothy game like bears, wolves, or alligators.[64] When a *Harper's* correspondent asked Dan Griffin, a professional hunter from Louisiana, what he thought of shooting birds, he insisted that he had "never made feathers fly, nor with powder and lead broke a bone that *hadn't marrow in it.*" Proudly he explained that "Confessor," his rifle, "would blot such a bird perfectly out of existence."[65]

Because inexperienced hunters often relied upon trophies as proof of their masculinity, they frequently placed the integrity of their trophies above enjoyment of the hunt. After killing his first buck, the young Frederick Gustavus Skinner waded across a frigid stream and proposed standing guard over the body while the other members of his party continued their hunt. "What did I care," he asked, "for marked trees or the scenery of the glades or anything else in comparison with this noble trophy of my prowess?"[66] He eventually relented, but only when his mentor convinced him that it would remain safe until their party picked it up on their return from perambulating through the Maryland woods.

Even experienced hunters depended upon trophies for the maintenance of their prestige. After an unsuccessful encounter with a panther in the White River valley of the Arkansas Ozarks, German sojourner Frederick Gerstäcker's friend and hunting companion old man Konwell insisted on taking the field as soon as possible so that the two men could redeem their reputations as hunters. "If we did not," he reminded Gerstäcker, "the neighbors would begin to believe that we were no longer good enough to kill even a deer."[67]

This pressure made some hunters rather contentious when awarding credit for a kill. When a deer dropped dead after running a gauntlet of Mississippi hunters, it left some doubt about who had drawn first blood. One of the hunters fell to his hands and knees and began examining the ground around his position, desperately searching for a single drop of blood, "as that would entitle him to the hide and horns — the meat being common property." Hunters could share the meat, and therefore the praise of their subordinates, but as a symbol of prestige, the trophy itself remained indivisible. The inedible portions of the game — hide, teeth, claws, tail, ears, and antlers — became the property of whoever dealt the mortal blow.[68]

As a supplement for physical trophies, some hunters created virtual trophies with their imaginations and rhetorical skills. When hunters composed hunting narratives, they usually featured their own triumphs. In essence, storytelling acted as another form of trophy taking — one that could potentially appeal to a national audience. Under layers of humor and adventure, almost every hunting story celebrated a triumph. Through spoken and written narratives, these hunters promoted their accomplishments as surely as any taxidermist. Those who commemorated their triumphs in words or in print preserved the memory of their achievements and communicated it to a wider audience. Whether related around a campfire, printed in a local newspaper, or published in a national periodical, hunting stories celebrated the prowess of their authors and their companions. The authors of hunting stories customarily identified themselves with their initials or with pseudonyms. These modest steps concealed their identity from a national audience, but for the audiences that southern hunters really valued (their fraternities and families), the identity of these authors probably remained clear.

Whatever their motives or their attitude toward the game they pursued, white hunters rarely discarded their kills. Hunters always told stories of the "one that got away," but the meat and trophies they brought home provided proof of the "one that didn't." Hunters took great pains to display this irrefutable evidence of their masculinity to the widest possible set of audiences. When they returned from the field, hunters displayed their kills by looping them around their necks, throwing them across their pommels, or hanging them from the front of their carriages.[69] When they engaged in these displays, hunters never forgot about the visceral products of the hunt. Even if it required backbreaking labor (at least on the part of slaves), they brought the meat and hides of their kills in from the woods and distributed them among their family, friends, and neighbors. By appealing to every conceivable audience, the dead animals that hunters brought home satisfied notions of "hunter as provider," while simultaneously affirming peer-oriented notions about the display of prowess, self-control, and mastery.

3. Hunting and the Masculine Ideal

Our sports are various, surpassingly exciting, and every way, manly.

A Mississippi hunter, 1839

SET APART from the everyday world but still intimately associated with it, the hunt created a stage for the performance of an evocative drama of white manhood. Thus it provided fertile ground for antebellum authors to create a varied but coherent image of the hunter as a masculine ideal. The particulars of this iconic image varied from author to author, but it retained a core set of characteristics that remained remarkably constant throughout the antebellum era.[1]

These characteristics included prowess, self-control, and mastery. The first usually emerged through competition. Manifest in hunting skill, it facilitated success in the field. It was attractive to men of all classes, colors, and communities because of its efficacy and simplicity. The second quality, self-control, supplemented prowess with a gloss of rationality that elevated the accomplishments of hunters above mere physicality. It added the triumph of the mind to that of the body. Mastery composed the third, distinctively southern, element of the ideal. Representing control over other people, animals, nature, and even death, this multifaceted concept helped white southern men define themselves as patriarchs and even, in some cases, as paternalists.

By blending these elements, hunting narratives offered up the image of an idealized hunter whose actions and demeanor fortified both the righteousness of slavery and the dominance of white males. This ideal gradually developed a class component based upon the idea of sport; nevertheless, it remained remarkably inclusive. Predicated on whiteness and maleness rather than wealth or ancestry, this image of the masculine ideal appealed to white men throughout the antebellum South. It made them, one and all, potential members of a "master class."

The role of the hunter as a masculine icon diffused into southern culture through a variety of channels. The polar ideals of noble savages and European hunter-aristocrats informed popular perceptions of the hunt throughout the eighteenth and early nineteenth centuries, but an important shift in popular culture came in the late 1820s when a number of developments made hunters an increasingly popular model of white manhood. During this period the appearance of James Fenimore Cooper's fictional "Leather-Stocking," Natty Bumppo, the proliferation of biographies of frontiersmen like Daniel Boone, the boisterous national presence of Indian fighter–turned–politician Andrew Jackson, and the dissemination of hunting narratives through the various books and periodicals of the sporting press infused the South with images of the hunter as a model of masculinity. This idea gathered strength and influence throughout the antebellum era, and white southerners embraced the image of the hunter with growing enthusiasm. The clearest descriptions of these expectations appeared in the sporting press, but the private writings of southern hunters revealed comparable conventions.[2]

Foremost among these characteristics was a carefully crafted form of competitiveness and an attendant desire for display. Few white hunters celebrated the merits of solitary travail; instead they glorified open competition with other white males because their triumphs and defeats in the field meant little unless observed by others. The desire for competition sprang from deep roots, which extended back into the colonial era. Historian T. H. Breen noted the importance of this aggressive competitiveness in his examination of horse racing among the gentry in the colonial Chesapeake. Competitiveness flowered in this young, dynamic society because it provided plenty of situations for the display of prowess. This bundle of masculine qualities, which (in the words of historian Nancy Struna) consisted of "strength, skill, bravery, and even gallantry," provided a solid, easily recognizable foundation for masculinity. Associated with the ability to achieve wealth and power, prowess not only differentiated successful hunters from women (the essential definition of masculinity), it also elevated them above less capable men.[3]

Rather than turning hunters against one another, competition actually bound them together. They were united by a common challenge: the pursuit of game. In his editorial for the initial issue of the *American Turf Register,* J. S. Skinner described competitiveness as an effective instrument of community building. He contended that while "sympathy springs from habits of association and a sense of mutual dependence on each other, the true estimate of character, and friendly and generous dispositions, are under no circumstances more certainly acquired, nor more assuredly improved and quickened than by often meeting each other in the friendly contentions and rivalries that characterise field sports." As a form of recreation, hunting transformed the "contentions and rivalries" that might ordinarily inspire animosity into the raw material upon which friendship and community could be constructed. Hunters celebrated competition because it helped them identify worthwhile companions—companions who could accurately judge their own achievements in the field. Other hunters acted as competitors, but their most important function was as an audience.[4]

Because competition often inflamed the passions, it provided an excellent catalyst for the display of self-control. The romantic celebration of a passionate temperament appealed to some southerners, but others worried that fierce competition might collapse the barriers that they had assiduously erected around their passions. White southerners occasionally reveled in their passions, but most feared the dangers of excess. Everard Green Baker, a thoughtful young planter from Panola, Mississippi, recognized his own internal struggle between passion and reason. He privately hoped "that God will give me grace to put down anything like passion—that my unclouded reason may always be triumphant, for I never give away to a burst of passion towards any one that I do not regret afterwards."[5] Most white southerners would have echoed Green's private homily. Self-control was an extension of an individual's will and demonstrated his capacity for mastering his own passions.

Self-control became particularly important for white males because they wielded such tremendous power. Steeped in an Old Testament vision of household patriarchy, many believed they held a divinely sanctioned monopoly on authority and leadership. In the words of historian Donald Mathews, they styled themselves as "Lords of Creation." By reinforcing the subordination of white women, slaves, children, and the natural world, the institutions of marriage, slavery, parenthood, and property ownership all supported this conclusion.[6] In the eyes of most white males, other southerners simply lacked the biological prerequisites for self-control. When white women or slaves appeared in hunting stories, for instance, white males almost invariably described them as weak-willed dependents. This ascribed inferiority also helped justify the dominance of white males over black males. As historian Dorothy Ann Gay has aptly noted, white men "never questioned the propriety of ruling over those they considered incapable of ruling themselves." Hunting gave them the opportunity to prove themselves worthy of this mantle of power.[7]

Believing they were charged with the protection of the weak and dependent in their midst, white men viewed "unclouded reason" as a prerequisite for fulfilling their divinely sanctioned responsibilities. Influenced by this ideal, as well as strains of evangelicalism that preached self-reliance, many whites advocated self-control because they realized that the excesses of unbridled passion could transform their allegedly benevolent patriarchal authority into the tyranny of petty despotism. Maintaining that the ability to restrain one's passions came from within, these southerners felt that a man who displayed self-control reinforced his claims over his household and property, justifying the perpetuation of patriarchy.[8]

In the field these patriarchs were interested in displaying not only their self-control but also their physical prowess in competition with other hunters. These goals of self-control, prowess, and competition balanced each other. Indeed, by the 1830s self-control had become an important component of prowess.[9] Self-control aided the display of prowess for two reasons. The first was strictly pragmatic: it increased a hunter's chances for success — calmness improved marksmanship, coolness prevented hasty decision making, and silence concealed the hunter from his prey. This concern for self-control was not related to class or status because anyone with experience in the field easily understood the functional benefits of self-control. Ozark subsistence hunters valued self-control for the same utilitarian reasons that Black Belt planters did.[10] Raucous valor was only appropriate on foxhunts, where dogs and drivers performed most of the actual work. In this case recklessness could intensify a foxhunter's display of horsemanship, but it never helped make a kill.

The second benefit of self-control involved display. Hunters appreciated the effectiveness of restraint in the field, but self-control gradually became important in its own right. In an article appearing in the *Spirit of the Times* in 1851, Charleston's S. L. C. recommended composure both before and after the kill. "You feel an exultation beside the fallen deer which many have failed to experience in the moment of much more important triumphs," he noted. "But of course you will take care to conceal this when your comrades come up—of course it is nothing to you to kill a deer."[11] Those who dispensed death with poise improved their chances for making the kill, but if they presented a sufficiently cool and competent demeanor, actual success became almost unnecessary. In some circles the emphasis on display meant that simply appearing competent became as important as actual ability. These dual benefits ensured that hunters who developed control over their passions improved their standing among all audiences. Fellow hunters could admire a hunter's composure in the field, while his dependents took note of more tangible accomplishments like the acquisition of meat.

Prowess and self-control appealed to men throughout the United States, but white southerners appended a third critical element to these qualities: mastery. Many northern hunters valued their ability to influence their social subordinates, but these sentiments paled when compared with the eager confidence with which their southern brethren pursued this essential component of southern masculinity. Whether it was expressed as dominion over women, slaves, domestic animals, property, nature, or death, southern hunters craved proof that they could control the world outside of themselves. This wide-ranging desire fixed itself upon every feature of the southern landscape with one exception: other white men. Implicitly equal in their whiteness and maleness, hunters never questioned the legitimacy of another man's independence and autonomy. Wealthy sportsmen might grouse about the depredations of pothunters, but the importance of maintaining white supremacy prevented them from deriding their manliness or their authority over their own households.

White hunters predicated mastery of others upon mastery of the self, and if a hunter could control his passions, his sphere of potential mastery quickly expanded. Once hunters sampled this mastery of self, they began seeking the expansion of their power and influence over others. This often began with dogs and horses. Because they played critical roles in most hunts, dogs and horses provided hunters with the opportunity to develop and display an essential preindustrial skill: the mastery of domestic animals.[12] Born of simple necessity, this form of power also created superb opportunities for display. Obedient dogs and horses provided evidence of mastery, and advice about how best to control them regularly emphasized the power of the individual will. Differences of opinion arose, however, about the appropriate way for a hunter to assert his will over his animal auxiliaries. One school of thought, championed by *American Turf Register* editor John Stuart Skinner, instructed hunters to "never let your dog have a will of his own."[13] The proponents of this school believed hunters should crush the will of their animals, which would subsequently obey their masters only out of fear. Other hunters, notably Alabama editor and sporting aficionado Johnson Jones Hooper, advocated the moderate use of the whip but discouraged breaking dogs entirely. "After all toying or coaxing fails," Hooper advised, "then you must try the virtue of the lash, remembering always to use it in moderation, and be very careful that you do not cow your puppy." Although he encouraged a light hand, he felt that those who discarded the whip entirely "are persons who would not in the field, among dogs which found and pointed birds, know the difference between a perfectly well-broken pointer and a 'pot-hunting cur.'"[14]

Hooper and Skinner disagreed about the intensity of corporal punishment, but neither questioned the efficacy of the whip because they both felt that without the firm hand of a capable master, dogs became a liability. Poorly trained dogs could wreck an outing in any number of ways. In 1838 a Virginia hunter testily explained that with a dog that was "self-willed, intractable, and unsteady, no really good sport can be had." He complained that when such a dog took the field, "the legitimate pleasures are marred and converted into unspeakable vexations. The sportsman becomes exhausted with fatigue in his efforts to control his dog, and loses his temper and his patience, and almost vows never to take gun in hand again when he finds all his efforts unavailing."[15] On the other hand, dogs that obeyed their masters proved invaluable aids in most forms of the hunt. They also displayed their owner's mastery before an appreciative audience.

Although hunters everywhere sought control over their animals, the powers of mastery and command over chattel were particularly prized in the South because of the presence of slaves. Indeed, many slaveholders dealt with their slaves in the same manner as their animals. Hunters never fully amalgamated their ideas about mastery of domestic animals and mastery of slaves, but they did employ remarkably similar language. Many hunting narratives blended the descriptions of dogs and slaves, making one almost indistinguishable from the other. Arriving at his host's plantation home in western Kentucky, the author of "The Big Buck," an 1854 *Spirit of the Times* story, described a scene in which dogs and slaves tumbled together in a display of eager fealty. "Such a hullaballo as greeted us when we alit at the gate!" he wrote. "The hounds had first discovered us, and, to the shout of their master, gave us a reverberating echo. Then the picanninnies came pouring in sooty legions out of the cabins of the extensive 'quarter' which flanked the mansion in the background—their black, shiny faces, stretched in yells and grins, exhibiting an ivory ecstacy of delight at the return of 'Massa Jack'—while the hounds nearly tumbled us into the dirt with their rude gambols."[16]

Several such stories aggregated slaves and domestic animals or sandwiched descriptions of slaves between those of dogs and horses. Some made this association with casual indifference. After a group of Mississippi hunters killed more deer than they could eat in 1840, one of them remarked, "We kill so much venison here that we are obliged to give it to the niggers and dogs to keep it from spoiling." When the WPA interviewed Ruby Mosley of San Augustine, Texas, in the early 1930s, she showed little hesitation in remarking that she and her family regarded slaves "as people of today regard dogs and livestock. We were good and kind to our slaves, took care of them as if they were fine horses."[17]

Embedded in a culture of racism, slaveholders readily associated the behavior of dogs and slaves regardless of the latter's undeniable humanity. As human beings, slaves presented their owners with a much wider range of responses and forms of resistance than dogs, but white hunters still judged the performance of slaves and dogs with remarkably similar criteria. Many slaveholders even believed that slaves required the firm hand of a master because, like dogs, they lacked the capacity for self-control. Without the lash, slaveholders felt that they could expect nothing but trouble and disappointment from their slaves.

Because white hunters created a parallel between dogs and slaves, many believed that hunting provided an excellent primer for the development of the habits of authority and the tones of command expected of a slave-holder. Capable control of the "equipment" of the hunt translated into a potential for mastery in the wider world. The direction of slaves on the field provided young slaveholders with some of their first lessons in utilizing slaves' knowledge and labor for their own ends.[18] As they grew more experienced, young white men could use the hunt as a showcase for the display of their growing capacity for mastery. Prize dogs, horses, and especially competent slaves all reflected favorably upon the character of their owners. Slaveholders especially appreciated slaves, dogs, and horses that took action with a minimum of prompting and total disregard for self-preservation. They attributed this reckless eagerness as a demonstration of the depth of their owner's power.

Slaveholders could easily adopt the advice of Hooper and Skinner on dogs as policy in slave management. Slaveholders and dog trainers alike promised that willingness to use the lash made its actual use increasingly unnecessary. They argued that the mere threat of punishment could be effective as long as it was backed by force. This made controlling slaves (or dogs and horses) without corporal punishment the ultimate proof of mastery and a necessary prerequisite of paternalism. Whatever their methods, slaveholding hunters confidently translated their command of a handful of trusted slaves in the field into proof of a permanent, preeminent mastery over all African Americans.

By marshaling an array of equipment (often including guns, slaves, dogs, and horses), hunters demonstrated their mastery of their property. This assisted them in their attempts to prove their dominion over the natural world. Surveying, clearing, fencing, and planting all provided visible proof of their power over the land, but without the physical evidence of stumps and ordered rows that represented mastery over their fields, many struggled in their attempts to prove their mastery over the forests, swamps, and marshes that surrounded their farms and plantations. Mastery over uncleared land proved a difficult proposition, but nothing dramatized this dominion more effectively than killing. Even if hunters could not exert their control over the terrain, they could prove their power over the lives of individual animals. By dispensing death with cool composure, hunters proved their dominion over discrete but symbolically important elements of the natural world with dramatic finality. Nothing demonstrated mastery as unequivocally as the taking of life, so for many the kill and the delivery of the trophy to the hearth became an essential act of domination.[19]

Nothing revealed the character of a hunter better than the moment of the kill—a neatly bundled moment of prowess, self-control, and mastery. Hunters exuded hearty masculinity when at rest, but they appeared their manliest after killing an animal. Describing a hunter who finished off a wounded deer with his knife, Florida planter William Stockton exploded with praise. "While the red knife in his hand told that lead and steel had both done their duty," he marveled, "I could not help thinking that I never had seen a finer figure and attitude as he stood firm and erect, the cap thrown slightly back, and high excitement marked on his face, giving clearness to his brow and brightness to his eye."[20]

White hunters always congratulated novice hunters when they killed because it illustrated the emergence of their incipient mastery. When Geordy, an inexperienced hunter, killed his first buck, William Elliott advised him, "You have done well to *kill*—let it grow into a habit."[21] He made it clear that a good hunter killed; he did not simply wound, and he certainly did not miss. Most hunting narratives thus concluded at the moment of the kill. Prowess, self-control, and mastery all converged in this satisfying climax.

Hunting was never easy; it usually required a measure of experience, some skill, and more than a little luck. Not surprisingly, some novices struggled in their quest for their essential first kill. A Mississippian remembered his first deer hunt as an exercise in frustration. Visiting a friend's plantation in the Yazoo hills outside Vicksburg in 1840, he took the field with a party of four. "The two standers, besides myself, were young at the business, and I was a perfect tyro," he recalled. "Before that day I had never killed but one deer, and had only been hunting three or four times in my life. However, I could kill partridges well enough, and thought that as the deer was larger than a partridge it was so much the more easily killed. Never was I more mistaken in my life." While the hunt's pack coursed the wood, he waited in his stand. Time passed, but he finally heard and then saw a wounded buck crashing through the underbrush. He mastered his beating heart and "let him have it, right and left,—bang! bang!—20 buck-shot in each barrel, but, alas! no venison. Then came the jokes." His host scolded him for missing, while his companions demanded an extra measure of marksmanship and complained that his shot "rattled all around them," endangering their lives. Shaken, the members of the hunt "patched up the peace by taking sundry strong pulls at our bottle."[22]

The day following his conspicuous lack of success, the frustrated Mississippian's ill fortune continued. In the midst of a chase after deer, his horse bolted. After regaining control, he wrote the day off and headed for home, but here his luck turned. Riding through the forest, he came upon a strange tableau: an unwounded buck fighting several slave dogs. Unaware of his presence, the buck kicked several of the dogs, and "after finding that he has impressed them with a suitable respect for his dignity—he walked slowly up the hill towards me with as much complacency as if he had won a noble and most gallant action." The hunter felt he "should in all probability have let him pass without even giving a salute," but his memories of the "jeers of Sunday" drove away his feelings of compassion. He no longer possessed any desire other than "that of having the laugh this time on my side—for the others I knew would get nothing—so I up gun and let him have it." After he fired, the dogs turned upon the stricken buck and fought in earnest. The novice, with his blood up, waded in and dispatched him with his hunting knife. Tasting triumph and shaking off the derision of his peers, he became an enthusiastic hunter, claiming that he killed sixty-eight deer in the following twenty days. Enticed by the varied delights of the field, he concluded his letter with a request for some foxhunting pups.[23]

Having proved themselves with innumerable victories, a few extremely confident hunters illustrated the totality of their command over themselves and others by restraining themselves at the moment of the kill.[24] J. S. Skinner's grandson, F. G. Skinner, proved his self-control and reinforced his claims of mastery through temporary restraint. On an outing in western Maryland in the 1830s, he and his mentor, Campbell, came upon an isolated pool covered with waterfowl. Caught by the beauty of the moment, they watched the birds moving across the surface of the water. Transfixed, Skinner described the changing tenor of their feelings as they viewed the scene: "We were in no hurry to convert this idyl of the wilderness into a scene of slaughter and terror, but the angel of mercy who havored over us for a moment fled away on drooping wing before the fierce venatic instinct to kill." Unleashed, they poured in shot with their ten-bore shotguns, killing ten blue-winged teal. Their spaniels also proved their quality (and the power of their masters) by remaining "motionless and as silent as if turned to stone" until released.[25] Displays of even momentary restraint remain remarkably rare, even though the sporting press discouraged wanton killing. Hunters saw self-control as an instrument in achieving the kill, not as its equivalent. When other hunters judged these moments of restraint, they took the hunter's previous accomplishments into account, but because uninformed observers might accidentally mistake a moment of self-control for the nervous inaction of the "buck ague," hunters rarely restrained themselves. Even for an experienced white hunter, the kill remained the quintessence of the hunting experience; it distinguished hunters from the less worthy ranks of spectators and dependents.

Killing and the effective use of violence remained popular and potent demonstrations of masculinity throughout antebellum America, but they were especially important for white southerners. The southern penchant for violence took many forms, but contemporary observers and later historians agree that the antebellum South was by any measure an exceptionally violent place. Explanations for the pervasiveness of southern violence vary. Some blamed the persistence and proximity of the lawless frontier, while others located the wellspring of violence in white southerners' obsession with honor. Convoluted motivations and local variation make this a skein that defies easy untangling, but whatever the manifold sources of violence, the presence of slavery certainly played an important role in its expression and ubiquity. Thomas Jefferson blamed the presence of slavery for its pernicious influence upon the character of young slaveholders. Raised as tyrants in an atmosphere of "unremitting despotism," he believed that they almost inevitably matured into violent and tempestuous adults.[26]

Slavery may have nurtured a preternatural predilection for violence among certain individuals, but it also encouraged the coolly rational use of violence as an instrument of social control. Because most southern whites respected the efficacy of violence, the mastery of death became an integral component of white masculinity. As long as violent behavior served acceptable ends, it remained a useful tool of the master class. Because of this, many linked the mastery of violence to the concepts of

prowess and self-control, which together reduced the potential for irra-
tional volatility. The violence of a carefully aimed rifle shot that brought
down a prize buck was a far cry from the volatility of an angry mob.

White southerners' preoccupation with violence sprang from their place
at the pinnacle of a slave society. Maintaining the stability of their position required constant vigilance and the decisive use of force in moments
of crisis. Nothing displayed the presence of these instruments of social
control as effectively as the orchestrated, organized, and tightly focused
violence of the hunt. Hunting not only provided training for such moments, it also revealed the willingness and ability of white southerners to
use force in a very public way. The imagery of a group of white hunters
and their dogs returning from the forest with a dead deer resonated with
meaning, especially for the population of enslaved African Americans. For
a slave contemplating escape or insurrection, it was a stark reminder of
the power of white hunters to track down and kill their defenseless quarry.

The pervasive violence of southern culture fed a predilection for mili-
tarism. Many writers associated it with hunting because the presence of
guns, horses, and killing provided opportunities to display a semblance
of martial valor. Whatever the game (with the exception of foxes, opossums, and raccoons, which were commonly hunted with dogs rather than
guns), hunting developed the mental concentration, dexterity, and strength
necessary for good marksmanship. Unlike the raucous, drunken ineptitude of militia musters or the unhurried staginess of target shooting, hunting (with its deployment of forces over varied terrain, long, boring lulls,
uncertain pace, and sudden moments of wrenching action) at least hinted
at the rigors of combat. Southern elites valued the homegrown martial
abilities of frontiersmen and backwoodsmen, but when they described
various hunting skills and their martial application in the sporting press,
they created a measure of class distinction. The most aristocratic forms
of the hunt, like foxhunting and deer driving, emphasized the development of the skills expected of officers: horsemanship, land navigation,
and leadership. For these forms of the hunt, success often relied as much
upon the effective deployment of forces across the field as on basic skills
with horse and gun. On the other hand, the forms of hunting most often
associated with poor whites (such as stalking game on foot, raccoon and
opossum hunting, and firehunting) stressed marksmanship and endurance

—the skills of the foot soldier. Still, it is important not to overstate such class distinctions, as they were never rigorous.[27]

The association between hunting and war encouraged the use of military metaphors in the descriptions of hunting expeditions. The hunt became "the campaign," and the action of the dogs and hunters became that of maneuvering troops. The cry of the hounds reminded one Baltimorian of "the roar of artillery at the battle of Austerlitz," while an Arkansan likened the movement of the dogs in the field to that of light troops. Hunters with no apparent military experience—at least with the campaigns they cited—favorably compared their hunts with the great battles of the Napoleonic Wars, which "were never half so exciting."[28] Many writers placed themselves in the center of these fantastic battles by assuming officers' rank. Hunting stories were populated with majors, colonels, and generals. Some drew these titles from the militia or from past military experience, but many of these titles were strictly honorary. A group of Memphis hunters who took the field in 1859 conferred commissions upon themselves with unbridled enthusiasm, but after appointing their "Captain-in-Chief" and naming themselves "First Lieutenants," they realized that the single slave who accompanied them "made up the rank and file, sutler, and man of all work" of their little army.[29]

Regardless of such comic-opera moments, most white hunters still considered hunting legitimate training for war. By portraying the hunt as a war game, they drew it further into the male domain, strengthening their claims of masculinity and clothing their accomplishments in the garb of martial glory.[30] Hunters reinforced their association with the masculine world of the military by describing nervous shooters as "hysterical women" and identifying accomplished marksmen as cool, competitive, and masterful models of masculinity.[31] Women watched and listened on the margins of this warlike world, while boys yearned for the day they could cross over into it.

A story entitled "A Panther Hunt on the Blue Ridge" summarizes the qualities that made the hunter a masculine ideal. Written by the pseudonymous Seebright of Virginia and published in the *Spirit of the Times* in two parts over the winter of 1837–38, the story features a model hunter, Moreland, who displays almost all the virtues of white southern manhood. Physically

an Adonis, he is "the very picture of health and activity. . . . He was tall
and well-made, compact in every limb; there was not one ounce of superfluous flesh about him: all was muscle and sinew." Active and healthy, he
seems incapable of idleness, but his constant motion never lacked purpose.
Easily demonstrated and instantly recognizable, prowess provided Seebright with an excellent foundation for Moreland's masculinity.

Mentally, Moreland effortlessly alternates between the two often competitive qualities: passion and self-control. Seebright astutely set them in
opposition—this tension intensified each quality. He first drew attention
to Moreland's proclivity for action, noting, "He was a high-spirited fellow,
incapable of restraint, impetuous in the extreme." Yet in the course of the
narrative, Moreland repeatedly reins in his passions, strengthening the display of his self-control. The depths of his "mastery of self" appear in the
climax of the story, when he faces a fierce, wounded panther with deadly
poise. In calmer moments Moreland consistently displays his mastery over
others with ease and practiced self-confidence. No one ever questions his
authority. Moreland's confidence makes him a jovial companion. Socially
adept, "he was the life and soul of every party for ten miles round" and
moves easily among his peers and subordinates.[32]

Moreland's total command of the three elements of masculinity—
prowess, self-control, and mastery—have one final effect: they give him
enough confidence to act the paternalist. As an avatar of the masculine
ideal, Moreland competently achieves this summit of white male accomplishment. Manifested as a sense of noblesse oblige and Christian charity,
Moreland's paternalism depends upon his absolute self-confidence and
the security of his position. He defends the weak, cares for the members
of his household (black and white), and freely shares his time and riches
with his friends. At its acme, Seebright reminded his readers, mastery beget
the self-confidence that allowed one to become truly "generous and hu-
mane." In Seebright's eyes Moreland was truly one of the "Lords of Creation." Healthy and capable, passionate but restrained, masterful and
paternalistic, such hunters provided ideal building blocks for southern
society. Their masculine virtues strengthened the ideal of democratic relations among free white men and the dominant ideology of household-
based patriarchy.[33]

Because hunting dramatized masculinity so effectively, these paragons of white masculinity achieved their standing without any overt representation of their sexuality. Rather than pursuing the incontrovertible proofs of marriage or fatherhood, many hunters displayed their manhood through an alternative path to masculinity — the hunt. Bachelors could use hunting as a substitute for marriage, but they could also employ it to substantiate their worthiness as suitors. Married men had already achieved a level of masculine display, but they could still use the drama of an occasional kill to reinforce their status as heads of household. Because hunting provided such a wide variety of opportunities for the display of masculine virtues, most white men could use it to broaden and deepen their masculine image. Few filled the mold as ideally as Moreland, but when taken together, the hunters who appeared in the sporting press provided an inclusive trope for white masculinity which remained remarkably consistent throughout the antebellum era.

Taken up during boyhood, hunting provided white men with much more than a salve for boredom. By mixing the straightforward efficacy of prowess, the critical leaven of self-control, and the multifaceted elements of mastery, white hunters transformed hunting into an elaborate exhibition of masculinity. Of the three, mastery had the greatest impact on southern society. Predicated upon control of individual passions, mastery potentially included dominion over women, slaves, domestic animals, property, nature, and (through the effective use of violence) death. The confidence born of control created the potential for paternalism and a secure justification for patriarchy and white supremacy. Little wonder that boys and men surged into the field with such eager enthusiasm.

4. Finding Peers:
The Criteria of Exclusion

I need only add, that the shooting of game birds, over pointers and setters, has been, time out of mind, the gentleman's amusement; so much so, that I would hardly hesitate to make some guess concerning any man's antecedents, who should cross a stubble with me one of these crispy, brown October mornings.

Johnson Jones Hooper, *Dog and Gun,* 1856

HUNTERS, looking for comradeship and validation of their masculinity, often hunted in groups. Hunting companions provided an appreciative audience for a hunter's demonstration of prowess, self-control, and mastery. Hunters, therefore, selected their companions with care, excluding those who were not congenial or knowledgeable enough to judge a hunter's exploits. In the process hunters created informal fraternities of like-minded peers. These fraternities customarily excluded women and slaves, but most also excluded various white men. Many fraternities sought legitimacy by drawing on the idealized images of white masculinity promoted by the sporting press, but when they excluded other hunters from their outings, fraternities also did so because of local traditions and the personal idiosyncrasies of their individual members. This allowed every fraternity to fashion its own unique sense of identity, which in turn created various criteria of exclusion. Fraternity members rarely expressed their preferences openly—they simply did not hunt with the people who failed to meet their qualifications.

In most communities fraternity boundaries remained fairly porous. Judging the worthiness of kin, friends, and neighbors remained straightforward, but most hunters still required some kind of introduction before they associated with strangers. Because of this, strangers often depended upon invitations or letters of introduction. This ensured that a hunt would usually remain exclusive. This was particularly important in the oldest parts of the South. Ralph Ranger's story "Sporting at the South," which appeared in the *Spirit of the Times* in 1846, illustrates the importance of personal relationships in the South Carolina low country. The story begins with a conversation between a Charleston gentleman and a slave messenger named Cudjoe. The narrator asks after his owner, a low-country planter. Cudjoe replies that "massa berry well, sir. Day aint nobody wid um—him say him dam' lonesome—him tired—hunt by himself—ax you fur come up, and bring any body you kin ketch." The narrator fulfills this request by bringing along an acquaintance from New York. Upon their arrival, their host quickly dispels any sense of formality among the members of the party. "We are to be together at least a week, if not longer," he says, "and as I detest formality of every description, if you have no objection, we will call each other by our christian names."[1] This tone of comfortable bonhomie came easily because existing friendships cleared the way. The New Yorker had been vetted in advance. Even though isolated planters were not above using the promise of good hunting as a lure for visitors, they still required a filter. Southerners rarely extended their hospitality without proof of a guest's social standing.

On other occasions a letter of introduction sufficed. Seated outside his hotel in a small town in the North Carolina piedmont in 1843, a traveler overheard several locals planning a deer hunt. An hour after meeting a member of the local gentry to whom he presented a letter of introduction (from a friend of his who knew some of the families in the neighborhood), he received an invitation to the hunt. His host loaned him his double-barreled shotgun and provided an introduction to five others hunters—all "fine looking fellows of 'real grit.'" Although he was not a hunter and had never "ridden in the saddle ten consecutive miles" or "seen a 'living saddle of venison,'" the traveler launched himself into the hunt with great enthusiasm. Engaged in a drive for deer, he waited in his stand, but he could barely remain still and "yearned to pour out my full spirit in one cheering answering cry to the merry pack." Fortunately he restrained his passions, and when a prize buck emerged before him, he came into his own. "Up goes 'Old Betsey'—bang—bang—a smart pain in my shoulder—a little claret from the right nostril, tells me 'Old Betsey' had done her part." Success brought friendship, and he passed that night pleasantly with his "companions of the day," whom he found "well-bred and intelligent gentlemen."[2]

The geographic and economic mobility of white society ensured that few fraternities possessed the organizational rigidity or aristocratic pretense to codify their criteria of exclusion. Spottily enforced and sketchily articulated, these criteria usually appeared when hunters strengthened the bonds of their fraternities by denigrating those whom they deemed unworthy of meaningful association. Sexist outbursts, racist remarks, ethnic jokes, displays of conspicuous consumption, and explanations of sporting (and unsporting) behavior made preferences clear by distinguishing outsiders (the objects of derision) from the insiders (the audience). Because most of the episodes where this occurred included a scapegoat in the form of a blundering hunter, it appears that many fraternities allowed white male strangers a trial run.

Hunters who promoted a strong rural identity fortified their image by denigrating urbanites. Popular among the rural gentry, this prejudice often appeared in the sporting press, which regularly presented urbanites as the weak and emasculated victims of the feminized, unhealthy, and avaricious city. This often tinged them with enough otherness to set them apart from their country cousins and provided writers with good examples of bad sportsmanship. When these pitiable creatures ventured out into the countryside, their weakness became all too apparent. Writers like Daniel R. Hundley who reveled in the romance of southern rural life stressed the alienness of urbanites in a rural milieu: "Ah! it is impossible for your pale denizens of the dusty town, whose horizon on every side is bounded by dull brick walls and flaming sign-boards, to appreciate the wild delight of a steeple-chase ride through brakes and briars, over gullies and fences, adown green lanes and under the overshadowing boughs of majestic forests, with a whoop and halloo, and hark, tallyho!"[3]

Unlike the quietly competent rural sportsman, urbanites frequently appeared in hunting narratives weighted down by their excessive baggage and seemingly more concerned with their voluminous wardrobes than their guns and horses. In a recollection of his youth, Frederick Gustavus Skinner described a group of Baltimore deer hunters who decamped in western Maryland with a wide array of extravagant equipment. They were particularly comic because they took the field "rigged out in the most extraordinary hunting suits; coats with multitudinous pockets, all of which had to be searched before getting what was wanted; caps and headgear of odd construction, but supposed to be absolutely necessary in hunting such noble game." He concluded with a snide description of their buccaneer-style outfits: "Every man had a broad belt, with a great shining buckle such as the stage brigands wear in a melodrama, and in these belts were

"Mr. X. hastens to get a shot at a deer." Overeagerness yields poor results. From Porte Crayon [David Hunter Strother], *Virginia Illustrated: Containing a Visit to the Virginian Canaan, and the Adventures of Porte Crayon and His Cousins* (New York, 1871), 42.

hunting knives — for close quarter, they said, with a dangerous buck at bay — long and heavy enough to decapitate a bison."[4] Skinner's mentor, Campbell, enticed this comical group into a drive for deer, in which the hooting drunken Baltimorians acted as the pack. Guilelessly, they drove the deer toward Campbell and one of his friends, each of whom killed several of the deer. At the conclusion of the hunt, the shooters magnanimously bestowed their venison upon the rowdily unsuccessful urbanites as a demonstration of their unequivocal superiority.[5]

Resourceful urbanites avoided such obvious pitfalls by securing proper tutors. A Baltimore native himself, Skinner became an able critic of urbanites by following the lead of his rural tutor. Such dedication on the part of urbanites remained relatively rare, and as the sporting press grew in size, sophistication, and influence, inexperienced urbanites increasingly relied upon it for their introduction into the world of the hunt. Because many of the submissions in the sporting press were from experienced hunters who often omitted the essentials of method, much of the material lacked direct applicability for novice hunters, but it was still a useful assortment of narratives and debates which, if read with care, could provide a novice with a good introduction.

Tapping into this growing market, several publishers began releasing instructional manuals for "young sportsmen." Many Americans relied upon English manuals and handbooks, but domestic presses began adapting English texts for American audiences as early as 1734 with the publication of *The Sportsman's Companion*.[6] Periodic reprints kept this manual in circulation, and by the 1840s a number of domestically produced books also provided instruction for the beginning hunter. Pitched toward boys, these manuals could also supply inexperienced adults with a wealth of valuable information. Some hunters concealed their lack of practical experience, but others apparently revealed their novice status without hesitation. When Nat L. of New York City embarked upon his first deer hunt in the South Carolina low country, he mixed his considerable enthusiasm with the anxiety of a greenhorn, confessing, "I have enjoyed sporting excessively in *books,* but, as I never was in the field, I cannot say whether the practice is as agreeable as the theory." In hunting narratives these "carpet hunters" usually acted as scapegoats and comic relief, but when shepherded into the field by rural hunters or competent urbanites, they could become regular members of a sympathetic fraternity. Urbanites often played the fool, but when they met the expectations of other hunters, they simply rounded out the party.[7]

Many fraternities considered certain urbanites worthy companions, but inexperienced urbanites who took their cues from the charming pastoralism of romantic novels and the wild exaggerations of the Crockett almanacs and other frontier fantasies rarely received a sympathetic reception. Because these accounts, which became popular in the mid-1830s, owed more to the overactive imaginations of writers who lived in the cities of the eastern seaboard than to actual conditions in the West, they made more exciting reading than the often pedantic instructional manuals, but few offered much in the way of applicable information. Lured by fantastically inaccurate visions of the hunt and stoked by Crockett's swashbuckling exploits, urbanites eagerly blazed into the southern countryside in search of venatic glory throughout the antebellum era. Their ignorance ensured that they made convenient whipping boys for more experienced southern hunters.

Ethnicity provided many fraternities with another useful signifier of otherness. Distinguished by outlandish names and ridiculous accents, the recognizably French-American and German-American characters appearing in the sporting press were customarily relegated to the role of the fool. Characterized as incompetents who possessed little control over their passions or their subordinates, they provided a stark contrast for the noble actions of the implicitly Anglo-American protagonists who appeared alongside them. The most colorful and detailed example of ethnic buffoonery appeared in the pseudonymous Seebright's 1837 story, "A Panther Hunt on the Blue Ridge," which features the meek schoolmaster Hans Von Schullemberger. Ordinarily a homebody, he becomes a part of a panther-hunting party when its leader, Moreland, sees him nervously peering from his window the morning after a panther attacked some nearby livestock. Intent on the death of a marauding panther but eager for a laugh, Moreland and his companions dismount and form an ad hoc press-gang. When they knock on his front door, Schullemberger hides in the bedroom, while his wife, "a sleek, comely looking dame," lets the party in and directs them toward his hiding place. As the hunters enter the room, Schullemberger feigns a deep sleep, but when one of them suggests dumping a bucket of water upon him, he opens his eyes, turns toward his wife, and begins burbling fearful excuses.[8]

Recognizing the authority (and masculinity) of the hunters, she betrays her husband because of his cowardice. Stepping aside, she asks, "My dear husband, if these gentlemen insist on it, how can I help it?" Her actions give the hunters all the recognition and power that Seebright believed they should hold. As Schullemberger woefully gathers up his fowling piece (he did not own a rifle because he believed bullets were dangerous), Seebright managed one last insult with an offhand comment regarding Schullemberger's "very fat children, of all colors and sizes, which he called his own." By questioning the paternity of his "comely" wife's children, Seebright completely undermined Schullemberger's claims to the mastery of his own household.

Once in the field Schullemberger cringes and jumps until he becomes a nuisance, so the party finally leaves him behind. As the rest of the party beats a nearby thicket, they hear the barking of the pack and a startled shout from Schullemberger — "Oh! mine Got!" — then the report of his gun and an agonizing cry. Returning at a run, the other hunters witness the panther disembowel Cudjo (a loyal slave), but they can find no sign of the unfortunate Schullemberger. Although the party mourned Cudjo's death, Schullemberger's disappearance was comedic. The awkward sorrows of his wife and children encouraged tears, but Seebright (who inserted himself into the action) admitted he "was forced to bite my lips together to repress my laughter." The following day, while exploring the area around the site of the panther attack, the party discovers the scratched, bloody, and disheveled schoolmaster hiding in a tree, keeping the local wildlife at bay with pathetic whimpers of "boo-oo-oo---shoo-oo."[9]

Retrieving Schullemberger, the party resumes the hunt and engages the panther in a final battle. In the midst of a chaotic fight, Schullemberger temporarily blinds the panther with an expeditiously placed charge of bird shot, saving Moreland's life and providing him with the opportunity to kill the panther with his knife. This act endows Schullemberger with a small measure of respectability, but as they return into town, he remains an emasculated outsider. When Moreland covers Schullemberger's torn clothing with his own hunting shirt, Seebright reaffirmed the spirit of inequality and paternalistic benevolence that structured their relationship. Moreland shields Schullemberger from the gaze of his neighbors, but he simultaneously confirms his own irreproachable masculinity and Schullemberger's apparently permanent status as his subordinate. As a caricature of ineptitude, Schullemberger provided Seebright with a perfect foil for Moreland, his avatar.[10]

White immigrants from continental Europe, like urbanites, could gain admission into certain fraternities as long as they modified their behavior to fit local expectations. In fact, ethnicity rarely appeared in hunting narratives because most hunters who belonged to recognizable European ethnic groups quickly assimilated themselves into white society. By downplaying their distinctiveness, they could become acceptable companions and fraternity members. Once approved by his companions, a hunter could safely reveal the shadow of an all-but-assimilated ethnic identity (say, the quirky pronunciation of a few words or a taste for roast opossum) while remaining a desirable companion. Unlike southerners of African descent, who faced almost insurmountable barriers, the relative ease with which most ethnic whites could assimilate themselves made them all but invisible.

A handful of free blacks made social contacts with whites when they hunted, but even William Johnson, a wealthy barber from Natchez, who hunted and drank with whites on numerous occasions, discovered a variety of barriers that prevented the development of a fraternal bond between him and his white hunting companions. Johnson's frequent outings in the company of his good friend Robert McCary, another free black barber of Natchez, and various other free black acquaintances revealed the creation of a loose free black hunting fraternity, but these bonds always recognized the unquestioned dominance of the color line.[11]

In most hunting narratives whites squarely placed free blacks under the umbrella of white patriarchy. Some whites recognized that free black hunters often owned their own dogs, carried their own guns (sometimes better guns than those the whites carried), and engaged in the market economy, but rather than fearing these demonstrations of autonomy on the part of African Americans, contributors to the sporting press blithely incorporated them into their paternalistic model of southern society. Constructed as efficient and compliant auxiliaries of white society, these "free gemmen of color" could safely be described as "real Leather-stocking looking sort of fellows" without endangering white supremacy.[12]

Slaves received more attention from white writers, but they certainly never appeared in hunting narratives as equals. Although slaves accompanied many white hunts, their presence almost never created anything approaching a sense of interracial camaraderie. White hunters customarily isolated slaves in a corner of the camp, except when they brought them forward to show them off as loyal huntsmen or foolish jesters. Rare moments of fleeting and ostentatious color blindness aside, few white hunters acknowledged the possibility of breaking down barriers between themselves and their slaves. Slaves performed a wide variety of useful and symbolically significant duties, but their owners ensured that the divisions between black and white remained robust and unquestionable.

Some white hunters used the hunt as a venue for the display of their wealth, which in turn made class an important criterion of exclusion. The increasingly democratic tenor of southern politics after the rise of Jacksonian democracy and the indispensability of maintaining the unity of white males in the face of slavery, however, made this a difficult proposition. Rather than creating boundaries according to the possession of a certain amount of wealth and property, many white hunters relied upon a more innocuous form of class distinction: conspicuous consumption. By taking the field with numerous dogs, horses, slaves, and guns, these hunters expended a good deal of productive capital without an equitable return. Such wastefulness was an effective (but indirect) illustration of their wealth.

Conspicuous consumption took many forms. Because most white hunters combined it with a measure of utility, they could make their position clear without directly invoking the shade of aristocratic privilege or "money power." Dogs provided hunters with both an effective instrument for display and a useful tool for the pursuit of game. A few mutts could be had for the asking, but because a well-trained dog could fetch up to $50 (a substantial sum), the acquisition of breeding stock could require a substantial outlay of resources.[13] The costs did not stop with acquisition. A well-maintained pack required food, shelter, and constant care. Many slaveholders saved some effort on their own part by remanding care of the pack to slaves and feeding their dogs on table scraps, but these measures withdrew slaves from the available labor force for at least part of the day and eliminated a source of feed for swine or slaves.[14] White hunters also used horses in their hunts. Like dogs, horses possessed a great deal of utility, but their expense could outweigh any possible return. Many white hunters spent much time and energy breeding horses for racing and hunting. Even when hunters rode less-specialized breeds or simply saddled up a plodding draft horse, they could accumulate substantial expenses from feed, care, and housing.

Domestic animals could represent a considerable expenditure of wealth, but the slaves who accompanied white hunts created the largest and most visible drain on a white hunter's resources. Absent from the fields and workshops, these slaves illustrated their owners' worldly success by proving the measure of their wealth. The presence of slaves certainly degraded the standing of men who owned no slaves, but it was also especially important in drawing distinctions between men who owned numerous slaves and those who owned few. The latter needed the labor of their slaves on their farms, so they rarely brought them into the field.

Hunters also spent a good deal of money on their guns. If properly cared for, a single weapon could serve several generations of hunters, but many wealthy hunters took pride in owning and using up-to-date weapons. Some hunters upgraded because newer guns incorporated various improvements in firearms technology (such as the percussion cap). Others bought expensive guns primarily as a form of lavish display. The finest and most expensive guns were English. In *Dog and Gun,* Johnson Jones Hooper repeatedly extolled the virtues of English rifles and fowling pieces. Purchasing domestic arms was unthinkable, and he dismissed potential concerns about cost (custom-made English guns usually ran from $300 to $500). When considering cheap American guns, Hooper asked "how any man of sense, should risk his life forty times a day with such a weapon." Some, like Marcus Gaines of Virginia, maintained that American guns achieved the same quality as English guns at half the price, but devotees of high-quality English firearms dominated the pages of the sporting press.[15]

Although Hooper and others of his ilk special-ordered their guns from abroad, less wealthy (or less pretentious) hunters purchased their weaponry from American gunsmiths. Prices were considerably lower (made-to-order guns ran around $110 to $125, and cheap guns cost around $30), but they were still beyond the means of many southern whites. Market hunters and slaveholders could equip themselves with firearms, but their prohibitive cost ensured that many southern hunters relied upon less expensive instruments like dogs and traps. Gun-hunting never became the exclusive preserve of the wealthy, but it did carry a mark of distinction.[16]

When white hunters took the field, they not only displayed their wealth, they also expended it. Certain kinds of hunting could be dangerous for domestic animals and slaves. Placed between hunters and game, dogs suffered the most. Stray gunshots, frightened horses, and angry bears ended the career of many a prize dog. Horses also suffered occasional casualties. Spurred on by enthusiastic hunters, many horses broke their legs in frantic jumps. Slaves also often found themselves in harm's way. Although most slaves took great care to avoid injury, they often remained close to the action and occasionally faced cornered pumas and desperate bears with nothing more than a knife or an old flintlock.

Finally, white hunters made a supreme gesture of conspicuous consumption by putting their own physical health in jeopardy. By placing themselves in harm's way, white hunters demonstrated both their masculinity and their indifference to personal injury. Aside from foxhunting, which encouraged hard riding through forests and over fences and streams, most forms of the hunt lacked real physical peril, but if hunters took enough unnecessary risks, any form of the hunt could become dangerous. By risking injury, white hunters could display their independence from physical labor and financial want. A few weeks mending a broken arm meant little to a wealthy slaveholder, but for a yeoman farmer it could economically cripple his family.[17]

Any kind of hunting could consume large amounts of a hunter's resources, but extended hunting expeditions were the ultimate expression of conspicuous consumption. Unlike the "long hunts" taken by Daniel Boone and other frontiersmen who sojourned at some distance from their homes in search of marketable skins and furs, these expeditions emphasized the gratuitous expenditure of time, provisions, and labor. Usually undertaken by a small party of wealthy planters (and an entourage of slaves), these expeditions quickly dispensed with any pretext of utility. Instead, they focused on copious consumption of liquor, rousing displays of masculinity, and strengthening of fraternal bonds. One of the white members of an expedition to Blackbeard Island near Darien, Georgia, proudly explained that "it is only the sportsman in easy, independent circumstances, who can fit out a successful expedition to Black Beard." By making the trip, he and his four companions proved their status as "four independent planters, as noble and generous souls as ever broke bread, and all good shots and experienced hunters."[18]

Hunters who achieved this degree of extravagance often gathered together in formal hunting clubs. These organized and chartered fraternities lay along the Atlantic seaboard, and they unapologetically demanded massive displays of wealth on the part of their members. When the St. Thomas Club of Berkeley County in low-country South Carolina organized in 1800, it required that its members make a tremendous outlay of money, food, and alcohol by hosting regular meetings for "Dinner & Liquors." The feasts grew more and more lavish as the proud and competitive members steadily increased the expected contributions of wine, liquor, and other provisions. Eventually club members required a prodigal feast consisting of "a barbecued Shoat or Sheep, a Ham or piece of Salt Beef, a Turkey, two Fowls or two Ducks, two loaves of Bread, and in the Season Potatoes, half a bushel of Rice, Pepper, Mustard and Vinegar, one bottle of Rum, half a Gallon of Brandy, and one dozen of good Wine, Pipes and Tobacco or one hundred Segars, one dozen Tumblers and two dozen Wine Glasses." By requiring such great expenditures, the clubs provided an opportunity for the display of wealth and power while excluding all but the wealthiest of planters.[19]

Conspicuous consumption provided an easy instrument of exclusion, but outside of the low country (with its relatively dense concentration of wealthy planters), few communities could afford the extravagant displays of the St. Thomas Club or the Blackbeard Island excursionists. Without the wealth and stability of the plantation communities scattered along the Atlantic seaboard, the establishment and maintenance of exclusive clubs became impossible. In other parts of the South, most white hunters found other avenues for the exaltation of themselves and their companions above the mass of white hunters.

Few areas of the relentlessly mobile and boisterously democratic South could support rigid class barriers, so most members of the gentry who sought to differentiate themselves from the mass of white men who regularly took the field did so by observing the strictures of sport. Those who observed the rules of sport constructed a social identity for themselves by promoting the idea that while a hunter was a man, a sportsman was a

gentleman. Sport provided a perfect instrument for the exclusion of undesirable whites because it strengthened the illusion of white male solidarity by artfully sidestepping the crudeness of conspicuous consumption
while bestowing a sort of ultramasculinity upon its devotees. Without directly invoking the question of wealth or challenging the integrity of white
male democracy, sport embellished the skills expected of any hunter with
the luster of aristocracy.

Imported from Great Britain and quickly adapted for American audiences by the sporting press, the concept of sport elevated the act of hunting and the concomitant display of prowess, self-control, and mastery
over the simple accumulation of corpses. Sport sketched a hazy boundary around its elitist advocates without directly invoking the question of
class. By elevating challenge above results, it clearly discriminated against
poor whites who needed game for provisions and trade. Already divorced
from purely economic concerns, hunting became an increasingly rarefied
activity. Killing remained central, but the advocates of sport insisted that
true sportsmen placed proper form above indiscriminate slaughter. The
advocates of sport insisted that real men (that is, those welcome in their
fraternities) killed in certain specific ways.[20]

Few white hunters denied the effectiveness of unsporting methods, and
most still recognized the importance of nonhunting audiences, so most
descriptions of unsporting methods included the caveat that hunters
should stay away from them unless everything else they tried failed. This
concession recognized hunters' needs for an occasional kill, but it still
pricked at their consciences. When hunters recorded their use of these
methods in their diaries and personal correspondence, they never expressed any moral uneasiness, but their entries often included a note of
desperation. These are the accounts of those who, when faced with a
shameful lack of success, turned toward otherwise unacceptable methods.[21]

Lacking the egalitarian tone of most other advice pieces, descriptions
of unsporting methods in the sporting press often took on a patronizing
tone toward their audience by referring to them as urbanites or "young
hunters." P. Z. of Alabama recognized that wild turkey often provided too
much challenge for some novice hunters (considering the bird's caginess
and the difficulty in mastering birdcalls) and offered advice for the bene-

fit of "city friends." "After days of vain toil in this pursuit," he counseled, "when you have sounded your most insinuating notes in vain, finding it unheeded; after you have, in sheer desperation, tried the impossibility of creeping on them whilst feeding, or the equally hopeful scheme, of dashing on the flock at full speed, all, in vain, then, and not *till* then, do I hold you clearly justified in adopting the following method of capture." He instructed unlucky hunters that instead of hanging up their guns at night, they should use the darkness as an opportunity to position themselves between turkey feeding grounds and their roosts. He promised that if the hunter remained quiet and calm, the turkeys would eventually fly to their roosts in low-hanging tree branches. Once they settled in for the night, a hunter could walk under a tree, take his choice, and make an easy kill. The others would immediately fly away, but one trophy would assuredly remain.[22]

Firehunters who submitted their experiences to the sporting press usually distanced themselves from the action and characterized themselves as observers or curiosity seekers. Some admitted that they enjoyed firehunting (Audubon wrote, "There is something in it which at times appears awfully grand"), but most included some form of qualification.[23] Most of these hunters insisted that they only took the field after being enticed by poor white or African-American hunters who promised an assured kill. Whenever a member of an exclusive party suggested a firehunt, another member usually provided the story of his first, disastrous firehunt as a cautionary tale. Generally stories of high expectations and inevitable disappointment, these narratives often include the unintentional killing of livestock, self-inflicted injuries, embarrassment, and ignominy. Yet, due to its undeniable effectiveness, firehunting remained a relatively common practice and a highly charged topic that hunters and sportsmen debated throughout the antebellum era.[24]

Hunters in different sections of the South used a variety of unsporting methods including (but not limited to) luring deer with salt licks, placing upright stakes beside low stretches of fences, putting traps underneath the surface of the water at the crossing places of streams, shooting hibernating bears, baiting ground, and shooting whole flocks of birds with massive, cannonlike punt guns. The least challenging of these methods was turkey trapping. An unscrupulous hunter constructed a cage out of sticks and placed it in a likely area of the woods, Digging a short ditch under one side of the cage, he scattered grain throughout the area, especially in the ditch. Then he went home. Enticed by the grain, turkeys browsed the area; eventually they discovered the grain in the ditch. Heads down, they worked their way into the cage. Once they ate all of the grain inside the cage, they looked up. Being rather dim, the birds continued searching for an opening in the cage at their eye level (for they could see between the slats of the cage) until the trapper came along and collected them. Battery shooting was another questionable method that received a good deal of criticism. Practiced in the bays and inlets of the Atlantic coast, it involved specialized equipment and a great deal of discomfort on the part of the hunter, who lay flat on his back in a contraption resembling a floating coffin stabilized by half-submerged sails. In this undignified but relatively concealed position, he barely broke the plane of the water. Carefully listening and watching the sky, he waited for the approach of unsuspecting waterfowl. When he detected their approach, he sat up and shot at whatever startled game presented itself.[25]

Sport provided an excellent instrument of exclusion. A few white hunters took sport to heart, but many used it for little more than self-aggrandizement and as a pretense for condemnation of others. Sport occasionally restrained hunters' behavior when they were around strangers, but it rarely dictated hunters' behavior when they were in a group of friends and relatives. Hunters used sport in the same way that they used the other criteria of exclusion: as an initial filter. Once an outsider proved himself in the eyes of his companions, they allowed him much greater latitude in his actions. Even the most rule-bound sportsman allowed himself and his fellows an occasional infraction.[26] One of William Stockton's stories, "Snipe Shooting in Florida," illustrates how easily some fraternities bent the rules of sport for their own convenience and pleasure. Traveling in northern Florida, he came upon a group of local hunters led by "the General." They had just finished killing a flock of twenty-three blue peters, and when Stockton asked the leader about the group's methods, he proudly replied: "'Oh! all military science! it *will* tell! I discovered the flock in the cove there, at daylight, arranged the hunters at once, an ambuscade was formed surrounding the cove, and at the signal, the whole battalion, I should say, partly fired. Only three escaped!' he proclaimed proudly. 'As we shall be here several days yet and it will not do to risk their spoiling' he wondered, 'what had we best do with them?'" Stockton thought he saw misgiving creeping over the entire party. He stoked it with the sarcastic reply, "Hide them, as soon as possible, lest some sportsman should pass this way."[27] Undaunted by Stockton's ridicule, the Floridians continued their hunt. As an outsider, Stockton's veiled disapproval proved ineffectual against the group consensus. Because the members of the shooting party apparently had suspended sporting restrictions against wasteful slaughter, Stockton abandoned his sanctimonious stance and joined in with gusto.

By altering his behavior and following the cues of the other hunters, Stockton strengthened his bonds with their temporary community. As the sun set they continued shooting whatever birds silhouetted themselves against the sky without any hope of recovering their kills. Only the splashes of the downed waterfowl told him that "we were doing execution." The next day, wearied by either the scale of waste or the repetitiveness of the killing, one of the Floridians expressed some doubt about continuing the slaughter. He proposed the reimposition of the strictures of sport. Because the party already had as much game as they and their friends could possibly consume, he suggested, "To continue is murder; let's go home." The rest of the party consented. As a member of the fraternity, he accomplished what Stockton could not.[28] Remarkably, Johnson Jones Hooper, editor of the *East Alabamian* and a prominent promoter of the sporting ideal, included this story in his book *Dog and Gun,* which also featured a series of vehement attacks on the pothunting practices of poor whites, boys, and slaves. The story appeared without editorial comment because Stockton had firmly established his reputation as a sportsman through his correspondence with Hooper and his previous pieces in the sporting press. Insulated by the corpus of his published stories, he transcended the label of pothunter even though he cheerfully engaged in pothunting practices himself.[29]

Because self-professed sportsmen often bent the rules of sport to suit their own needs, many of the southern contributors to the sporting press developed the character of the pothunter as an aid in identifying unworthy hunters. Unlike the frontiersman and the backwoodsman, pothunters provided nuance-free scapegoats. They lacked both the potential usefulness of the backwoodsman and the frontiersman's capacity for heroism. As the antithesis of the sportsman, they provided a negative role model against which all hunters could measure their achievements. Foremost among pothunters' shortcomings was their lack of community spirit. They had no interest in building fraternities or networks of gift giving and reciprocity. Unlike backwoodsmen, pothunters rarely acknowledged the authority of southern elites. This rebellious attitude alarmed members of the gentry when it was manifested among their poorer, armed neighbors. But rather than couching their censure in terms of class antagonism, most writers who described pothunters condemned them for violating the rules of sport.

Many prolific and widely disseminated writers created a detailed case against the perfidious pothunter, but few spewed as much vitriol as Johnson Jones Hooper. Most of Hooper's early stories describe the travails of a sly cracker protagonist named Simon Suggs. Lured into tight situations by his unremitting greed, Suggs usually managed to muddle through. He lived by his favorite aphorism, "It is good to be shifty in a new country," and fleeced every slow-witted Alabamian who came his way. Boisterous and deceitful, Suggs lived "as merrily and as comfortably as possible at the expense of others," including his own mother (whose pipe he once loaded with gunpowder). He swindled without prejudice and cheerfully bilked slaves, Indians, and Methodists out of their money and their dignity. Yet, despite his eye for dishonest opportunity, he never remained on top for long because his unflappable overconfidence usually undermined his own devious efforts.[30]

While Hooper's fiction painted the wily cracker in a humorously derogatory light, his nonfiction work often contained a forceful attack on poor whites. Unlike his Simon Suggs stories, his short book, *Dog and Gun,* was intended as a serious work. First published in 1845 and bereft of humorous anecdotes, it took the form of an instructional manual for "gentlemen." The product of a lifetime of firsthand experience in the field, *Dog and Gun* also revealed Hooper's thorough command of the sporting press. He bolstered his own knowledge of hunting with citations from various august authorities from both sides of the Atlantic, in particular Henry William Herbert, who received the dedication.

In his book Hooper reviled the lowly (and probably illiterate) pothunter in order to elucidate the lessons of sport. Hooper's descriptions of pothunter foolishness instructed through inversion. If Hooper's readers avoided the behavior he described, they could become sportsmen by default. Hooper made his lesson clear by attacking the masculinity of his pothunter scapegoat. Hooper compared pothunters to squirrel-hunting boys because they followed the "vulgar idea" that "a shot-gun is effective in proportion to the amount of powder and lead crammed down it." Unlike sportsmen, pothunters ignorantly blasted away without art or craft. "Ignorant and irreclaimable," pothunters could never lay aside their childish things.[31]

Hooper deepened his critique by reminding his readers that pothunters cared nothing for the constructed challenges of sport. Intent upon harvesting as much game as possible, they used whatever methods proved most effective and economical. Sportsmen like Hooper found all of these methods equally reprehensible not only because they demolished the pretense of sport but also because they took a heavy toll on wildlife. He feared that if pothunters continued their effective slaughter unmolested, sportsmen would have nothing left to hunt. The lack of prowess, self-control, and mastery revealed by their indiscriminate and undisciplined shooting clearly signified their unworthiness as companions.[32]

While Hooper concerned himself with pothunters' unremitting and wasteful assaults upon local wildlife, South Carolina planter-politician William Elliott took a much more alarmist view of pothunters. His cautionary tale "The Fire Hunter" features a shiftless overseer, Slouch, whose unremitting greed threatened the integrity of the race politics lying at the heart of southern society. Set on a South Carolina plantation, the story opens with Slouch berating a slave messenger who had informed the absentee owner about the deer that regularly browsed the plantation pea field. After receiving this piece of information, the owner sent a message back to Slouch announcing his intention to hunt the deer with a few of his friends. Slouch was not invited. This turn of events angered Slouch because he wanted the deer for himself. Expressing his dismay over his social and economic position, Slouch complains that "here he's been writing to me, as if I was a nigger; telling me to keep them bucks till he comes over with his friends to hunt them." "Dang me, if I do," he curses. "Who gave them to him? were they born in his cattle-pen? have they got his mark and brand upon them? all that have white tails are in my mark, and I'll shoot them as I please, and ask no odds."[33]

In an unusual fit of activity, Slouch sends for Pompey, a slave hunter, and accuses him of poaching. Fearing exposure and enticed by Slouch's offer of a forequarter of deer, Pompey casts in his lot with the overseer. Solely concerned with results, they agree that firehunting seems the most efficacious method, and after sealing their pact, they make plans for a night of hunting before the owner's return. Once darkness falls, they stealthily make their way into the pea field frequented by the deer. Pompey has brought along a skillet (or "fire-pan") full of lightwood and catches the eyes of a deer, which appear as "globes of greenish flame." The deer stares, transfixed, providing Slouch, who is carrying the gun, a stationary target.[34]

The excitement of the moment overcomes Pompey's earlier reluctance. Eager for action, he exclaims, "Got, Mass Slouch, dat 'ill do! . . . S'pose you gee me the gun—I'll slam um ober, I tell you!" Apparently an old hand at firehunting, Slouch replies, "When did you larn, pray?" Eyeing Pompey "keenly and not over kindly," he asks, "How do you know the distance?—you'd fire before you had got close enough, or scare him by getting too near." Even when describing the most reprehensible members of the white community, Elliott, like Hooper, maintained his commitment to white supremacy. Unlike the excitable slave, Slouch possesses at least a measure of self-control. He creeps closer and fires. After the deer falls, he and Pompey begin dressing and dividing the animal. In the midst of their labor, Slouch hears a noise. He looks up, sees another set of glowing eyes, and fires. Unfortunately, the eyes belonged to one of his employer's colts. Fearful of his wrath, Slouch mutilates the colt to camouflage the gunshot wounds and encourages Pompey's complicity in his escalating crimes. "Pompey! keep this close, and I'll make it up to you! You needn't know anything about it, nor miss the colt, till day after to-morrow; and, by then, I reckon, my shot-holes will tell no tales!"[35]

Here, in a short story of poaching, Elliott summed up one of the darkest nightmares of large slaveholders, a conspiracy between slave and overseer. Without respect for the plantation owner's property or orders, Slouch and Pompey had poached his deer, killed his colt, and then entered into collusion, obscuring these events from the slaveholder's patriarchal eye. Never content with subtle touches, Elliott continued layering on his admonitions with a heavy hand. Eager to convert his share of the deer into cash, Slouch entices the plantation driver, Snug, into his conspiracy with a cut of the meat. In exchange, Snug helps him carry the remaining venison into a nearby town where Slouch sells it. Returning to the plantation by a different route than Slouch and Snug, Pompey discovers a skillet full of dying embers — evidence that another firehunter was afield that night. He immediately suspects the greedy Slouch, but here Elliott surprised his readers by revealing that the other firehunter was actually a neighboring plantation owner. And instead of merely killing a deer or a colt, this hunter had accidentally shot and mortally wounded Pompey's brother, Toney. Pompey stumbles upon them as the firehunting planter exacts a promise from the dying Toney that he will not identify his assailant. Afraid of recriminations from his absentee neighbor (now out a deer, a colt, and a slave), the guilty planter hastily exits before Pompey can see his face, and his identity remains a mystery. Toney never breaks his vow, and after a final melancholy monologue, he dies.[36]

In these final pages Elliott echoed Hooper and indicted would-be sportsmen for their complicity in the continued existence of unsporting and potentially destructive activities. Thus he transformed discussion of sport into pointed social commentary. Losing a few deer was merely the thin edge of the wedge. In his hands firehunting symbolized what he perceived as a dangerous weakness in southern society. It not only increased the depletion of game, it also undermined the cohesiveness of the white community. The first fissure appeared when Slouch entered into a conspiracy with the slaves under his nominal control, but the second came as a surprise because Elliott struck at the top of the pyramid. By destroying his neighbor's valuable property (Toney) and showing his cowardice (by running away from Pompey), the firehunting planter betrayed white supremacy. With a single illicit night of firehunting, he threatened the cohesion of his community and shattered the image of benevolent white patriarchy.[37]

Such an alarmist description of pothunters was rare. While Hooper strutted and Elliott fretted, most sporting writers considered pothunters thick-witted, greedy fools rather than actual threats to the antebellum power structure. In his story "My First and Last Fire Hunt," southern humorist William Tappan Thompson presented his pothunting companion, Samuel Sikes, as a thoroughly incompetent backwoodsman, rather than an underhanded conspirator. Like most backwoodsmen, Sikes "delighted in no other pursuit or pastime" than hunting, "though he pretended to cultivate a small spot of ground." He spent so much of his time in "the pursuit of game, that his agricultural interests suffered much for the want of proper attention." Because of his fascination with the hunt, Sikes neglected his six "tallow-faced" children and earned the scorn of his wife.[38] His gable featured a huge pair of antlers along with ten or twelve tall fishing poles. Thompson noted that if these and the conspicuous display of drying skins "did not convince you that the proprietor was a sportsman, the varies and clamorous music of a score of hungry-looking hounds, as they issued forth in full cry at every passer by, could not fail to force the conviction." Thompson referred to Sikes as a "sportsman," but he did so sarcastically because Sikes clearly ignored the constraints of sport, even those that had been enacted into law. Thompson explained that "the Fire-Hunt was Sam's hobby, and though the Legislature had recently passed an act prohibiting that mode of hunting, he continued to indulge, as freely as ever, in his favorite sport, resolutely maintaining that the law was 'unconstitootional and agin reason.'"

In describing his first firehunting experience, Thompson took the pose of a neutral observer, carefully distancing himself from the action. Noting that he did not carry a gun himself, he insisted that he accompanied Sikes for the experience alone. Despite Sikes's assurances of great excitement, the firehunters spend most of the night bumbling around in the dark. The only action occurs when Sikes accidentally shoots his mule, Blaze. The situation further deteriorates when Sikes mislays his gun and gets lost. When it starts raining, the sodden pair takes shelter under an overhanging oak and sits in silence until Thompson turns and says, "I think this will be my last fire-hunt, Mr. Sikes."

Even in the face of defeat, Sikes keeps up his misplaced confidence. "The fact is," he reassures Thompson, "this 'ere aint very encouragin' to new beginners, major, that's a fact — but you musn't give it up so. I hope we'll have a better showin' next time." Around daybreak they recovered Sikes's musket and finally emerged from the forest. Despite their dismal lack of success, the sight of Sikes inspired Thompson's compassion, which he tempered with black humor. "I contemplated, for a moment, the ludicrous appearance of my unfortunate companion. Poor Sam! — daylight, and the prospect of home brought no joy to him — and, as he stood before me, with the saddle and bridle of the deceased Blaze girded about his neck, his musket in one hand and pan in the other, drenched with rain, his clothes torn, and a countenance that told of the painful conflict within, I could not but regard him as an object of sympathy rather than ridicule."[39]

Sikes's ignorance and his complete lack of prowess, self-control, and mastery helped dramatize the divide between sportsmen and pothunters. Crafted and refined through numerous appearances in the sporting press, the image of the pothunter became an easily recognizable literary trope, which sporting writers referenced whenever in need of a negative role model or a piece of rough humor. The product of gentry fears and aspirations, the pothunter became the most easily recognizable trope of exclusion by the 1840s. This popularity kept pace with the depletion of game. If hunters in a particular area noticed a decline in the amount of available game, the pothunter provided them with a convenient scapegoat (often for good reasons—poor whites did kill a lot of game). By the 1850s the *Spirit of the Times* fairly boiled over with strident condemnations of pothunters and their wasteful ways. Spearheaded by writers who lived along the eastern seaboard, these attacks charged pothunters with the vicious destruction of various game species.[40]

White hunters sought the company of their like-minded equals, but the mobility of southern society could make the identification of peers a difficult proposition. By constructing and subsequently denigrating the "other," fraternities strengthened their coherence and their collective identity. Through the failings of these outsiders, fraternity members refined a shared concept of masculinity. Descriptions of outsiders helped define the character of the insiders. The sporting press was key in creating and disseminating various criteria of exclusion. These ideas influenced the behavior of many southern hunters, but they were never truly hegemonic. Rather than creating a set code of conduct, the sporting press laid out a smorgasbord of characters. These aided individuals and groups in their search for peers and scapegoats.

Every hunting fraternity chose its own reasons for including or excluding other hunters. The most basic contours of masculinity—prowess, self-control, and mastery—remained fairly constant, but myriad local variations remained. Some fraternities never addressed questions of ethnicity or urbanity, while others dispensed with the idea of sport. Most simply used whatever criteria seemed convenient, and often they only imposed these criteria when they took the field with strangers. The outsider in any hunting party carried the onus of proving himself to his companions, and the sporting press could only provide him with cues about appropriate behavior in the field. If he tread carefully, appeared sufficiently masculine, modified his behavior to fit with the expectations of his hosts, and appeared congenial, he could become a de facto member of the group. On the other hand, if he appeared inept or failed to modify his behavior, he would forever remain a stranger to his companions in the field.

5. The Community of the Hunt

It is such trips as these that give new energies to the mind and body; they bring about social feelings, and a day or two's relaxation from business arouses inclination to attention to it, and to work on in anticipation of new sport. Excursions of this sort bring out the character of man; they tend to warm his heart and soul.

A Baltimore hunter, 1850

WHEN WHITE HUNTERS chose their companions from the pool of possible associates, they created and refined their personal image of masculinity. When hunters banded together into a fraternity, they combined these individual notions into a shared image of masculinity, which manifested itself in the composition of their criteria of exclusion. When they synthesized from personal experience, tradition, and the sporting press their particular definition of masculinity and an accompanying vision of the ideal companion, most fraternity members valued flexibility over sporting dogma. Although many fraternities adopted the standards for exclusion that appeared in the sporting press, few followed these guidelines rigorously.

A variety of social forces, including personal idiosyncrasies, kinship networks, and land-use patterns, created a wide range of acceptable behavior. Some fraternities elevated the daylong pursuit of a single, inedible fox to the zenith of masculine experience, while others dispensed with the rules of sport and emphasized killing a large amount of game. These standards depended upon geographic location and the character of a given fraternity's members. Demographic variables like duration of settlement, supply of game, proximity of towns, and intensity of agriculture created tremendous diversity in the composition and orientation of hunting fraternities across the South. Whatever their structure at any given moment, fraternities remained almost infinitely malleable in terms of their numbers, intensity, and composition. Rather than denoting weakness in the

organization, strength, or importance of hunting fraternities, this muta-
bility proved their resilience and universality.

Fraternities expressed ideas about masculinity and exclusion in different
ways. Although distrust of urbanites, ethnic whites, and pothunters provided many fraternities with sufficient criteria to limit the pool of possible
candidates, initiates faced a final test. Hunting companions in the end were
judged, not by their hunting prowess or their standing in the community,
but by the expression of a rather subjective quality: congeniality. This
sense of affinity and mutual agreeableness played a decisive role in the
construction and maintenance of fraternities across the South. It bound
men together and provided the critical ingredient that transformed groups
of hunters into fraternities. Letters of reference, fine marksmanship, and
an encyclopedic knowledge of sport might help initiates make some important connections, but neither wealth nor ability trumped congeniality. An initiate might present impeccable credentials and kill with ease, but
if no one enjoyed his company, neither of these otherwise useful signi-
fiers carried much weight.[1]

Hunting nurtured the development of congeniality by providing a
venue for the deepening of trust, the promotion of homogeneity, and the
expression of intimacy. Once these were attained, the stridently professed
criteria of exclusion faded in significance. Each of these factors played an
important role, but trust was of paramount importance. Every manifes-
tation of congeniality included the presence of trust. Group hunts made
excellent proving grounds for this admirable quality because they forced
interdependence upon its participants. Replete with guns, shared hardship,
and the challenge of the kill, hunting depended upon a measure of co-
operation between the participants.

A typical drive for deer provided numerous opportunities for the deepening of trust. Before casting the dogs (who were directed by their owner
or one of his slaves), each hunter manned a stand that overlooked a game
trail leading away from the drive (the stretch of ground that would be
coursed by the dogs). Most stands were nothing more than a gap between
thickets, and enthusiastic hunters usually knew every stand in their neighborhood well. Many even named their favorite stands and ranked them according to preference. The hunt began when the dog drivers released the
pack and directed them through a section of woods in the hope that they
might rouse some deer. If everything went as planned, the deer, driven by

the sound of the pack, would begin running toward the stands. This brought the deer well within the effective range of the hunters' waiting guns. Every hunter hoped that at least one deer would attempt an escape through his particular stand so that he would have the opportunity to make a kill. Because stands often lay some distance from one another, hunters let each other know if they hit their targets by shouting or (among the better equipped) blowing their horns. Depending on these signals, the other hunters would either stay in place, rush for other stands, or converge on the shooter's position. If he shot and missed, a conscientious hunter reloaded and kept his place, so that others might have a shot at his fleeing target or at any other deer roused by the pack. If he wounded his target, he signaled his intention to chase it down (often on horseback). The other hunters usually joined him in the exciting pursuit. This sense of teamwork ensured that even though they relied upon the efforts of individual marksmen, deer drives possessed a definite sense of collective effort and shared benefits. Even though the skin, antlers, and prestige of felling a deer went to the individual who brought it down, every hunter benefited by sharing in the division of meat and the thrill of the hunt.[2]

At every step these hunters placed considerable trust in their companions. The mechanics of the hunt demanded that they trust one another to remain at their stands and shoot with effect. In terms of masculine display, they trusted one another to provide an appreciative audience and subsequently relate an acceptable version of events. Hunters also expected a fair division of meat and a proper apportionment of credit for whatever they killed. Without trust, this web of interdependence quickly unraveled. Hunters who pursued individual gain, misled their companions, or shot without effect could shatter the spirit of congeniality that bound fraternities together.

Hunters' love of tall tales illustrated the tangled relationship between trust and congeniality. These stories became extremely popular because they boldly exceeded the limits of the possible. Rather than posing as the truth, these stories exaggerated the truth with such unrivaled and unapologetic intensity that few ever questioned their veracity. They enthralled and entertained; they did not inform. When related in person, this sort of easy play with the truth required a strong sense of community; if everyone, teller and listener alike, shared a similar understanding of the world, intentionally outrageous lies became obvious. Hunters could safely revel in wildly inaccurate campfire tales because of the nature of their audience. The danger arose when someone (be it an untrustworthy slave, unreliable relative, shyster lawyer, litigious neighbor, or unscrupulous merchant) presented a member of the party with a mundane (and therefore less detectable) lie.[3]

Hunters resented anyone who took advantage of this trust. In one case a white hunter from Augusta, Georgia, became increasingly irritated with one of his acquaintances — a duck shooter named Tom — because he inflated a story of his prowess to ridiculous proportions. Ordinarily acceptable, this behavior became threatening because Tom told the story to anyone who would listen. While tale-telling among friends and family was agreeable, Tom insisted upon boasting about his unlikely prowess to strangers. If they expressed doubts, Tom called upon one of his companions for corroboration. Eventually the companion complained, "Look here, Tom, if you add another duck, I'll be d—d if you must not get a new witness!"[4] In this case their fraternity initially eliminated the danger of the lie, but as it drifted into wider society, it took on new power and potency. If a lie escaped into the wider community, it could threaten the standing of the entire fraternity. Tom became problematic when he told his lies to an audience made gullible by the corroboration of his companion.

Hunters loved tall tales, but they remained suspicious of yarn-spinning strangers because a lack of familiarity made it more difficult to detect their lies. Once they escaped from the intimate circle of fraternity, these lies could lead to lawsuits, fights, and duels rather than laughter and good cheer. This concern with the imperceptible lie helps explain hunters' distrust of braggarts. Because a surreptitiously inflated tally of kills or a believable tale of triumph could easily evade detection, most hunters preferred quiet modesty or ridiculous flights of fancy. Writing in 1830, a correspondent of the *American Turf Register* remarked that "first rate shots never brag. If ever you hear a bragger; mark him down a junior sportsman, or second rate."[5]

Even though most hunters respected modesty, an individual could always brag about the abilities of others, especially his regular companions. Many stories told in the first person included glowing descriptions of the other members of the hunting party, praising their prowess, self-control, or mastery. When a Mississippi hunter killed an elk near Vicksburg in 1843 (a rare feat by that time), the lucky hunter spread the credit around, acknowledging dog, gun, and hunting companions alike. Like gift giving, this sort of ostentatious display remained acceptable because it masked as generosity. Because the only worthy praise was unsought and unexpected, most considered this sort of "indirect bragging" appropriate.[6]

Most white hunters predicated trust upon homogeneity. Few white hunters sought much variety among their hunting companions because they wanted companions who resembled themselves. The common practice of excluding hunters who seemed markedly different revealed a pervasive fear of untrustworthy otherness. Because appearances could be deceiving, most depended on introductions or firsthand experience when assessing strangers. With trustworthiness resting on a foundation of familiarity, a dearth of references could scuttle an otherwise attractive prospect. Stereotyping provided a useful instrument for the creation of homogeneity, but most fraternities made their final determination in the field.

Whatever the alchemy of the particular moment or the exact composition of the group, most white hunters enjoyed time spent in the exclu-

"Hunter's Camp on Meadow Mountain." By Edward Stabler, from Meshach Browning, *Forty-Four Years of the Life of a Hunter; Being Reminiscences of Meshach Browning, a Maryland Hunter,* rev. and illustrated by E[dward] Stabler (Philadelphia, 1859), opp. p. 386.

sive company of their peers. Trust and homogeneity created an exclusive space that allowed relaxation and a degree of intimacy that most men balked at in wider society. Once fraternity members established a certain level of trust and confidence in one another, the brittle formality of white society evaporated. The absence of women, an abundance of liquor, and what a Mississippi hunter described as "an infinite quantity of laughing at jokes, new and old, witty and dull," created a relaxed atmosphere. Other hunters expressed similar sentiments. In 1841 a white hunter from Alabama described a deer-hunting expedition in the *Spirit of the Times.* "Never, Mr. Editor," he wrote, "can you realize in all their liveliness and *haut gout,* the joyous delights that wait on dog and gun, until you shall have made one of a party of good, hearty, social fellows, to 'camp out' for a deer-hunt—men who can give and take, as they come round, either a horn or a joke, and maintain for days together the keenest rivalry for the honors of the field, all in honorable fairness and gentlemanly good humor."[7]

Class certainly played an important role in the selection of companions, but in the end congeniality rather than wealth or status determined whom white hunters considered their peers. Even as they studiously maintained divisions of color and gender, white hunters often allowed class lines to fade into insignificance in the field. Planters who lived along the Atlantic seaboard could create and maintain exclusive clubs, but in more recently settled districts with a large percentage of small farmers, white hunters rarely became very particular about the social stature of their companions. When Mississippi planter Zenas C. Preston went hunting in 1844, he thought nothing of taking the field with his trusted overseer Saxon Adams. Members of the gentry who published accounts of such "egalitarian" hunts in the sporting press often represented their participation as a kind of paternalistic condescension, but most of those who recorded these outings in their diaries did so without posturing.[8]

Some hunters seemed to meet all the obvious prerequisites for membership in a fraternity, but they still found themselves excluded because they could not align their behavior with the expectations of their companions. Congeniality and trust only came if an individual modified his behavior to fit with his hosts. Only then could a hunter begin the slow process of familiarization that would gradually endow him with a sense of trustworthiness. Demographic similarities alone could not ensure a spirit of congeniality. A series of stories appearing in the *Spirit of the Times* in 1849 describe a manic hunter from Arkansas named Mr. Catchpenny. These stories exaggerate for comedic effect, but they also illustrate the effectiveness of the hunt as a proving ground for the demonstration of congeniality.

Catchpenny secures an invitation to join a hunting party by virtue of his white skin, gender, age, and native birth. He quickly exposes the quality of his character, however, when he reveals that he considers bear hunting an "indispensable accomplishment" that will aid his political ambitions. Such blatant social climbing makes him immediately suspect to his companions. Although hunting with a group certainly provided opportunities for cutting deals and discussing politics, most hunters rarely appreciated those who approached the hunt as an opportunity for the overt promotion of their personal agendas.

Catchpenny is even more suspect once the extent of his hunting skills becomes apparent. He cuts a ridiculous figure, appearing in the field equipped with an assortment of gaudy hunting paraphernalia and riding a mule that "resembled a plump, half fledged squab in its early efforts to fly."[9] In the forest Catchpenny quickly becomes disoriented and panicky, imagining hungry predators behind every tree. When a bear appears he runs away, his gun dangling forgotten in his hand. Increasingly emasculated and alienated from the other hunters, Catchpenny becomes obsessed with making a kill. After a night's rest he rides back into the fray on the author's charger, "eager to retrieve his lost reputation," but he remains "oblivious of the process of rough joking" at his expense taking place among the other members of the hunt. During the party's next encounter with a bear, Catchpenny hides in fear, but once his companions have brought it down, he acts out a vicious travesty of hand-to-hand combat in a foolishly brutal display. "His mighty soul seemed suddenly aroused by the intense excitement of the scene. In a voice of thunder, he cried, 'kill him! kill him! kill him!' and, as if all the courage of all the Caesars animated his single arm, he rushed furiously up. Panting, he paused to collect all his energies for the desperate struggle, then, with clenched teeth, and fiercely protruding eyes he recklessly threw himself upon the foe. Fast and strong descended the blows of Mr. Catchpenny's reeking knife, and at each blow he muttered with vindictive satisfaction, 'oh y-e-s, damn you.'"

In the story these excesses are attributed to the previous day's humiliation. Constructed as the antithesis of southern masculinity, Catchpenny revealed the personal nature of congeniality. This effeminate, oblivious, self-interested, vicious, inexperienced lout showed the southern readers of the *Spirit of the Times* a twisted and brutal reflection of their own worst tendencies, but they only became apparent in the course of the hunt.[10]

Most of the narrative focuses upon Catchpenny's unworthiness, and although it proves this time and again, it also reveals something about his hosts. Because the story also features positive images in the form of the narrator and his companions, it throws Catchpenny's failings into stark contrast. Unlike Catchpenny, these hunters shoot with effect and maintain an admirable level of self-control (especially in light of Catchpenny's foolishness and incompetence). By generously shepherding Catchpenny through his grievous errors and frequent gaffes, their good humor verifies the depth of their masculinity and the strength of their fraternity.

If an initiate appeared capable of congeniality, he could begin striving for masculine achievement within the context of a fraternity. As always, the kill remained at the center of such displays. Some white hunters, particularly those with a romantic or particularly elitist bent, insisted on commemorating a novice's first deer, bear, or fox with a rite of passage. Some established fraternity members seemed particularly taken with these ceremonies, but most novices remained more intent on achieving their first kill. These rituals varied from fraternity to fraternity, and a few became quite theatrical. The most melodramatic initiation rite—blooding—included smearing the face of the initiate with the blood of his first kill. Established fraternity members used this as a ritual of inclusion, which symbolized the verification of a novice's manhood, but because congeniality only developed over time, many fraternities stopped short of making this a sign of true equality.

One of William Elliott's accounts of a drive for deer in low-country South Carolina, "A Day at Chee-Ha," contains the most detailed and nuanced account of blooding in the sporting literature of the antebellum South. In this story Elliott rides into the swamps surrounding his plantation accompanied by his neighbor Loveleap (an enthusiastic and experienced hunter), "two sportsmen who had not yet 'fleshed their maiden swords,'" a pack of twelve hounds, and two slave drivers who minded the

dogs. In the course of the drive, one of the novices, whom Elliott nick-
named Tickle, dropped a deer with the second barrel of his shotgun in full
view of the rest of the party. The other hunters quickly rode in and congratulated him on his "first exploit in sylvan warfare."[11] As Tickle stooped
to examine his trophy, Loveleap "slipped his knife into the throat of the
deer, and before his purpose could be guessed at, bathed his [Tickle's] face
with the blood of his victim." "This, you must know," Elliott explained,
"*is hunter's law* with us, on the killing [of] a first deer." Elliott's favorite
driver, Robin, instructed Tickle on the importance of blooding.

> As our young sportsman started up from the ablution, his face glaring like an In-
> dian chief's in all the splendor of war-paint—Robin the hunter touched his cap
> and thus accosted him: "Maussa Tickle, if you wash off dat blood dis day—you
> nebber hav luck again so long as you hunt." "Wash it off!" cried we all, with one
> accord; "who ever heard of such a folly. He can be no true sportsman, who is
> ashamed of such a livery." Thus beset, and moved thereunto, by the other sage ad-
> vices showered upon him by his companions in sport, he wore his bloody mask
> to the close of that long day's sport, and sooth to say, returned to receive the con-
> gratulations of his young and lovely wife, his face still adorned with the stains of
> victory.[12]

In this short passage Elliott conveyed a wealth of information about his
particular vision of the hunt. From the outset "Tickle" is clearly something less than a man in Elliott's eyes. His nickname alone sets him apart
as an immature, subordinate member of the party. In front of this discerning audience, Tickle's marriage, which ordinarily would have connoted
a substantial degree of masculinity, means nothing. In Elliott's world of
the hunt, Tickle remains an untested virgin who has not yet "fleshed his
maiden sword." Elliott further reduced the young hunter's stature when
he pushed Robin into the foreground. Elliott and Loveleap signify the
temporary transfer of their authority to Robin by supporting his lecture
with occasional shouts of affirmation. This momentary inversion owes
everything to Elliott, who basks in a glow of preeminent mastery and paternalistic benevolence. Robin's status as Elliott's slave makes his actions
and knowledge an extension of Elliott. He considered himself such a fine
sportsman that even his slave possessed a master's understanding of sport.

Significantly, even after enduring an ablution of blood and a battery of
hectoring lectures, Tickle remains subordinate. In this case "initiation" did
not create equality. For Elliott, blooding was just another test of Tickle's

worthiness. Even as he directed a celebration of Tickle's accomplishment, Elliott reinforced Tickle's inferiority by undermining his success. Elliott revealed that "the claims of our novice, to the merit and penalties of this day's hunt, were equally incomplete, for it appeared after inspection, that Loveleap had given the mortal wound, and that Tickle had merely given the 'coup de grace' to a deer, that, if unfired on, would have fallen of itself, in a run of a hundred yards." "It must be believed," he acknowledged, "that we were quite too generous to divulge this unpleasant discovery to our novice, in the first pride of his triumph!"[13]

By denying Tickle the kill in print while keeping his peace in person, Elliott reinforced the power of his own position (and that of Loveleap) and heightened the exclusivity of his fraternity. As experienced hunters who stood comfortably at the center of their small fraternity, Elliott and Loveleap easily adapted the situation to suit themselves. By anointing Tickle on their own terms, they asserted their absolute control over the hunt and their chosen companions. Such benevolent generosity further strengthened their masculinity. By affirming their power over Tickle, they also strengthened the bonds of congeniality that bound them together.

For the most part blooding remained the rite of the excessively romantic. It carried more weight in literature than it did in daily life. Despite Elliott's assertions, blooding was no "hunter's law." In fact, it only existed in a handful of communities. Few hunters even bothered recording narratives of their own first kills. Because diaries and personal correspondence rarely note these moments, Frederick Gustavus Skinner's memories of killing his first deer are exceptional. He remembered that after shooting it down, he became "hungry for the congratulations of my friend and teacher," because of his eagerness "to be formally admitted into the noble fraternity of Woodsmen." No stranger to romantic allusion, he explained that he "felt like a young squire of the Middle Ages who had gallantly won his spurs and was about to receive the accolade of knighthood from a Bayard or a Duguesclin." His mentor shared in his excitement and wished they were in Germany so they could have a triumphal ceremony including a march of the "sons of St. Hubert," libations in honor of the "jolly god of the Rhine," and "dancing and general festivity." After their shared joy in the young hunter's accomplishment, the mentor patiently listened as his protégé expounded upon the details of the kill.[14]

Unlike young Skinner, most initiates preferred liberal doses of alcohol to blood rituals when they and their companions marked their first kills. After a night of heavy drinking in 1857, a Louisiana novice succeeded in killing his first deer. Elated at his success, he tied the trophy to his saddle and joyfully led his companions back into camp where he drank "a thumping dose" of liquor, which unexpectedly turned his stomach. Staggering into the tree line, "he commenced spouting in a way very much resembling a fire engine, the nozzle of which is chocked up!"[15] Few fraternities encouraged such dramatics; in fact, most hunters experienced their first kill with relatively little fanfare. After a morning's hunt in 1850, wealthy South Carolina rice planter Keating Simons Ball recorded in his diary: "Hunted before breakfast. Francis M. Waring, a lad, killed a deer, the first he ever shot." The boy's accomplishment was worthy of comment, but scarcely so.[16] Whether terse or crudely slapstick, these brief notices of a hunter's first kill usually lacked ritual and pageantry. They did, however, demonstrate the willingness and ability to kill, which remained the bedrock of any hunter's character. Killing provided many fraternities with an excellent litmus test for their initiates, and the rituals associated with it by sportsmen like Elliott and Skinner were less important than the event itself.

Indeed, the best evidence of inclusion and acceptance is not found in these rituals. Congeniality usually sprang from routine interactions among hunting companions that often led to continued socialization off the hunting field. Because of its physical and ideological separation from the domestic sphere, the hunt provided an effective testing ground for new male members of a community. If initiates proved themselves worthy in this rather rarefied space, they could then gain an entrée into other, more private aspects of their hunting companions' lives. By passing muster in the world of men, an aspiring hunter became an acceptable risk in more domestic situations. The diaries of Everard Green Baker chronicle a young bachelor's efforts to establish himself in a new home near Natchez, Mississippi. Although cotillions, church, tea, visits, and dinner parties eventually rounded out his social scene, he first entered the local community through hunting. Once his hunting companions assessed his character and found him congenial, he was allowed to meet and socialize with the female members of their families.[17]

In other situations congeniality could appear fairly rapidly. When they hunted away from home, most white hunters who sought out companions and altered their behavior to fit with local expectations forged temporary

friendships with other hunters rather easily. A group of hunters might take
the field in relative isolation, but even in sparsely settled areas, prolonged
action in the field usually attracted local hunters. When they visited the
campsites of extended hunting expeditions, most of these visitors simply
spent an evening around the campfire drinking liquor and telling stories,
but on other occasions inquisitive locals became regular members of the
hunt.[18] It usually did not matter whether these local hunters were plantation owners or poor whites; traveling hunting parties invariably welcomed
the newcomers because they could provide an intimate knowledge of
the terrain and the wildlife. Even a backwoodsman could find a place
by the campfire of a well-moneyed hunting expedition if he increased the
chances for their success.[19]

Once an initiate proved himself capable of congeniality, he could count
himself a member of the fraternity. Thereafter, he became a mediator of
acceptable behavior and an arbiter of the criteria of exclusion in his own
right. Membership also allowed considerable leeway in personal conduct.
However strictly fraternities policed their boundaries, they usually became
rather flexible when assessing the behavior of their members. After a certain point fraternity members no longer needed to provide constant affirmation of their prowess, self-control, and mastery.

When hunters took the field with trusted companions, it appears that
the rules of sport could safely fall into disuse. Even impeccable sportsmen like F. G. Skinner's mentor, Campbell, maintained an unsporting salt
lick for local deer. This practice contradicted the spirit of his own definition of sport because it eliminated the "manly and legitimate" contest
"between the instincts of the game and the skill and woodcraft of the
hunter." The salt lick meant that instead of pursuing deer, Campbell could
simply set himself near the lick and wait for their approach. Lured by the
taste of salt, they presented him with a variety of easy targets. Campbell
defended his actions by explaining that he did not kill all the deer attracted
by the lick, "for it was too much like assassination" and lacked the proper
challenge of "true sport." Unsatisfied with this explanation, his budding
pupil asked, "How is it, that though you apologized for using a 'lick' as unsportsmanlike, you could bring yourself to establish one?" Confronted by
his student, Campbell thought for a few moments and admitted that although the lick did "prick his conscience every now and then when he

happened to think of it," he maintained it because it assured a steady supply of summer meat.[20]

In some cases fraternity members even altered the display of masculinity by redrawing the particulars of prowess, self-control, and mastery to fit the specifics of their situation. Of the three, self-control became the most subjective. Once a group became sufficiently congenial with one another, self-control became increasingly tractable. In some cases even the previously reprehensible demonstration of passionate excess could actually become an important component of masculine display. If properly timed and placed in a suitable context (that is, in a stable fraternity), the release of passion could become an exercise in the display of self-control.

Hunters sought to repress their passions, but most recognized that excitement remained an essential ingredient in the hunt. For many southerners a man who seemed devoid of passion appeared incomplete. White southerners feared the excesses of passion, but many also believed that when properly harnessed, passion could stoke the fires of ambition and fuel the engines of progress. Hunters with the cold perfection of automatons recast the hunt as cold-blooded murder or (even worse) poorly remunerated labor.[21] For these reasons hunters sought the control of passion, rather than its annihilation. All hunters attempted to achieve a delicate balance of cool detachment and vigorous excitement because a hunter who did not temporarily lose himself in the excitement of the chase had no heart, but the hunter who repeatedly lost control of his passions lacked a head. In the eyes of antebellum observers, the balanced tension between these two elements — the vigorous heart and the rational brain — created a competent and powerful man, but the proper ration and expression of these elements varied from fraternity to fraternity. When in doubt or when hunting with strangers, hunters restrained their passions and focused their energies on presenting a cool and competent demeanor.

Passionate release could have beneficial effects. For many it became an important aspect of the hunt. For a contributor to the *Norfolk Herald,* it made hunting a transcendent experience. When he hunted, he became absorbed in the excitement of the moment, forgot "the pains of body, or of mind diseased," and lost "the recollection of distresses that had almost borne him to the earth."[22] Other white hunters glorified the primal

excitement of the hunt. After killing his first buck, Frederick Gustavus
Skinner "became a lunatic uttering a war-whoop wild enough to resusci-
tate the countless generations of dead Indians who had hunted in ages
past." Some hunters defined their excitement as a kind of temporary madness. Skinner's grandfather John Stuart Skinner explained, "There is certainly, as the Frenchman says, a je ne scai quoi or excitement, a sort of
hallucination, about the *chase,* that borders on madness, delightful madness!" Consumed by the rapture of the chase, William Elliott cheerfully
inquired: "'Huntsmen, is it not charming? Does it not make your pulse
quicken? Is there not a thrill of pleasure shooting through your frame?
Can you tell your name? Have you a wife? A child? *Have you a neck?*' If you
can, at such a moment, answer questions such as these, you do not feel
your position and are but half a sportsman!" For Elliott (an extreme case)
excitement obliterated whatever concerns he brought into the field. Properly elicited, his passion temporarily displaced his reason; it elevated him
above every possible concern. Other forms of recreation provided a
respite from the cares of daily life, but only hunting offered him the complete (if temporary) annihilation of these concerns.[23]

Once he took the field, any number of events could inflame a hunter's
passion. The sound of a pack in full cry, for instance, had the power to
render some hunters speechless—"insensible"—lifting them up into tran-
scendental states of bliss. For the Charlestonian who wrote as Ralph
Ranger, a pack of dogs barked "with music far sweeter to mine ear than
all the German or Italian that ever was played or sung." Greenwood believed that upon hearing the "full chorus" of a pack, "Handel himself, had
he been present would have admitted was music." An Arkansan who gloried in the music of the pack considered its effect an accurate barometer
of manhood. "Shakspeare may talk about a man whose soul is not moved
by a concert of sweet sounds being fit for treason, stratagem, and spoils,"
he explained, "yet men of refinement have been known, who were insensible to the melodious screeching of cat-gut, and who could discover
no particular charm in the opera. But he must be *without* a soul who could
be insensible to the soul stirring music of nature's own choir—a fine pack
of dogs."[24]

The "savage music" of the pack made hunters capable of extremes in
athleticism and foolhardiness. It made a group of Mississippians cast caution to the wind. Pursuing the pack, one of the excitable hunters wrote,

"we fly—we are omnipotent—we dare and surmount any obstacle—performing feats, which, in cooler moment, we shudder to contemplate."[25] Many expressed their joy when this heightening of the passions temporarily overwhelmed their sense of self-preservation and decorum. They delighted in this feeling that recast foolhardiness as bravery. In pursuit of a fleeing deer, a Louisiana hunter explained, "so great was our excitement, and so intense our anxiety, that we did not stop to calculate probabilities; But on we dashed, our whole souls in the chace."[26] Randolph Spalding of Georgia explained that he and his friends hunted foxes by moonlight because in the darkness they could not see the gopher holes. Not being able to see the danger, they didn't "care a d—n" and drove their horses forward without fear.[27]

Fraternity and congeniality proved critical in each of these cases (except Frederick Gustavus Skinner's Indian "war whoop," which his mentor accepted as youthful excess) because passion only became acceptable when hunters lost control of their passions as a group. Congeniality facilitated the creation of a tacit understanding between fraternity members, and it transformed passionate release from a universal failing into an integral element of the hunt. Fraternities could safely and privately regulate the release of passion because they carefully excluded outsiders who might confuse healthy and invigorating passion for its close relative—deleterious and disruptive passion. Socially and physically isolated, the hunt created a special cultural space that made this rather subjective distinction possible. Like the duel, the hunt directed passion into orderly channels through which it could be released. By sharing in an episode of "temporary insanity," each hunter released his individual passions, which in turn drew the group together, making it both stronger and more cohesive.

In contrast, when a hunter lost his composure and his companions did not share his immoderate zeal, his actions were often censured by the other members of the group. In a story entitled "The Enthusiastic Hunter" that appeared in the *American Turf Register* in 1833, Nimrod of King William County, Virginia, described an ardent foxhunter who pursued the fox with what his companions considered an excess of passion. When the exuberant hunter pushed his mare too hard, she fell and broke her neck, leaving him dismounted. After depositing the saddle and bridle at a nearby farmhouse, he continued the chase on foot and soon encountered his younger brother, "who was so much shocked and alarmed at the accident just passed, that he was going to walk his horse, towards home, saying that he had concluded to quit." Already out of the chase, he offered his horse to his overzealous brother, who immediately mounted and sped off in pursuit of the pack. Nimrod noted that "most of the company" were equally shocked and "absolutely quited and went home." Other groups of hunters might welcome such enthusiasm, but a hunter's behavior was always judged in the context of his fraternity, and in this case the foxhunter's companions viewed his fervor as wretched excess.[28] Thus the exact ratio of excitement and self-control always remained a local variable. Most white hunters cultivated this tension throughout their hunting careers, and as they became more experienced, most struck a balance between the thumping heart of a tyro and the cool efficiency of a market hunter that matched the expectations of their companions.

Most hunters eventually acquired calm self-assurance with experience, but even veteran hunters occasionally revealed an unacceptably passionate nature. Hunters constantly sought the reaffirmation of their ability to kill, and when presented with a shot after a long drought of disappointment, many hunters could easily lose their composure. Hunters commonly referred to such a moment of anxiousness as an attack of the dreaded "buck ague."[29] In an 1851 article for the *Southern Literary Messenger,* S. L. C. of Charleston described the moment when an apprehensive hunter anticipates taking a shot at a passing deer. "The heart thumps harder," he wrote, "the throat parches, the sight seems dim and glazed, the hands shake violently, the knees totter, and there is an undoubted case of *Buck-ague.*"[30] Any hunter can experience this moment of immobilization, and it marks a hunter's inability to control his own passions. He is unable to contain his anxiety or excitement enough to take the shot. Unlike a hunter's release of passion, however, there were no positive aspects to buck ague. It simply marked a hunter's inability to achieve his stated aim — a kill. Everyone censured a hunter who endured these moments because they demonstrated his individual lack of self-control and his ineffectiveness as a hunter.[31]

When white hunters lost their coolness and composure without the approval of their companions, their mask of self-control cracked and split, so most of them concealed their momentary weakness. Hunters who offered their own experiences with buck ague for publication usually set their stories in the past or framed them with accounts of their recent successful hunts. A litany of past successes outweighed a few awkward failures. Most hunters, however, simply kept their peace. After describing the symptoms of buck ague, S. L. C. offered a postscript regarding confidentiality: "Many a one has felt it, and confessed it, while a great many men have felt it, but have been wise enough to keep their own secrets."[32]

A few fraternities placed so much emphasis on congeniality that some hunters (especially those who did not depend on hunting for their provisions) came to value socialization more than the excitement of the chase. Virginian Alexander Hunter explained that "it is a matter of indifference to me whether or not my companions are good shots, as but a fraction of the time spent on the trip is spent in actual shooting." When putting together an outing, he always tried to have three companions. This ensured that should the hunt prove disappointing, they could always pair off and make a full whist hand.[33] A South Carolinian who wrote in 1841 emphasized the social and gastronomic pleasures of camp life. After partaking in a satisfying feast that followed a day's hunt, he observed: "Many good and true men, and orthodox sportsmen, too, are of opinion that this is the *best part of a day's hunt*. Without wishing to settle the question, . . . I am free to confess it is by no means to me an *unwelcome part of it*."[34]

Sociability among like-minded men often took precedence over the actual hunt in the wealthiest and most stable fraternities. This was particularly true of the hunting clubs of the South Carolina low country. As game became depleted in their neighborhoods, many of these clubs gradually became little more than steering committees for elaborate neighborhood barbecues. In his sketch of the St. John's Hunting Club, Robert Wilson maintained that by the 1850s a majority of the club's members rarely hunted, and "quite a number" of them could not load a gun or sound a horn, though most showed up for neighborhood gatherings. Few of these clubs even mentioned hunting in their written rules. Instead, they concentrated on the particulars of the monthly club supper, eventually becoming, by the end of the antebellum era, supper clubs in all but name. In these cases the desire for socialization and conspicuous consumption overrode any limitations in the availability of game.[35]

Not surprisingly then, in 1849 Floridian William Stockton could admit that membership in some hunting clubs had little to do with hunting ability. One poor shot remained a member of a club because "he was one of the best and most amusing fellows in the world." Regardless of his poor marksmanship—"he never could learn to shoot"—he always turned out on hunting days because he enjoyed the company. His companions accommodated his shortcomings by assigning him the worst stand—keeping him away from most of the action and keeping themselves safe from any stray shots.[36] In the rarefied world of low-country clubs, hunting companions might make allowances for such incompetence, but in other contexts bunglers would not be tolerated. This was especially true among poorer white hunters who relied on game for provisions. In these cases the weak link in a string of deer stands could find himself the butt of jokes and insults. Repeated failures could result in ostracism.

The value that low-country hunting clubs placed upon congeniality was exceptionally high, and few other fraternities ever achieved their level of stability and continuity. Yet the members of many of these clubs continued to reenact the practiced drama of the hunt because it remained a perfect venue for the display of their masculinity. Most fraternities, including some of the seaboard clubs such as the Camden Hunting Club of Camden County, Georgia, continued to stress the kill over socialization. An 1838 correspondent of the *American Turf Register* described the Camden group as "one of the best regulated clubs of the kind in the United States." As evidence he presented the club's rule sixteen, which stated that "any member who shall fire at a deer less than 40 yards distant, and not *hit* or *kill,* when the *opportunity is fair,* shall be fined.—No deer shall be considered hit unless *killed,* or unless *blood is seen.*"[37] Meek but sociable hunters could simply hold their fire, avoid the fine, and enjoy the society of the clubhouse or campfire.

The exclusivity that hunters expressed in culling their potential hunting companions was in the name of congeniality. In so doing, it provided them an effective instrument for the creation of coherent white communities. Whatever the exclusiveness or stability of their hunting fraternities, hunters congratulated themselves when they could dispense with invitations altogether. Hunters enjoyed knowing that they could quickly assemble their neighbors, dogs, and slaves with a handful of messengers and a few blasts of a hunting horn because it dramatized the power and coherence of white society.[38]

A hunter in west Florida illustrated the power of this communitarian feeling when he described the change that overtook himself and his neighbors every year in late October. Describing the members of his hunting fraternity, he excitedly explained that "a desire to hunt became *instantly* a strong feeling with several of us, as if there was some necessary conexion between these first chilling winds of autumn and that state of mind."[39] Needing neither plans nor encouragement, his neighbors instinctively knew when to turn out for a drive for deer. Invitations became superfluous because this group of friends shared something approaching group consciousness born of familiarity and habit.[40] This degree of coordination and cohesiveness illustrated more than the élan of a particular hunting fraternity. It made visible the lines of power and control that crisscrossed southern society. At the sound of a hunting horn, field hands did not drop their hoes and join the chase; women did not rush for their riding boots; and poor whites remained in their fields unless called upon as guides. Only members of the fraternity in question responded to the call. This routine event continually reenacted the hierarchy of power upon which southern society was constructed. It reinforced the white hunters' sense of mastery over their subordinates, and it strengthened their cohesiveness as a master class.

Hunting was an eminently social activity. Regardless of their social standing, all white hunters wanted to display their masculinity, but the drama of the hunt remained unfulfilled unless performed before an audience of appreciative peers. This desire for validation underpinned the creation of fraternities and the subsequent imposition of various criteria of exclusion. Hunting fraternities desired exclusivity because hunters placed a great weight on the approbation of their peers. Hunters took great pride and satisfaction in their companions, so they selected them with care, because without the presence of congeniality, the display of masculinity became wasted effort. Hunting fraternities looked to the sporting press for ideas and inspiration, but in the end their understanding of the hunt, masculinity, and sport depended upon the encouragement and validation they received from each other. Thus, white hunters established and enforced a variety of criteria of exclusion. By excluding undesirables and encouraging a degree of order and conformity within their ranks, hunting fraternities became peer communities. Trust, homogeneity, and intimacy revealed the presence of congeniality, which in turn signified the existence of worthwhile companions and a stable fraternity of hunters.

Congeniality bore other fruits as well. The feeling of community that it helped create bound white males together. These ties supported abstract notions like white supremacy by providing concrete representations of white power. By displaying white masculinity to such varied audiences, the hunt provided a dramatic affirmation of white supremacy and the tremendous power wielded by white males. This was true in terms of both the hunt and what the hunt represented. Just as killing an animal could dramatize the wide-ranging mastery of white patriarchy, the gathering of a hunting party could represent much more than a merry day of male bonding. An assembly of white men on horseback with guns and dogs could track a runaway slave as easily as they could set out on a hunting excursion. In either case it was an unmistakable exercise of white power. In the eyes of white hunters, and indeed in the eyes of all southerners, participation in the hunt made them more than men; it made them a master class.

6. Slavery, Paternalism, and the Hunt

Sam was the Chief's alter-ego and he was universally admitted to be a first-rate judge and manager of farm stock generally, but far above this the old darkey prided himself on his knowledge of and skill in hunting raccoons, and other nocturnal "varmints." . . . He seems to me to have retained in a greater degree than any of his race I have ever seen, the more useful instincts of his—not remote—savage ancestry; instincts nearer to infallibility as regards the interpretation of the simpler laws of nature than much of our boasted knowledge.

Frederick Gustavus Skinner, hunter and essayist, 1887

SLAVES and slaveholders hunted together throughout the antebellum South. Unlike the adventures of Huck and Jim, these hunts rarely created an atmosphere of egalitarian camaraderie, nor did the usual absence of women create the opportunity for a color-blind "boy's night out." As historian Kenneth S. Greenberg has noted, "An integrated hunt was not an egalitarian hunt."[1] Instead, as so often happened in the Old South, slaves and slaveholders sought different goals and ascribed different meanings to one another's actions while working and living in intimate proximity. They participated in the same hunts, but they occupied radically different positions in the antebellum power structure, utilized different knowledge of the natural world, and even employed different criteria of success. Whether cognizant or blissfully unaware of these differences, slaveholders incorporated slaves into their hunts and their hunting stories.

In most hunting narratives slaves were usually mere supernumeraries. Working quietly in the background, they performed the unacknowledged labor that made it possible for slaveholders to adopt the pose of men of leisure. While slaveholders acted out their dramas of masculinity and mastery, slaves hauled, tracked, cooked, cleaned, and chopped. It was a rare traveler or slaveholder who recognized the vital role that slave labor played in allowing southern elites to enjoy the recreation and gratification of sport. Most authors relegated slaves to the margins of their narratives. Like house servants and field hands, slave huntsmen were usually unseen and unacknowledged.[2]

In reality, slaves performed a variety of tasks at every stage of the hunt. Much of this labor occurred before anyone even took the field. Slaveholders depended upon slave farriers, grooms, and stable hands for the training and care of their dogs and horses. These slaves often accompanied the animals into the field as handlers and whippers-in. The initial stages of most organized hunts also depended upon slave labor. On many occasions slave couriers carried the messages that brought the white hunters together. Once white hunters agreed on a time and location, slaves usually facilitated transportation. If traveling by water, white hunters depended upon slave oarsmen. Even if they rode horses or carriages, a slave usually brought up the rear with a wagon full of supplies.[3]

Whites continued relying on slave labor once they reached the field. If a hunting outing stretched overnight, slaves performed the "rougher work in camp," which included such domestic chores as preparing meals, gathering firewood, and cleaning the campsite.[4] Slaves also performed active roles in the course of the hunt itself. They frequently tracked and located game, guarded stands, and directed the pack. After a successful hunt their labor continued; while whites relaxed, slaves dressed and cooked the game and looked after the horses and dogs. If the whites became bored with their own company, they might call on their slaves for a bit of fireside entertainment.[5]

The particular composition of these tasks depended upon the nature of the hunt—its size, duration, and quarry. Different kinds of hunting demanded a variety of special duties for slaves. A foxhunt, for instance, required slaves capable of driving dogs, caring for horses, and repairing broken fences. Deer drives, on the other hand, required tracking, driving, and butchering. Raccoon hunts called for yet another mix of skills. On these hunts slaves (who usually provided their own dogs) acted as dog drivers, torchbearers, and axmen.[6] Regardless of these variations, most slaveholders agreed with the English sojourner Captain Flack who recommended that every group of white hunters take along "a couple of servants . . . to perform all the little odd jobs about the camp, and to take charge of it during their absence."[7]

In many cases slave hunters were just another piece of equipment in the eyes of their owners. One slave hunter, John Finnely of Jackson County, Alabama, recalled this attitude when he described his duties in the field.

"De Marster used me fo' huntin'," he explained. "Him use me fo' de gun rest. W'en him have a long shot, I'se bend over an' put my hands on my knees wi'le de Marster put his gun on my back fo' to git a good aim." He continued, "Also, I's tu'n de squirrels fo' him. W'at I's do am to walk 'roun' de tree, den de squirrel watches me an' goest to de udder side f'om de huntah . . . den de squirrel watches me an' goest to de udder side whar de Marster am astandin' still. Den he gits de shot." He decided, "All dat am not so bad, but w'en he shoots de duck in de wautah an' I'se have to getch it out, dat gives me de worryments. So de whuppin' comes dis away."

> De fust time he tells me to fetch de duck f'om de pond, I's skeert, powe'ful skeert. I's stahts to git ready, tooks off my shirt an' pants but thar I's stands. I's steps in de wautah, den back 'gain, an' 'gain. De Marster am gittin' mad. He finally says:
> "Swim in dere an' git day duck!"
> "Yas sar, yas sar, Marster", I's says, but I's jus' keep steppin' in an' back. Finally de Marster cuts a switch an' gits behind me. Hie hits 'bout three good licks an' den in I's goes."

"I's could never git used to bein' de wautah dog fo' ducks," Finnely concluded.[8]

White hunters who wrote narratives of their hunts concentrated on their white characters and typically downplayed the presence of the vast majority of the slaves who accompanied their outings as simple laborers, but some writers described their slave companions in some detail. A few even created hunting narratives that feature slave protagonists. These narratives usually focus on the accomplishments of certain extraordinary slave hunters, or "huntsmen." Huntsmen performed a variety of tasks. Some spent most of the year hunting for their owner's larder while others only took the field in the company of their owner or his sons.

When slave huntsmen appear in white narratives, their actions usually support the ideology of white supremacy and benevolent patriarchy. Fixated upon the idea of mastery, these pieces sidestep the mundane utility of slave labor and focus on the symbolic relationships between slave hunters and their owners. As unapologetic advocates of white supremacy, these writers used their hunting stories as an instrument to promote the idea that slavery was a social good. The presence of slaves provided an opportunity for southern whites to demonstrate their mastery over slaves and (by association) free African Americans too. Toward this end white

hunters — be they diarists, essayists, or novelists — carefully tailored their
descriptions of slaves to resonate with the racist expectations of their
slaveholding friends, neighbors, and relatives. These narratives present
white visions of idealized black masculinity.

These images of slaves and this vision of slavery complemented the
contemporaneous efforts of the overtly political proslavery ideologues.
Beginning in the early 1830s, the recognized mainstream of proslavery
thinkers, which featured political writers such as John C. Calhoun, Roderick Dew, and George Fitzhugh and novelists such as William Gilmore
Simms and John Pendleton Kennedy, developed the proposition that
southern slavery was the most logical, moral, and economically effective
form of social organization.[9] Unlike these outspoken and often combative proslavery figures, authors of hunting narratives addressed the subject
of slavery indirectly. They rarely made the promotion of slavery the central feature of their stories, but in describing hunting practices and rituals,
they created an effective platform for the promotion of proslavery doc-
trines. Ostensibly apolitical national periodicals like the *American Turf Register* and the *Spirit of the Times* provided access to an excellent audience of
transsectional white males — an audience the proslavery ideologues craved
but found almost impossible to address.

Consciously or not, these writers discovered an effective instrument for
the dissemination of proslavery ideas. Never overtly political, they operated within the constraints of their medium. Editorial policies, the desire
of commercial publishers for a national audience, and the demands of
American readers for action and excitement meant that southern hunting stories were not polemical. The resulting innocuousness of most hunting narratives increases their value as a source for determining popular
ideas about slaves and slavery in the antebellum South. Because many of
these writers never even considered the political implications of their slave
characters, their stories reveal the pervasiveness of proslavery ideas among
members of the southern elite.

White writers presented a particularly sentimental vision of slavery. The
submission and obedience of the slaves appearing in these narratives represented the power of their owners. Few of these stories, however, describe the use of physical coercion by slave owners. Rather than illustrating
the brute efficacy of corporal punishment, white writers celebrated the

subtle controls of paternalism. Essentially a system of slave management, paternalism offered slave owners an effective and palatable alternative to the relentlessly brutal inhumanity of chattel slavery. By supplementing main force with a series of informal negotiations between themselves and their slaves, paternalists recognized a measure of humanity in their slaves. Antebellum advocates of paternalism insisted that if slaveholders recognized their slaves' abilities, they could reap the rewards of increased productivity, prestige, and satisfaction. The image of beneficent masters and loyal bondsmen also aided slaveholders in their defense of an increasingly embattled institution. By creating an image of slaves prospering under the benevolent umbrella of paternalism, these stories echoed the wishful thinking of proslavery ideologues.[10]

Blending utility and symbolism, nothing displayed the promise of paternalism and the power of white mastery as effectively as the huntsman did. By illustrating the effectiveness of paternalism, these idealized slaves promoted slavery as an ideal system of social organization and racial harmony. By creating huntsmen who were attentive, loyal, and capable while remaining simpleminded, slothful, and somewhat childlike, white writers provided their readers with a composite of the white image of the ideal slave. Unlike the numerous field hands who customarily accompanied white hunts, these slaves did more than simply labor; they dramatized a paternalistic vision of the South. Promoted from the ranks of ordinary laborers for their intelligence and ability, huntsmen provided an idealized vision of master-slave relations and, by inference, of a functional slave society. Highly valued by their owners, they repaid trust and affection with loyalty and attentiveness. Trusted with firearms, influence, and a measure of autonomy, huntsmen provided a powerful and easily digestible illustration of paternalism. These slaves acted as the black analogue to the romantic backwoodsman. Instead of threatening the stability of southern society, they reinforced it.[11]

Slaveholders rarely coddled their huntsmen, but many did allow them a great deal of latitude. Few slaves, however, could expect the freedom with which South Carolina planter-politician William Elliott's huntsman Robin shirked onerous or dangerous labor. On one occasion, while riding after the pack in pursuit of a fleeing deer, Elliott and Robin pulled up their horses at the edge of a dense thicket that had grown across a canal. As the dogs continued into the underbrush, Robin dismounted and climbed a tree overlooking the field of action. His eyes could not penetrate the "Serbonian bog" of the thicket, but both listened as the sound of the chase grew increasingly distant and excited. "Zounds, Robin!" cried Elliott, "they have him at bay there — there in the canal. Down from your perch, my lad, or they'll eat him, horns and all, before you reach him." Despite Elliott's enthusiasm, Robin maintained his position and observed: "What use, massa? fore I git dere, dem dog polish ebery bone." Infuriated, Elliott exclaimed, "You are afraid, you rascal! you have only to swim the canal," but before he could finish, Robin had interjected, "Got maussa, if he be water, I swim 'em — if he be bog, I bog 'um — if he be briar, I kratch tru um — but who de debble, but otter, no so alligator, go tru all tree one time!" Stymied by Robin's intransigence, Elliott wondered if he had, in fact, given an unreasonable order in the excitement of the moment. The incident passed, and the hunt continued without any punishment for Robin.[12]

Southern literature is replete with images of lazy and intransigent slaves. It was less common to portray an incident in which slaves were allowed to argue their way out of a task, and Robin was only allowed to do so at Elliott's pleasure. Robin never feared harsh retribution because of the special relationship that he and Elliott appeared to share. Robin knew better, however, than to question Elliott's orders in front of other whites. Thus, this idealized vision of the master-slave relationship required characters who knew their roles and the limits of acceptable behavior. Elliott never considered Robin's reluctance a threat to his power, so Robin acquired a significant degree of autonomy, but only because of Elliott's confidence in Robin's ultimate loyalty.

The image of the knowledgeable, capable, and loyal huntsman attained its purest forms in literature, but the huntsman was also celebrated by white hunters in their diaries and correspondence. Even if he fell short of literary ideals, a loyal huntsman reinforced the paternalistic vision of slave society, and so he was viewed by white hunters with particularly warm emotions.[13] A huntsman was valued because he represented more than just assistance in the field and an occasional brace of quail. Because paternalism exemplified the highest level of white mastery, a skilled and competent huntsman complemented the masculinity of the hunter who owned him. A huntsman's behavior represented his owner's masculinity by illustrating his capacity for the skillful mastery of others. The hunt was an ideal venue for such a demonstration because it often provided a convenient audience of peers.

In their search for masculine prestige, some hunters found the display of paternalism particularly enticing because when wielded with skill, it dramatized the personal power of the slaveholder who used it. Mastery without physical coercion never failed to impress other whites. Even when presented with the opportunity for escape and equipped with the instruments of rebellion, huntsmen appeared attentive and loyal. Huntsmen were perfect foils for white protagonists because they provided dramatic verification of white power, masculinity, and (not incidentally) the righteousness of slave society. Elusive and subtle, paternalism was difficult to display. Small wonder then that slave owners prized their huntsmen. They provided their owners with an unparalleled instrument for the dramatization of a quietly negotiated relationship.

Because of these qualities, white hunters placed huntsmen high in the hierarchy that they imposed on the slave community. Many white writers characterized them as members of a "slave aristocracy"—a stratum of the slave community that lived in close proximity to whites. The white understanding of this relationship appeared clearly in John James Audubon's idealized vision of southern society, which included generous and openhanded planters and loyal and capable huntsmen. Describing a hunt in low-country South Carolina, he wrote:

> Each pack of dogs is under the guidance of a coloured driver, whose business it is to control the hounds and encourage them in the hunt. The drivers ride in most cases the fleetest horses on the ground, in order to be able, whilst on a deer hunt, to stop the dogs. These men, who are so important in the success of the chase, are possessed of a good deal of intelligence and shrewdness, are usually much petted, and regarding themselves as belonging to the aristocracy of the plantation, are apt to look down upon their fellow-servants as inferiors, and consider themselves privileged even to crack a joke with their masters.[14]

Like the drivers who directed the labor of field hands on large plantations, these slaves possessed a measure of responsibility and autonomy; like house servants, they often worked in close proximity with whites; and like artisans, they possessed special skills valued by their owners. When they accompanied whites into the field, their skills and specialized knowledge increased their owners' comfort and chances for success. Because they were the most conspicuous slave hunters, their labors often emphasized the display of mastery rather than unadorned utility.

Huntsmen often acted as auxiliaries for white hunts, but they also often took the field alone in service of their owners. When they considered their huntsmen, slaveholders usually fixated upon the demonstration of their mastery, but another, more prosaic benefit remained foremost in the minds of many slaveholders: meat. The dramatization of mastery interested southern writers, but for many slaveholders huntsmen provided nothing more than a specialized form of slave labor. Relatively unsupervised and trusted with firearms, these slaves ranged through the fields, forests, and swamps that surrounded their owners' homes. By feeding their families and dependents with the game brought in by slave hunters, slaveholders simultaneously improved the quality of their diets and cut the cost of provisioning. Even on a relatively self-sufficient farm or plantation, it also provided a welcome respite from the otherwise incessant routine of pork and corn.[15]

When slaveholders sent their huntsmen into the field alone, they did so because they knew that huntsmen could provide a relatively steady supply of game for their own tables and the slave kitchens. By relying on huntsmen for provisions, slaveholders could maintain their sporting credentials. Rather than stooping to the level of market hunters themselves, these slaveholders hunted for the pot through trusted surrogates. When a huntsman returned from the forest with a brace of ducks, his owner was not concerned whether they were shot "on the wing." The rules of sport need not apply to slave hunters.[16]

Meat was much more than a meal, however. In a society dominated by ideas of ownership and control, it became a repository of power. Meat became charged with meaning when a slave huntsman returned from the field. Anxious to display his competence (for the privilege of hunting could easily be withdrawn), the hunter usually relinquished whatever game he killed to his owner or the cook. This ensured the owner's monopoly on meat. In the slaveholder's estimation he was entitled to the meat because of his position as the head of the household. Among whites the gift of game played with subtly paternalistic resonance, but when game passed between a slave owner and his slaves, it was a tangible reminder of the owner's power and domination. A slave owner who controlled food controlled life and death.[17]

In the eyes of their owners, huntsmen resembled other high-ranking slaves, but this special status cut in two directions. It provided huntsmen with greater autonomy and a marginally better standard of living, but it also made them more visible to their owners. Because of the huntsmen's special status, their owners expected more (in terms of labor and loyalty) from them than from other slaves. Proximity created a new set of tensions and responsibilities. In a society based upon forced labor and predicated upon white supremacy, anonymity could have its advantages.

Huntsmen led comparatively privileged lives, but they lived under the constant threat of demotion. Matthias, the designated duck hunter on a low-country South Carolina rice plantation, took the field six days a week during duck season, which lasted most of the winter. The overseer only trusted him with enough powder for a single shot, so every workday Matthias hiked into a nearby marsh, where he crawled through the reeds until he reached the water's edge. There he carefully sighted his heavy long-barreled musket upon the unsuspecting rafts of congregating waterfowl that rested on the water. Once his gun was sighted, he lay in the mud until the birds grouped themselves in a position favorable for a single, massively destructive shot. One year the overseer grew dissatisfied with Matthias's performance and switched him to the plantation's canal-digging crew. A few days later he inspected the construction site from his horse. He called out for Matthias, and when he appeared, he asked, "Do you think you can kill ducks now?" Matthias implored him, "Obshur, jus' try me, fur de Lord's sake, try me!" Satisfied with the chastening effect of Matthias's time as a field hand, the overseer restored him to his position.[18]

Even though slaveholders callously manipulated their huntsmen, few lacked confidence in the knowledge and abilities of these special slaves. Most even trusted their huntsmen with their lives. Despite some initial reservations, Georgia sportsman Randolph Spalding confirmed this kind of confidence while stalking deer with his huntsman, Davy. Preparing for a shot, Spalding warned him to keep close and mind his rifle. Davy replied, "Oh, I don't fraid ob me massa, you know I ain't gwine shoot you, and I ain't fraid you shoot me." Then he audaciously contrasted himself with other slaves and even with his owner's peers. "Massa Dent and massa Fennell, and dat dam rascal Sampson, people got to be fraid of—you and me hunt togedder dis twelve year, and we nebber shoot one-a-nodder yet." Elated with this unsolicited expression of fidelity and apparently unconcerned with Davy's somewhat menacing conclusion ("we nebber shoot one-a-nodder *yet* "), Spalding responded with a confirmation of his appreciation sweetened with a sliver of masculine respect. For at least a moment he did not consider Davy a "boy"—the customary term of address for male slaves. Instead, he worded his reply as if to an equal. "That is a fact, Davy, and I did you injustice when I cautioned you, for you are the only man that I will jump deer with."[19] Loyalty and submission earned Davy a glimmering instant of ephemeral, illusory equality.

Even though white and black hunters both appeared in hunting narratives making similar kills, there was no semblance of parity between the two feats. Narrators of hunting stories crafted a series of impermeable ideological barriers between themselves and their slaves. This was done with care and detail because slave hunters could actually outperform their owners in the hunting field, unlike in other arenas of masculine travail (such as politics or business). For example, when slaves handled guns with effectiveness, whites discounted their achievements in a number of ways. Hunting waterfowl in Florida in the 1830s, Charles Edward Whitehead, a sojourning New Yorker, magnanimously offered Scipio, his slave companion for the day, a shot with his spare musket. In his hands the episode became an illustration of Whitehead's mastery and power. He instructed Scipio to "take his own time, and fire as he chose," but Scipio could not wait long before he "fired as one wing of the army wheeled over us." Whitehead generously assessed the damage: "The aim was not a bad one, for a dozen ducks fell at the shot, and several more at intervals came slanting down from the flock." Yet Scipio's accomplishment was downplayed while Whitehead's "stronger shooting gun bored a hole through the black mass and twenty-seven ducks fell on the open water, and two or three went down aslant into the reeds."[20] In this brief episode Whitehead condescendingly proved that not only could he trust Scipio with a gun, he could also outshoot him with ease.

Once white hunters had proved their dominance in these hunting narratives, they could describe slave accomplishments without threatening their own positions. A story entitled "Bear-Hunting in Louisiana," which appeared in an 1851 issue of the *Spirit of the Times*, features a huntsman named Joe who shoots and kills a wounded bear, which his white companions describe as the largest bear ever killed in that part of Louisiana. Even though Joe delivers the killing shot, the white hunters reserve the credit for themselves. The author explained that the bear "had received one or two mortal shots, which almost every gentleman who had fired, asserted to have been his own." Rather than crediting Joe, the author opted to give one of the white hunters "the credit of stopping her," because his shot allegedly prevented the bear's escape. The writer justified this appropriation by explaining that the shots fired by the other whites brought the bear to bay. This, he argued, was the turning point of the hunt. Joe's final shot became incidental. In white eyes Joe acted as nothing more than an executioner; he might just as well have killed a pig. If Joe had been a white hunter, this apportionment of credit would have been considered grand theft and vicious defamation.[21] By blithely ignoring slave achievements, slaveholders avoided the possibility of inverting the master-slave relationship and shored up the bulwark of white supremacy.

The restrictions that white hunters placed upon huntsmen prevented the opportunity for a real or symbolic inversion of power, but they could not entirely eliminate the possibility that huntsmen could occasionally outperform their owners in the field. Confronted with the threat of slaves who might exceed their owners' accomplishments but reluctant to exclude slaves from their hunts, slaveholders created a hierarchy of game. By declaring certain species (bear, deer, and most species of wildfowl) off limits to slaves, slaveholders eliminated much of the potential for competition between blacks and whites. Beginning in the 1830s, the contributors to the sporting press drew an increasingly sharp line of demarcation through the animal kingdom, in effect segregating game and reinforcing the boundaries between black and white hunters.[22]

White hunters began drawing these distinctions in the eighteenth century by indicating their partiality for hunting certain species of game. The preferred species changed over time and varied from fraternity to fraternity, but by the nineteenth century most whites recognized the boundaries William Elliott described in *Carolina Sports*. Elliott listed as appropriate objects of the chase black bear, deer, lynx, and fox. He appended to this list a note that "to these might have been added, some years back, the panther, the wolf, now nearly extinct; and, upward of a century ago, the buffalo." The principal birds he considered the objects of sport were wild turkey, partridge, dove, golden plover, woodcock, snipe, wild geese, ducks, sea plovers, and curlews.[23]

Some of these preferences arose because of the sentimental connection between southern sportsmen and the British aristocracy. Because English traditions verified the worthiness of hunters who pursued deer, bear, fox, and wildfowl, southern sportsmen adopted the North American varieties of these animals as their preferred quarry. This rather tenuous link survived throughout the antebellum era because the American sporting press freely borrowed much of their material from English periodicals. This policy kept southern sportsmen informed about developments in English foxhunting. It also provided a variety of descriptions of English adventurers who pursued big game in the far reaches of the empire. Because most southern sportsmen recognized the English aristocracy as the final arbiter of sport, these stories helped confirm their own chosen game.[24]

These distinctions also sprang from purely functional reasons. White hunters' desire for recreation and their constant search for opportunities to display their masculinity also played important roles in the segregation of game. Whatever their differences, deer, bear, and fox all ordinarily provided hunters with long, entertaining, and often arduous chases. As challenging trials of prowess and mastery, these chases provided an ideal stage for the demonstration of white masculinity. Too often other game, like opossum and raccoon, simply treed. Gray foxes also treed with frustrating regularity, leading many white hunters to prefer hunting red fox, deer, and wildfowl. Bears also regularly treed, but they were so useful and made such impressive trophies that they remained desirable quarry.

Professions of sport aside, white hunters also favored these animals because of their mundane concerns as farmers and agriculturists. Foxes and pumas were targeted because of their taste for domestic fowl. Besides posing a threat to crops and livestock, deer and bear provided ample meat and marketable skins. Most white hunters in newly settled areas did not consider themselves sportsmen, so they hunted whatever species made the most frequent raids upon their cornfields and chicken houses. Here the primary aim was not the prestige of killing; it was the utility of eliminating an economic threat.[25]

Unless animals such as raccoon and opossum posed a direct threat, sportsmen generally felt that they offered inferior sport, so they pursued them only as a recreational novelty or as a piece of local color from the slave quarters. As indigenous species with no European counterparts, raccoon and opossum fell within the slave's domain. When white hunters blundered into a raccoon or opossum, they killed it, but they often turned the body over to their huntsmen because they considered these animals more suitable on a slave's table. Solomon Northup, a free black from New York who was sold into slavery, took advantage of this distinction. During his imprisonment on a Louisiana plantation, he became proficient at raccoon and opossum hunting. His owner did not object, in part, because he felt that "every marauding coon that is killed is so much saved from the standing corn."[26]

Such gradations of game became more prevalent throughout the antebellum era. Writing in the mid-1840s, English naturalist Charles Lyell wrote that although he considered raccoon and opossum meat "too coarse and greasy for the palate of a white man, . . . the negroes relish them much." Discussing slaves' love of opossum in 1858, a writer calling himself Joe Manton of Turnwold, Georgia, noted that "the negroes have commenced hunting the opossum, and a fine time they have of it. They love the chase, but they love the meat of the opossum more; and so they do the meat of the raccoon."[27] The depth and complexity of this system of segregation developed alongside paternalism and the proslavery ideology. By providing a forum for the development of ideas regarding these racially ordered preferences, the sporting press helped create a remarkably uniform, if laxly enforced, system of game segregation by the early 1830s. By the end of the antebellum era, few whites would openly disagree with the South Carolina sportsman who declared that he considered raccoons and opossums "vermin too ignoble for the gun," properly hunted only with "clubs and curs."[28]

Although whites would never boast of hunting these "ignoble" creatures, game segregation was another principle of sport that was often discarded when hunters entered the field by themselves or in the context of a hunting fraternity. John Audubon, for instance, had an outsider's perspective on southern hunting practices, and he recognized the flimsiness of the barriers created by game segregation. Visiting a plantation in South

Carolina, he observed that "hunting the Opossum is a very favourite amusement among domestics and field labourers on our Southern plantations, of lads broke loose from school in the holidays, and even of gentlemen, who are sometimes more fond of this sport than of the less profitable and more dangerous and fatiguing one of hunting the gray fox by moonlight." Yet even with a measure of objectivity concerning his host's desire for excitement, he carefully distanced himself from those who hunted raccoon for food. "I prefer a live Raccoon to a dead one; and should find more pleasure in hunting one than in eating him," he declared. A sportsman might hunt a raccoon, but he would never deign to eat one.[29]

Game segregation created distinctions between the accomplishments of black and white hunters in the field. Racism served a similar function. Racist stereotypes allowed white hunters to create a barrier between their accomplishments and those of slaves. This eliminated much of the potential for rivalry. It also made the hunt an important workshop for the construction of white conceptions of race and black masculinity. Hunting narratives influenced broader conclusions about race, but they also reflected tensions particular to the hunt. Straddling two currents of racial stereotyping, white hunters preserved the dominant eighteenth-century version of African savagery, but they also promoted the emergent nineteenth-century ideal of slaves as overgrown children.[30] The highly charged atmosphere of the hunt and white hunters' preoccupation with mastery help account for the durability of this seemingly contradictory duality. The characterization of African Americans as savages became a perfect foil for the self-control of the white sportsman.

Many of these white hunters maintained that although a predilection for savagery ordinarily lurked under a slave's childlike mask of dissembling, the excitement of the hunt could force it to the surface. In many hunting narratives, when slave huntsmen were first confronted with danger (or "supernatural" threats like owls, blue jays, or Indian mounds), they jumped and cringed, but when they were aroused by the excitement of the chase, this fear could become displaced by bloodlust. Once manifest, such savagery provided a favorable contrast with the supposed self-control of white hunters.[31] The occasional outburst of slave savagery in these narratives was intended to remind readers that slaveholding was, in fact, a

"Osman." A maroon hunter. From Porte Crayon [David Hunter Strother],
The Old South Illustrated, ed. Cecil D. Eby Jr. (Chapel Hill, N.C., 1959), p. 148.

benevolent, patriarchal responsibility. By developing popular images of slaves (potentially savage but ultimately loyal), slaveholders (beneficent patriarchs), and slavery (a form of uplift and social control), hunting stories illustrated the redemptive power of slavery in general and white paternalism in particular.

The virulent racism that saturated white perceptions of African Americans throughout the nineteenth century made it easy for white writers to argue that huntsmen (and by inference all slaves) owed all of their skills to the careful training and effective management of their owners. This racist myopia meant that few whites acknowledged or praised the capabilities of the slaves themselves. But it also meant that when a slave did excel in the field, slaveholders never had to doubt the ultimate totality of their authority, or the righteousness of their power.

On a hunt in low-country South Carolina, Nat (a visiting New Yorker) expressed his admiration of Cudjoe (a huntsman) by complimenting his "perfect fearlessness" and his ability to penetrate seemingly impassable thickets. When Nat added that Cudjoe "never seems to *think* of danger," one of his companions, a local planter, explained: "That is the secret of his success. He does *not* think of it. Indeed, they generally seem to entertain more anxiety on their horses account than their own." Like a well-trained animal, Cudjoe became worthy of praise when he dissolved concerns for his own needs, and even his own safety, into an unconditional commitment to his master's pleasure. When a huntsman achieved this level of devotion, slaveholders beamed with pride, for they attributed the strengths of the slave to the steady hand of the owner. Nat's companion confirmed his praise by defining a good huntsman as "one who enters into the spirit of the sport, and takes a pride in always catching a wounded deer if it is within the range of possibility." Further, a good huntsman never let "his dogs get away from him." Thus, because, as Cudgoe's owner complained, he often saw a "whole day's sport spoiled by the negligence or fear of a new hand," Cudjoe gained importance, not as a man, but as a reliable piece of field equipment. Nat's compliments, while heartfelt, could just as easily have described a fine horse or dog as a slave. Dehumanized and stripped of their own motivations when they appeared in white narratives, huntsmen became little more than extensions of their owners' will. When huntsmen succeeded, slaveholders looked on with pride. When huntsmen failed, slaveholders could chalk it up to the stereotyped failings of the entire race.[32]

The presentation of huntsmen as noncompetitive "faithful retainers" maintained the dominance of white hunters — they remained at center stage in hunting narratives and in the field. Even when slaves played key roles in the drama of the hunt, they never acted as anything more than extensions of their owners' will. The existence of slave families, communities, or motivations all faded from view in these narratives, allowing the accomplishments of the white protagonists to remain paramount.[33] The story "A Panther Hunt on the Blue Ridge," which features both Ralph Moreland, the model sportsman, and Hans Von Schullemberger, the archetypal outsider, also features Cudjo, a huntsman who maintains a particularly close relationship with his owners. Born on the same day as his owner (Ralph Moreland's father), Cudjo remained his faithful companion throughout his life. He dandled young Ralph on his knee and considered him "his own flesh and blood." His owners repaid this fidelity by considering Cudjo a member of their extended family. Seebright, the author and narrator, portrayed him as a paragon of the loyal slave — happy, constant, and completely enmeshed in the web of paternalism.[34]

Cudjo unfortunately meets his untimely end while driving the pack during an ill-fated puma hunt. Drawn away from the pack and the other hunters during the course of a chase over broken and heavily wooded ground, Cudjo inadvertently confronts the puma at the brink of a chasm. It deals him a fatal blow and "laid his bowels bare" before escaping into the brush. Reeling from his fatal injury, Cudjo tumbles into the chasm, "striking each jutting cliff on his downward descent, till he was lost in the darkness below." Night falls soon afterwards, preventing the recovery of his body and the continued pursuit of the puma. The next morning the party descends into the chasm and finds the "mangled body of poor Cudjo." Temporarily overcome with emotion, Ralph Moreland grasps Cudjo's hand and weeps. Seebright magnanimously described his tears as "the genuine outpourings of a noble and manly heart" — thereby refocusing attention once again on Cudjo's devoted owner.[35]

Gathering up the body, the party marches back into town where they attract a train of spectators. They all admire Cudjo's fidelity and comment on the goodness of his heart. Once they return to the Moreland household, Cudjo's boyhood playmate and owner laments over his body and remembers the times when Cudjo nursed him through sickness, screened him from punishment, and even meekly bore his brief outbursts of temper. Equally overcome, another member of the family, the garrulous cousin Bob, exclaims: "I'm d—d if ever I thought I loved that nigger so. . . . Well, if that darky hadn't a white heart, my name's not Bob Jones!"[36]

Cudjo epitomized the fondest hopes of paternalists for their slaves. More than a convincing front of dissembling or quiet efficiency, he was fidelity incarnate. In Seebright's hands the master-slave relationship became a profound and heartfelt connection. Cudjo apparently had internalized the lessons of paternalism, and his submission and obedience were instinctive and inevitable. Force and coercion never entered into the equation. Indeed, physical punishment became an expression of excess rather than necessity. Cudjo obeyed out of devotion rather than fear. Proximity with whites sublimated his "primitive nature" into loyalty and sacrifice. Through a lifetime of intimate relations with his owner's family, Cudjo developed a "white heart," making him capable of refined emotions. These well-developed ties with the Morelands bleached out more than Cudjo's heart. Existing in the shadow of Moreland's effusive paternalism, the slave community faded into nothingness. In the story no slaves mourn Cudjo's passing; his family in the Big House had become his only family.

Cudjo provided an idealized image of the master-slave relationship and an extreme example of the ways in which huntsmen who tempered their knowledge and ability with loyalty and trustworthiness could acquire considerable influence over their owners.[37] White hunters recognized the danger of diluting their authority, but those who professed great faith in the power of paternalism and the abilities of their huntsmen proudly revealed these moments of interdependence. In part, this security stemmed from restraint on the part of huntsmen. In these narratives huntsmen cheerfully and capably kept themselves within the boundaries of acceptable behavior. Huntsmen never endangered other members of the party, nor did they intentionally mislead their masters. In fact, in these narratives they only rarely revealed their own desires because they concerned themselves exclusively with the needs of their owners. Slaveholders facilitated this loyalty by constructing a host of restrictions. Although whites never drew an explicit set of boundaries around a huntsman's influence, they protected the stability of the master-slave relationship by framing their power in terms of a finite event—the hunt. Any transfer of authority was partial and temporary. By clearly demarcating the time and space within which huntsmen could safely offer their opinions or operate without direct supervision, these hunting stories made it clear that the power of the white protagonists remained uncorrupted and absolute.

In his prototypical "plantation novel" *Swallow Barn* (first published in 1832), southern novelist John Pendleton Kennedy depicted another idealized version of the paternalistic relationship between white protagonists and a trusted slave. This relationship illustrated the interplay of lent authority and the inviolable power of white supremacy. The slave, Carey, entering the parlor, doffs his hat and reports that he has identified an opossum as the perpetrator of a series of raids on the chicken house. Carey asks Ned Hazard (the heir apparent) and his visiting cousin, Mark Littleton (the narrator), if they would enjoy a hunt. Hazard playfully inquires whether Carey, "as an old sportsman, thought it lawful to hunt an opossum at midsummer." This question "set the old negro to chuckling, and afterwards, with a wise look, to putting several cases in which he considered a hunt at the present season altogether consonant with prescriptive usage." Although opossums did not reach their fattest until persimmon time, Carey believed "it was a good law to hunt any sort of creature when he was known to be doing mischief to the plantation." Carey introduces, and quickly dismisses, a second proscription when he notes that game should not be hunted while carrying young. In this case, however, Carey notes, the opossum is a large male and "shocking fat." Thus, "Carey considered him as a lawful subject of chase."[38]

Satisfied with Carey's assessment, Hazard, Littleton, and Harvey Riggs (a visiting neighbor) agree that an opossum hunt can provide a pleasant diversion. Their party forms up after the rest of the family retires for bed. Consisting of the three gentlemen, six or seven slave men and boys, and a motley assortment of disorderly slave dogs, the party seems perfectly suited for the hunt of the "wild and disorderly game in which they were engaged." The party marches to the wood line near the chicken house and waits, silent and seated, for the arrival of the opossum, which they expect will launch another raid. After some waiting, one of the slaves, Big Ben, proposes a new plan. Because "Ben had the reputation of being an oracle in matters of woodcraft," the whites adopt his counsel and move out toward the opossum's home — a large gum tree.[39]

Fumbling through the darkened forest, the party finally reaches the tree, while the dogs course the forest for the opossum's trail. When their barking wanes Hazard wonders aloud if they have lost their way. Frustrated by this lack of confidence, Carey scolds him. "Never mind!" he exclaims, "that 'possum's down here in some of these bushes watching us." After

A slave climbs a tree in pursuit of game. From Charles Wilkins Webber, *The Hunter-Naturalist: Romance of Sporting; or, Wild Scenes and Wild Hunters* (Philadelphia, 1851), opp. p. 84.

rebuking Hazard for his pessimism and explaining the peculiar nature of their prey, he reassures him, "You trust big Ben; he knows what he's about." When the pack turns away from their position, Riggs takes his turn as a skeptic and shouts, "We have lost our chance!" Carey immediately admonishes him and explains, "It's only some varmint the dogs have got up in the woods."[40]

Finally the opossum arrives. Finding his way blocked by the party, he climbs a nearby tree, which the "canine rabble" quickly surrounds. Ben climbs after the opossum and shakes him off a succession of limbs, forcing him inexorably downward. When he finally plummets to the ground, the entire party becomes a bit unhinged. "The frantic howl, screech and halloo that burst from dog, man, and boy, when the object of their pursuit thus became distinctly visible, and their continued reduplications— breaking upon the air with a wild, romantic fury—were echoes through the lonely forest at this unwonted hour, like some diabolical incantation, or mystic rite of fantastic import, as they have been sometimes fancies in the world of fiction, to picture the orgies of a grotesque superstition." As the passions of the dogs and hunters reach fever pitch, Hazard "interposed himself and commanded silence." He wants the opossum alive, so the slaves secure the dogs and swallow their own enthusiasm.[41]

Once brought down, the opossum plays dead. The whites poke at him for awhile out of novelty, but "he was at length taken up by Ben, who causing him to grasp a short stick with the end of his tail, (according to a common instinct of this animal,) threw him over his shoulders, and prepared to return homeward." Upon returning to the plantation house at nearly three in the morning, Riggs expresses some regret at their "savage pleasure." Hoping to soothe his anxiety, Hazard promises the release of the animal, hypothesizing that this night of terror will keep it from returning to the poultry yard. By twice asserting Hazard's final authority over the trophy, Kennedy subsumed the accomplishments and desires of Carey and Ben under the pinnacle of their master's authority. Operating in concert, Carey and Ben located the opossum, organized the hunt, drove the dogs, and finally secured the animal, but all at Hazard's behest. Even though he wielded mastery with a light (almost negligent) hand, he appropriated Ben and Carey's recreation in the forest as surely as their labor in the fields.[42]

By freely erasing and redrawing the limits of Carey's influence, Kennedy accomplished two ends. At an elementary level he provided his readers with an interesting piece of local color, but this bit of harmless fun was also a dramatic display of paternalism in action. Throughout the episode Carey acted as an effective extension of Hazard's will. Initially he became a second set of eyes and ears, observing events around the plantation and relaying interesting tidbits of information to his owner. This provided an opportunity for the display of Carey's knowledge of sport, and enmeshed in his owner's conceptions of hunting restrictions (seasons and pregnant animals), he carefully related a set of justifications for the hunt that satisfied his white audience. Rather than just parroting information, Carey proved his understanding of the rules of sport through application. Once the whites accepted the opportunity for a hunt, Carey swung into his third role and became a sort of majordomo. By directing the dogs and slaves, Carey insulated his white companions from the labors of the hunt. Following Carey around the field, they essentially became passive observers rather than actual actors. This distance reinforced their class position and increased the level of Carey's responsibility. When the excitement of the hunt eventually slackened in spite of Carey's expertise, the whites began fidgeting and complaining, acting the part of boys out on a lark. This earned a few choice rebukes from Carey, but all within the limits of the game. Carey's borrowed authority justified his outbursts, but Kennedy reaffirmed the dominance of the white protagonists when Hazard decisively redrew the boundaries of his authority. The appropriation of the trophy reminded Kennedy's readers that Hazard had never actually relinquished his power.

Although whites were loath to recognize it, the possibility also existed that despite the best efforts of slaveholders (and the huntsmen themselves), the delegation of authority could put slaves in the position of directly challenging their superiors. Whites avoided this uncomfortable situation by denying their huntsmen's ability to think for themselves. White hunters adroitly defused the danger of symbolic inversion by characterizing slave agency as nothing more than an indirect expression of white desire. Carefully scripted around a racist vision of slave character, a huntsman besting his owner in the field did not threaten the social order.[43]

Yet regardless of their sentimental portraits of the master-slave relationship and their protestations of confidence in the fidelity of their bondsmen, slaveholders never put themselves in a position that could test the loyalty of their huntsmen. Even in fiction slaveholders never tempted their huntsmen with an untoward measure of power or autonomy, nor did they knowingly provide any real opportunities for the inversion of power. Slaveholders made certain that armed slaves never outnumbered whites on any given outing. On the occasions when whites hunted alone, they rarely took the field with more than one armed slave companion. Even the largest outings, which could include a score of slaves, usually only included a single armed huntsman. Slaveholders also maintained the distance between slave huntsmen and white women. Slaveholders never overtly recognized the masculinity of their huntsmen, but as a drama of masculinity, hunting made this distance especially important. Slaveholders ensured that huntsmen never interacted with white women outside the presence of a white man — and then only rarely.[44] Slaveholders also circumscribed the movements of their huntsmen when they shot for the pot. When slaveholders sent them into the field, the huntsmen customarily carried written passes, which any white person might demand for inspection. Particularly suspicious slaveholders monitored the amount of powder and shot carried by their huntsmen by comparing the amount of ammunition they dispensed with the number of kills their huntsmen brought back home.[45]

Passes and bookkeeping reinforced the barrier between black and white accomplishment in the field, but nothing matched the pervasive influence of racism, which provided white southerners with a distorted lens through which they could view and evaluate their huntsmen's abilities and behavior. Whites presented themselves in hunting narratives as superior and expert while African Americans appeared at once savage and childlike: superstitious, slothful, and excitable. The southern fixation upon race shaped every hunter's perception of himself and other hunters. As the most dramatic denominator of identity and power in the antebellum South, race provided every hunter with the raw material for his conception of self. The centrality of race meant that it had a variety of meanings and effects. Whites who recorded accounts of slave hunters expressed a staggering array of impressions. Some saw slaves as nothing more than simple laborers, while others (especially those who characterized themselves as paternalists) boasted warm and sympathetic relationships between themselves and their slaves. Epitomized by the image of the huntsman, this relationship celebrated slave pliancy and the white capacity for mastery. Portrayed as being utterly dependent upon their white "benefactors," these slaves did much more than simply reinforce familiar stereotypes. Every action they took elevated their owners into the radiant light of triumphant paternalism. Huntsmen occasionally performed heroic acts, but for white observers their actions were only relevant within the context of this paternalistic relationship.

Some white writers apparently believed that even in death huntsmen remained nothing more than an extension of paternalistic sentimentality. An account of the funeral of Abba Ned, the huntsman on a plantation in the Georgia Sea Islands, illustrates the totality of this arrogant appropriation. Told from the point of view of a wealthy white houseguest, "Funeral of a Negro Huntsman" appeared in the *Spirit of the Times* in 1857. The story starts on a cold December evening. Wandering around the spacious mansion, the houseguest begins listening to the "dreary" singing that rose up from the slave quarters.

> He war de fuss on de coon an' de bar track,
> Poor Abbah Ned!
> Cuter 'an de fox in de up country woods,
> Poor Abbah Ned!
> Gwine hum now.

The singing commemorated the life of Abba Ned. He had died a few hours before from the mortal wounds he suffered on the morning hunt. Wallowing in maudlin sentiment, the white houseguest laments his death. With no thought for Abba Ned's family or peers, he proclaims a fraternal bond between himself and Abba Ned. He cries, "Poor old soul! good brother! had I left him to be buried by others?" Yet he remains within the house and assuages his grief by presenting a dubious transcription of the spiritual that accompanied Abba Ned to his grave.[46]

In these stories racism, paternalism, and the various barriers that prevented direct competition between white and black safely relegated slaves into a permanently subordinate position. In their enthusiasm some white writers stretched the paternalist vision of master-slave relations beyond the limits of plausibility. Indeed, this idealized version of slavery had little to do with the realities of slave life. Fortunately documents like the Works Progress Administration ex-slave interviews, the transcripts of court records, and archaeological excavations provide a contrast to the planter vision. It becomes apparent from these sources that in the field, even as black and white participants often occupied the same spaces, the meanings each ascribed to the activity varied greatly. Despite all of the techniques that whites employed to maintain a distinction between their accomplishments and those of their slave huntsmen in the field, they never fathomed that their slave auxiliaries brought a different set of motivations and expectations that made white distinctions irrelevant.

7. Slave Perceptions of the Hunt

What I et? Anything I could get.

Elisa Doc Garey, a freed slave from Hart County, Georgia

WHEN WHITES portrayed huntsmen in their hunting narratives, they sought to strengthen the association between themselves and a masculine ideal grounded in white supremacy and black dependence. Slaves saw things quite differently. When slaves took the field, they primarily saw hunting as an opportunity to ameliorate their condition. In their own accounts of the hunt, slaves rarely spent any time worrying about a symbolic interaction with their owners, the display of mastery, or the intricacies of sport. Rather than concentrating on these abstractions, slaves focused on the products of the hunt. Game provided them with a supplementary food source, an item for trade, and a measure of autonomy. This did not preclude the development of complex meanings within the slave community. Slave hunters consumed much of the game they killed themselves, but slaves who shared their kills with their friends and family strengthened the power and cohesion of the slave community as a whole. By denying the totality of white power, generous hunters refuted their owners' vision of mastery. They also contributed to the development of an African-American ideal of black masculinity.

When they described the drama of the hunt, slaveholders invariably placed themselves (or their fictionalized representatives) at center stage where they bask in the warmth of loyal slaves and grateful white women. But when whites appear in slave narratives of the hunt, they usually seem remote and relatively unimportant. Whites draw boundaries and set limits on slave hunters, but they rarely act as a source of slave identity. The slaveholders' drama of the hunt often featured huntsmen or, more frequently, silently loyal slave supernumeraries. When these huntsmen, whippers-in, and laborers spoke for themselves, however, they revealed a different drama, one equally tied to ideas of masculinity and community but anchored in family and subsistence rather than fraternity and display.

Like their white counterparts slave men learned how to hunt during boyhood. The restrictions of slavery meant that slave boys took their lessons whenever and wherever they could. Most acquired the essentials of woodcraft through simple trial and error. Simon Stokes of Guinea, Virginia, never received any formal instruction; he learned how to hunt by chasing opossum with other boys from the quarter. Other slave boys picked up the basics by assisting their owners. Johnson Thompson of Rusk County, Texas, learned through observation—he accompanied his owner whenever he went squirrel hunting. Bob Mobley of Crawford County, Georgia, received hands-on instruction. His owner, Henry Mobley, even taught him how to shoot.[1] Because able-bodied men spent the vast majority of their time laboring for their owners, slave boys who learned from adult slaves usually received instruction from older men who no longer rated as full hands. Aaron Ford of Lake View, South Carolina, learned how to set traps from his grandfather.[2] These men rarely evoked a saccharine sentimentality from their black students to equal the maudlin paeans composed by white hunters about their slave mentors. Concerned with the usefulness of the lesson rather than the relationship it represented, slave students focused on the transmission of knowledge.

Like many of their white counterparts, slave boys also picked up the essentials of hunting from other boys—black and white. Unlike adults, when black and white boys hunted together, they often did so in relatively color-blind conditions. Unless they had finicky parents, young boys customarily played with one another regardless of their color. Silvia King of Fayette County, Texas, described a playfully chaotic situation in which "all chilluns played together, w'ite and black. I'ze had er dozen at er time er rollin' roun' on der kitchen floor u'nner foot black an' w'ite. Day fished, an hunted togedder an' played ball and rode de plough stock, effen de get er chanct, an' git in debblemint all de time."[3] Black and white boys frequently met one another as playmates, but with its sex specificity, danger, and departure from the quotidian, hunting created an opportunity for intense socialization among boys. These relationships could blossom into

lasting friendships. Describing his childhood in Lincoln County, Mississippi, Abe McKlennan explained the friendship between himself and one
of his owner's sons, Jim: "We loved each other mighty, an' we plays to-
gethah' all th' time." The relationship between the two boys rested on a
foundation that at least superficially was egalitarian—whenever they went
fishing, they evenly divided the catch between themselves. Fortunately for
McKlennan, their bond provided more than fish; on at least one occasion,
it saved McKlennan from a whipping at the hand of the overseer. Sum-
ming up, McKlennan simply stated, "Me an' Jim loves each othah like hogs
did corn."[4]

Such friendships could provide slaves with a great deal of privilege.
When Mose Davis grew up near Perry, Georgia, his owner, Colonel Davis,
did not require any work from him because he "was play-mate and companion to Manning, the youngest of Colonel Davis' five sons." They spent
most of their time fishing and hunting together and became so close that
they often slept in the same bed.[5] Descriptions of such color-blind friendships appear throughout the WPA ex-slave interviews, but slaves who enjoyed such relationships clearly saw themselves as special cases. Such love
and trust could temporarily insulate particular slaves from many of the
harshest aspects of slavery, but the effect of their race and bondage was
ultimately inescapable.

Some white boys had little difficulty denying the humanity of their
slaves. Empowered by their privileged position (which provided free time,
equipment, and power) and desirous of an opportunity to emulate their
elders, white boys often facilitated slave boys' participation in the hunt.
These associations could nurture boyhood camaraderie, but white boys'
incipient desire for mastery inevitably characterized the relationship between black and white boys in the field.[6] Even so, slaves still preferred
hunting to working in the fields. Mark Oliver of Washington County, Kentucky, accompanied his young owner on wild turkey hunts on the plowed
fields around their home, but the two never became friends. Still, this emotional distance never precluded Oliver's enjoyment of the hunt. Oliver's
account lacks the warmth of the friendship described by Abe McKlennan,
but he insisted that "me and him sure had good times."[7] Even in poor
company a turkey hunt provided a welcome respite from the demanding
routines of drudgery and coercion that characterized plantation life.

Most male slaves never had an intimate relationship with their owners or with members of their owners' families. This did not preclude slave boys from hunting on their own, but it did make it more of a challenge. The opportunities for hunting varied widely, and because of their considerable power over slaves' lives, slaveholders exerted an inordinate influence over these opportunities. As slave boys aged their owners' demands on their time and energy rose, but while they were young, their responsibilities were less onerous. Some slave children began performing chores once they turned six years old, but even on crisply managed plantations, most succeeded in finding some time for amusement and recreation between toting water, picking up chips, watching infants, and gathering firewood.[8] Whatever the sources of their knowledge and opportunity, slave children pushed into the outdoors with great eagerness.

Apparently hunting became an index of masculinity at a relatively early age. The beginnings of gender differentiation began appearing when boys took the field in search of game. Girls might fish with great enthusiasm, but they rarely hunted. As a child, Acie Thomas spent much of his time in the company of other slave children roaming the broad acres of the Folsom plantation in Jefferson County, Florida. They waded and fished in a nearby stream, chased rabbits, and collected wild berries and nuts. Because Thomas enjoyed the tutelage of an older male relative, he quickly mastered "all the wood lore common to children of his time."[9] Such freedom from constraint varied from settlement to settlement, but even H. C. Bruce's brutal owner in Chariton County, Missouri, allowed a few years of relatively carefree youth before putting him to work. Because four or five other boys about Bruce's age also lived on the farm, they spent their days hunting and fishing together.[10] Like Bruce and his companions, most boys spent at least some of their free time hunting. Like their white counterparts, slave boys usually lacked firearms; undeterred, they relied upon a variety of slingshots and traps.[11] When he was a boy, Robert Wilson and his friends just used rocks. "Weuns don't kill of much of de game but 'twas good fo' to pass de time 'way."[12]

Whatever their relationship with particular slaves, slaveholders eventually exercised their prerogative and replaced the license of youth with the obligations of adulthood. The exact timing of the transition from childhood depended upon a variety of factors, including the character of the slaveholder, local custom, and the economic and political development of the area, but whenever it came, this shift imposed tremendous demands upon slaves. A relentless schedule of hard labor customarily consumed every daylight hour for five and a half to six days a week. Plowing, planting, weeding, chopping, and harvesting the diversified crops that grew on southern farms and plantations allowed a few lulls in the work routine, but enterprising slaveholders filled even these with a variety of tasks including ditchdigging, wood gathering, and construction jobs. In many cases this relentless cycle of labor left precious few opportunities for anything but sleeping, eating, and a bare minimum of child care. Because forced labor consumed most of the time and energy of adult slaves, the onset of adulthood severely restricted hunting opportunities.[13]

Despite their exhaustion and lack of free time, many slaves discovered and exploited the interstices of their owners' power. Whether snippets of time or moments of independent thought, these chinks in the oppressive structure of slave society provided them with the material and opportunity for the creation of a rich and varied slave culture. This patchwork of various African traditions, Euro-American influences, and New World innovations created and sustained a vigorous African-American identity that transcended the limitations of bondage and gave slaves a powerful instrument for survival and resistance.[14]

Slave culture drew upon a wide variety of sources, but its maintenance depended upon three complementary elements: the utilitarian exchanges of the internal economy of slavery, various leisure activities, and slaves' conception of the spaces that they shared with whites. The product of slaves' cleverness, tenacity, and opportunism, each of these elements helped create feelings of autonomy, cohesion, and resistance within slave communities. The effort and imagination of slaves were essential for the construction of slave culture, but the success of these efforts often depended upon a combination of white beneficence and disinterest. Because hunting involved aspects of every element of slave culture, it provides a useful instrument for the analysis of slave culture as a whole. It also provides an excellent illustration of how slaves constructed a rich and vibrant culture from stolen moments and subversive meanings.

Slaves participated in the internal economy whenever they worked for themselves. By exchanging goods and services with others, slaves accrued

a variety of tangible benefits, including wages, liquor, housewares, livestock, vegetables, fish, hides, and game. The acquisition and distribution
of these goods endowed many slaves with a spirit of resistance. Whether
weaving baskets, tilling their own gardens, or hunting game, slaves who
participated in the internal economy denied the totality of their owners'
control over their labor.[15]

Slaves found several uses for game, but in most cases they simply ate
it. Because slaves rarely received much domestic meat from their owners,
game provided an important supplementary component of many slave
diets. Loaded with an assortment of vitamins and proteins, it provided
slaves with a nutritionally significant dietary variation.[16] The slaves who
lived on Tom Asbie's Virginia plantation prized the rabbits and opossum
that they caught themselves because, as Silas Jackson remembered it, "we
did not get anything special from the overseer."[17]

On some occasions, especially in the summer months when meat
spoiled quickly, slaves received some of the game from white hunts. But
even then, slaveholders generally provided their slaves with inferior cuts
and the meat of whatever species they found unpalatable.[18] Thomas Cole
of Jackson County, Alabama, remembered that his owner's family ordinarily reserved beef, fish, venison, goats, chickens, wild turkey, and the best
pork for themselves. Slaveholder preference meant that slaves usually ate
only certain species of game; however, game segregation did not prevent
slaves from occasionally hunting the favored species. When the smoked
pork that made up slaves' usual meat ration ran out, Cole recalled, the
slaves would either "kill a beef or goats or some men would be sent out
ter git some wild turkeys or deer." Because "dey allus brings em back," this
proved quite effective. Making the most out of their situation, slaves also
exploited whatever species their owners disdained. Cole remarked that
"there was allus plenty of possums and rabbits and us young boys would
allus take de dogs and git plenty of possum ter cook wid sweet pertaters
and we brought in plenty of rabbits too." The combination of rations of
domestic meat, sanctioned hunts after "white" game, and the independent efforts of slave boys ensured that the slaves Cole knew "allus had
plenty of meat ter eat."[19]

The division between black and white game meant that the game
brought in by slave hunters often went through a process of apportionment. In the case of Victor Duhon, a slave huntsman who lived on a

Louisiana plantation, the division came in the central kitchen, which prepared food for everyone on the plantation. When he brought game in, the whites appropriated the partridge and ricebirds for their own table, but they left the owls, rabbits, raccoons, and opossums for the slaves.[20] Because most slave owners disdained raccoon and opossum meat, it usually made its way to the quarters regardless of who actually killed it.[21]

Scattered across the South and living in a wide variety of environments, slaves exploited and consumed a variety of wild game. In general, however, they relied primarily upon three animals — opossums, raccoons, and rabbits — for their game meat.[22] When they pursued these animals, hunters required little more than dogs, sticks, and enthusiasm. Most slaves prized a meal of raccoon or rabbit, but opossum held a special place in many hearts. Rachel Adams lived on a plantation near the town of Eatonton in Putnam County, Georgia, and she loved opossum. When asked about them, she excitedly replied: "'Possums! I should say so. Dey cotch plenty of 'em und atter dey was kilt ma would scald 'em and rub 'em in hot ashes and dat clean't 'em jus' es pretty and white. OO-o-o but dey was good. Lord, Yessum!" Solomon Northup of Louisiana agreed that "verily there is nothing in all butcherdom so delicious as a roasted 'possum."[23]

Even though many especially liked opossum, the harsh conditions of slavery meant that slaves had to consume whatever meat they could acquire. This allowed for considerable diversity in some slave diets. Growing up in Freestone County, Texas, Jeff Calhoun remembered eating a great variety of game. First, he explained, "if we want meat we went to the woods after it, deer, turkey, buffalo and some bear." His family supplemented these familiar species with an equally impressive array of unorthodox game. "I have eat a little of all meat I guess ceptin' dog. I eat some hoss and skunk, crow and hawk," but he drew the line at wolf and coyote. Although Calhoun's diet may have been particularly diverse, throughout the South slaves occasionally dined on songbirds, skunks, muskrats, rattlesnakes, and "robin gumbo and pie."[24]

Slaves also found that whites could change their preferences with irritating capriciousness. In times of need game that discriminating white hunters considered the rightful provender of slaves occasionally ended up on slaveholder tables. In Hall County, Georgia, Anderson Furr's owners routinely ordered their slaves out on hunts for opossum. He remembered that he and the other slaves "cotch lots of 'possums," but this did not benefit the hunters. As Furr crossly remembered it, "Day made Niggers go out and hunt 'em and de white folk et 'em. Our mouths would water for some of dat 'possum but it warn't often dey let us have none."[25]

Surplus game might eventually reach the quarters, but only after slave-holders took their pick of the choicest cuts. If slave hunters killed enough game, this might mean that some slaves and their owners ate remarkably similar meals. Remembering her childhood on a plantation in up-country South Carolina, Charlotte Foster felt that she received ample provisions. In fact, she and her family "got just what the white folks ate."[26] Few slaves professed this level of equality, but in the absence of reliable storage techniques, a sizable kill could benefit every member of a slaveholding household. Harriet Davis of Palestine, Texas, remembered her owner, Steve Glass, distributing game among his slaves. Whenever Glass killed a "big deer," he brought it back to the house where the slaves would "put it in great big pot and cook it."[27] Everyone partook in the subsequent feast. In this way hunts often provided an exciting variation upon an otherwise bland and unvarying diet.

Slaveholders' proclivity for confiscation encouraged a degree of secrecy among slave hunters. Furtiveness on the part of slaves and indifference on the part of whites kept many of the slave exchanges that supported the internal economy out of written records. Even so, archaeological evidence, the WPA ex-slave interviews, and an occasional white observer noted that slave hunters brought the game that they killed back to the quarters so that they could share it with their families and friends. White observers occasionally perceived the outer contours of this practice within the slave community. When John James Audubon accompanied an opossum hunt, he noted that the hunters remained in the field after they took their first opossum because they were "not yet satisfied, either with the sport or the meat: they have large families and a host of friends on the plantation." Slave observers noted the same concerns on the part of slave hunters. Georgia Baker of Taliaferro County, Georgia, praised the plantation huntsmen George and Mack because "when dey went huntin' dey brought back jus' everything: possums, rabbits, coons, squirrels, birds, and wild turkeys."[28]

Contemporary sources—including perennially suspicious sportsmen—never overtly addressed the possibility that slave hunters might selfishly withhold game for themselves. Because men trapped and killed much of their game in relative seclusion, they could consume it in secrecy or trade it off their owners' property without the knowledge of the other members of their communities, but few apparently did so. But even if slave hunters kept their kills to themselves, they opened a fissure in the suffocating structure of slave society. The confidence and independence born of a moment's self-sufficiency could bestow even a selfish hunter with a measure of self-esteem.

Many slave hunters traded their game with whites, but successful slave hunters who shared their game with other slaves advanced themselves in their struggle against physical and emotional bondage. At its most elemental level, game provided slave families with a source of supplemental provisions, which aided them in their daily struggle for survival. Property acquired by participation in the internal economy facilitated the stability of the slave family, which in turn strengthened the cohesion of the slave community. Diverse origins, high death rates, and periodic dislocation (from sale and inheritance) made the formation and maintenance of slave families and communities extremely difficult. By providing a valuable resource, hunting could help strengthen the bonds between slaves. In a society predicated upon the constant degradation of African Americans, a simple act of generosity like the gift of game could become a potent symbol of resistance. By sharing their kills with friends and members of their families, slave hunters affirmed and intensified the cohesion of their ties with other members of their communities. While an opossum bake might mean a few saved pennies for a slaveholder, for a slave it could represent a moment of power for a loving spouse, a capable parent, or a caring friend. By nourishing their bodies, game could also strengthen their sense of self-sufficiency and self-esteem. A meal that came from someone other than the slaveholder provided a dramatic and easily recognizable symbol of agency and power within the slave community. The slave community even drew strength from slave hunters who took the field at the behest of their owners because their accomplishments (if not always the game they secured) remained their own.

The exchanges of the internal economy could range beyond a slave hunter's immediate surroundings. Desperately short of other essentials, some slave hunters exchanged their game with their owners and nearby storekeepers for cash, guns, ammunition, household goods, or occasional indulgences like liquor and candy.[29] Such informal trade networks could become quite complex. When Gus Feaster killed rabbits and opossum around his home, he took them into nearby Union, South Carolina, where he sold them to a variety of townspeople. If he could not dispose of all of them through these personal contacts, he sold or traded the remainder to "Ole man Dunbar" who ran a local beef market.[30] When slaves relied upon towns to sell their kills, their trade in game could parallel their owners' trade in staple crops. Sam Ross of Putnam County, Georgia, trapped beavers in the swampy part of his owner's plantation and sold the pelts in Augusta and Savannah, where his owner sold cotton and corn.[31]

By strengthening slave families, creating a sense of slave agency, and improving the material quality of slaves' lives, the internal economy supported the development of slave culture. But the internal economy alone was not enough to nourish slave culture. It also depended upon a variety of leisure activities like singing, dancing, storytelling, and worship. Each of these activities created a space that was at least somewhat independent from the mastery of slaveholders. The world of work provided the raw material for slave culture, but leisure time gave those products and exchanges their critical meanings. As a world apart from work, leisure time became a critical repository for African-American identity, which stitched the scattered elements of the internal economy into a meaningful design capable of weathering the rigors of slavery.[32]

Despite their pragmatic focus upon hunting as a source of supplementary provisions, for slaves hunting was a hybrid that bridged the gap between the internal economy and leisure time. Many slaves thought of hunting as a practical necessity and an important aspect of the internal economy, but they also considered it a form of recreation. Recalling his youth in Washington County, Mississippi, Reuben Fox remembered that "the biggest fun what the men had on the place was going hunting." Like many white hunters, Fox recognized the recreational aspect of hunting, but he never overlooked the ways in which amusement dovetailed with utility. The hunters enjoyed themselves, but they also kept "the kitchen supplied with everything such as coons, possums, squirrels, and rabbits."[33]

Hunting also served as a source of entertainment by providing raw material for slave folktales. These stories illuminated as well as entertained because they preserved and transmitted an understanding of the natural world from African and African-American ancestors. Information regarding the behavior of wild animals recurs throughout slave folklore.

Most folktales from the Georgia and Carolina low country involve the activities of anthropomorphized animals such as Brer Rabbit. The actions of the various animal characters not only reflected the storyteller's knowledge of the human world through metaphor, but they also revealed an intimate understanding of the natural world. In some cases slave hunters shared their knowledge without storytelling. When hunters brought in information about the local landscape, they complemented the knowledge that slave women acquired when they entered the woods and swamps in search of firewood and medicinal herbs. In turn, this familiarity with the local terrain aided slaves who took to the woods for other leisure activities like clandestine religious services or nighttime visits to neighboring farms and plantations. Unnoticed by whites, and perhaps only of incidental interest for many slaves, this knowledge still provided a variety of benefits for the entire slave community.[34]

Every slave potentially benefited from this knowledge, but no one needed it as much as runaways. Celebrated runaway Charles Ball became well acquainted with the topography of the forest around his owner's Georgia plantation through frequent hunting outings. Familiarity grew with his skill, and he soon "began to lay and execute plans to procure supplies of such things as were not allowed me by my master." Emboldened, equipped, and increasingly familiar with southern forests in general and the local landscape in particular, Ball began planning his escape. Once he took to the woods, Ball, like many other runaways, relied upon his hunting abilities for an occasional protein-rich meal as he made his way north.[35] Rather than seeking sanctuary in the North or in Mexico, most runaways sought temporary relief from particularly harsh punishment and overwork by taking to the woods near their homes. These sojourns usually lasted only a few days, but some runaways might "lay out" for months or even years at a time.[36] Most relied on theft and gifts from friends and family remaining on plantation grounds, but hunting provided some of these runaways with an important source of food.[37]

The internal economy and leisure time provided slaves with essential components of slave culture, but in many cases slaves depended upon a third critical component. This aspect of slave culture concerned slave conceptions of the spaces (both cultural and physical) that they shared with whites. The often debilitating effect of white power marred this aspect of slave culture with overtones of powerlessness and degradation, but in some cases slaves' understandings of this shared world played as central a role in the construction and maintenance of their culture as the internal economy and leisure time.

Even though slave owners controlled their slaves' labor, they could not control their thoughts, and evidence of the vitality of slave culture became manifest in a variety of indirect ways. Subversive work songs, work slowdowns, and sabotage all affirmed the existence of an independent (or at least semiautonomous) slave culture. Huntsmen provide a useful example for the examination of this often ambiguous cultural phenomenon. Trusted by their owners and charged with numerous duties, huntsmen, unlike most other slaves, acquired a measure of their owners' authority. They gained this authority because whites saw huntsmen as extensions of themselves, but the actions of huntsmen, even as described in white sources, revealed an independent agenda. These moments usually evaded the historical record, but they did occasionally become apparent.

Georgia planter Randolph Spalding wrote a narrative of a heavily equipped expedition to Blackbeard Island on the coast of Georgia that was published in the *Spirit of the Times* in 1848. The account illustrated how even in the highly charged setting of a white hunting expedition some slave hunters exploited the interstices of their owner's power. Writing several years after the events it described, Spalding had to reconstruct his narrative from memory. Interestingly, Spalding's story revealed the existence of African-American agency even within the one world over which whites possessed absolute control—their narratives.

In the course of the story, the leader of the expedition, a wealthy low-country planter, repeatedly relies upon his huntsman, Dick, for confirmation of his own decisions. Endowed with a considerable measure of borrowed authority, Dick takes great care in backing up his owner's influence among other white hunters. When deciding the location for the first drive, several members of the party ask Dick's owner which part of the island he thinks is most likely to have deer. When he suggests the southern end of the island, one of the other hunters objects, "D—n the south end! I have never had any luck there." Dick's owner responds with confident assurance, "I think you will have it to-day, however; at all events we must try it." Reinforcing his authority, he consults Dick with an offhand "Don't you think so, Dick?" The faithful slave chimes in, "Yes massa, deer in da, for true, I see dem kack tick as ants, de las time I bin da!"

Presented with this expert witness and Dick's owner's intransigence, the contrary hunter assents. The planters fan out and take their stands while Dick leads the pack into the forest.

After an exciting hour of shooting, the planters regroup and begin comparing notes. Dick soon emerges from the underbrush "puffing with excitement and want of breath" and exclaims: "Good God amighty! I neber yeddy such a shootin; how much deer una kill now; one, two , tree, for, five, six, sebin!" Focusing attention upon his owner, he asks, "Mr. M, how much you kill?" "Three, Dick," the owner replies, holding his head up and looking proud. Doubly vindicated, Dick turns on the doubter: "Ah, ha! wen massa tell you for come to de souteen you say damn. Please God you ought not for git one single shot; I tell you, massa know ebry spot deer day an Blackbade." In this second confrontation Dick dared not rely exclusively upon his own authority, but he remained relatively secure from retaliation because he shifted the attention and the mantle of expertise back upon his owner's shoulders.[38] By reiterating his owner's earlier claim that he could produce deer, Dick reminded the other planters of his owner's ability. Dick also allowed a moment of otherwise immodest bragging when he asked his owner how many deer he killed. By seeming to spontaneously remind the other white hunters of his owner's prowess and skill, Dick helped increase his owner's status among his peers. He also defended his owner's prestige; in the case of an unsuccessful hunt, Dick's actions would have protected his owner from criticism. By confirming the decision to hunt the south end, he assumed some responsibility in case of failure. If there had been no deer, Dick's owner simply could have blamed Dick. By playing the herald, Dick could either exalt his owner's accomplishments or protect him from criticism. Endowed with a measure of borrowed authority, Dick buttressed his owner's reputation among the other hunters.

At a superficial level Dick's actions confirmed his owner's trust and simply reflected a paternalistic vision of the master-slave relationship. Dick did more than increase his owner's prestige by playing the role of the loyal bondsman, however. Rather than simply confirming his owner's decisions, he sheltered himself behind his owner's authority and insulted the contrary hunter—something neither he nor his owner could ordinarily do without the possibility of serious repercussions. In most situations this sort of insolence would earn a flogging, but Dick played the game carefully. Although he pushed the limits of acceptable behavior, he never left the protective shield of his owner's influence. Because he only reiterated his owner's opinions, he never acted as anything more than an extremely presumptuous extension of his owner. Because Dick never appeared to be expressing his own opinions, the presence of his owner precluded the possibility of immediate punishment from the contrary hunter. By carefully harnessing his insult — "Please God you ought not for git one single shot" — to a series of compliments for his prideful owner, Dick strengthened the bond of reciprocity between himself and his owner while dressing down one of his owner's peers.

Even though Dick played the game with skill, he always walked a razor's edge because his owner could retract his protection at any time. If, on a whim, he decided that Dick overstepped himself, he could punish him at will. Regardless of his borrowed authority, Dick remained a slave, and as such he remained entirely at the mercy of his owner. Because Spalding perceived Dick as an instrument rather than an actor, his actions explored the limits of paternalism, rather than challenging the social order.[39]

Few slave hunters discovered opportunities that rivaled Dick's experience on Blackbeard Island. Rather than redefining their roles vis-à-vis whites, most slave hunters concentrated on creating identities for themselves within the context of the slave community. Instead of relying on the judgment of their white owners, most slave men looked to other African Americans to affirm their masculine identities. By creating identities that depended upon the perceptions of other slaves rather than those of whites, these slaves reappropriated an important measure of cultural autonomy. Hunting proved a rare opportunity for slave hunters to demonstrate their masculinity while keeping their actions within the limits imposed by slaveholder power. For many slave hunters the most important element of this reappropriation concerned the definition of their gender roles. By sharing the game they killed, slave hunters assumed the patriarchal mantle of provider. Confirmed in this surreptitious usurpation of slaveholder power by their friends and family, these hunters tapped into two powerful cultural currents. The most immediate reference points often lay uncomfortably near the person of the slaveholder. By playing the role of the patriarch within their own family, these slaves asserted a sense of masculinity that mirrored that of their owners and, not incidentally, many African societies. By assuming the role of provider, however, slave

hunters challenged their owners' authority and refuted the often emas-
culating influence of slave society.[40]

White demands shaped African-American culture, but other influences
were also at least as important. By the antebellum era most slaves felt little more than a tenuous, mythopoetic connection with Africa, but elements of various African cultures still influenced the ways in which slaves
perceived the world. Some of the roots of the association between masculinity and hunting may rest in African soil because many Africans, like
Europeans, placed hunting in the domain of men.[41] Slaveholders frequently ignored slaves' gender when they dispensed work assignments —
they sent women into the fields without a second thought — but in the case
of hunting, their preference for male hunters meshed with their slaves'
own expectations in terms of the gender division of labor. Among blacks
and whites alike, the hunt defined its participants as men.[42]

Unlike many of their owners who focused on the act of hunting, most
slave hunters were more concerned with the products of the hunt. While
slave hunters provided their owners with two sets of benefits, one symbolic (mastery) and the other quite tangible (food), slaves remained almost
solely concerned with the latter. This made the gift of game rather than
the display of trophies the most powerful use of the kill. By ameliorat-
ing the harshness of slavery, meat both strengthened and created family
ties. During one period of his captivity in South Carolina, Charles Ball
shared the game he caught with the family he was quartered with, greatly
improving their quality of life, for until he moved in with them, they
lacked a regular supply of meat. After he pooled his kills with the other resources of the household, Ball could proudly assert that "all the people
on the plantation did not live as well as our family did, for many of the
men did not understand trapping game, and others were too indolent to
go far enough from home to find good places for setting their traps."[43] He
made it clear that his efforts benefited not only himself but others as well.
Isolated by his lack of any nearby blood kin, Ball made an important decision when he chose to supply his adoptive family with game. His ability and generosity bridged one of the gaps created by the dislocations of
slave trading.

Unlike Ball, most slave hunters had their own families. James Brittian's
father, Ben Brittian, served as the huntsman on a Mississippi plantation
owned by Joe and Charlet Benoit. Ben impressed his son as a capable

provider. James remembered that he "was always in the woods getting coons, possums, squirrels, rabbit, and game of all kinds. He never came home he wasn't loaded down with it."[44] Especially successful slave hunters could provide even extended families with an intermittent supply of game. When asked about the supply of opossum during her childhood on a plantation located in Floyd County, Georgia, Callie Elder exclaimed: "'Possums, Oh, mussy me! my grandpa hunted 'possums at night and fetched in two and three at a time. Don't say nothin' 'bout dem rabbits for dere warn't no end to 'em. Rabbits stewed, rabbits fried, and rabbits dried, smoked, and cured lak hog meat! I et so many rabbits when I was young I can't stand to look at 'em now but I could eat 'possums and gnaw de bones all day long."[45]

Men provided the key ingredient of game, but in most slave communities slave hunters depended upon the culinary skills of slave women when they brought their game back to the quarter. The relationship between a male hunter and a female cook might grow over time. Husbands and wives often divided the labor of hunting and cooking between themselves, but this partnership could also develop without bonds of kinship and marriage. When Charles Ball was quartered with a woman named Lydia and her indolent and irritable husband, Ball still brought her "as many rackoons, opossums, and rabbits, as afforded us two or three meals a week." Because she "understood the way of dressing an opossum," he provided "one for our Sunday dinner every week, so long as these animals continued fat and in good condition." When he presented her with game (such as "a quarter of a rackon or a small opossum"), she appeared "very thankful."[46] Evidence indicates that everyone, even children, habitually turned their game over to slave women for cooking. This gendered division of labor fit perfectly with slaveholder desires. Improved slave diets increased productivity and cut costs, while stable slave families reduced the number of runaways. Despite the fact that their actions often benefited their owners, they also strengthened the slave community and nourished slave culture—both of which helped shield slaves from the dehumanizing horror of broken families, forced labor, and casual brutality.

Fixated upon their own visions of the hunt, slaveholders rarely considered that the hunt could have a variety of meanings and benefits for the slave community. Because they only thought of slave hunters in relation to themselves (rather than in relation to other slaves), slaveholders ruled them with a relatively light hand. Because of this, as long as they brought in a steady supply of meat, most slave hunters took the field without direct white supervision. Carefully selected for their trustworthiness, slave hunters usually carried written passes from their owners, which they could then present to the slave patrol or any other inquisitive whites they met along the way.[47] Henry Barnes, a slave from Clarke County, Alabama, explained that "at night if any ob de men wanted to break a night's rest, he cud go 'possum an' rabbit huntin', so long as he got a pass from his boss, an' wuz in de fiel' de nex' mawning on time."[48] Slaves who hunted without passes might suffer for their troubles. Another Alabamian, Annie David, explained that as long as the men from her plantation carried passes, they "could hunt and fish on the plantation all they wanted," but slaves who hunted without passes might suffer serious repercussions: "if they slipped off and the 'patrollers' caught them, they sure were in for a good beating."[49]

Despite such dangers, hunting offered slaves enough benefits that many took the field even if they lacked official sanction from their owners. Although they usually operated with at least the implicit consent of their owners, these illicit slave hunters confronted several impediments when they decided to take the field without specific instructions from their owners. The first obstacle was time. Exhausting and time-consuming, the immense demands of forced labor circumscribed slaves' lives and consumed most of their waking hours. Nevertheless, highly motivated slaves discovered and exploited the brief and occasional lulls in the work routine.[50]

Plantations working on the task system (a form of slave labor that emphasized piecework) afforded slaves some flexibility in determining their free time. Because their owners and overseers demanded set results from their slaves (rather than working them a set length of time), slaves could conceivably finish their work assignments before nightfall, freeing some daylight hours for their own use. The task system predominated in the game-rich estuarine environments of the Georgia and Carolina low country, and many slaves living under this system used this opportunity for hunting. Most white observers recognized the effectiveness of this incentive and thought the task system lent itself to independent labor by slaves. Some travelers reported that slaves could finish their required labor as early as two in the afternoon, freeing the rest of the day for their own use.[51]

The task system provided slaves with flexible work schedules, but slaves who worked under the gang system, which predominated in other parts of the South, also found opportunities for hunting. Because slaveholders demanded their labor during daylight hours, these slaves often hunted at night. Even particularly avaricious slaveholders rarely worked their slaves after nightfall (except during harvesttime), so slaves made the most out of the hours between sundown and bedtime. Martha Colquitt grew up as a slave near Lexington, Georgia, and she recalled that "slaves never had no time to hunt in de day time, but dey sho' could catch lots of 'possum at night."[52]

Regardless of the form of work organization, most slaveholders also suspended labor on Sundays. Slaves used this opportunity to pursue a number of ends, which included prayer, gardening, dancing, singing, housekeeping, relaxation, fishing, and (quite naturally) hunting.[53] Free time varied according to the desires of individual slaveholders and the vagaries of the agricultural cycle. Nightfall and Sunday provided the most numerous and reliable breaks in the routine, but even these could evaporate according to the needs (or whims) of slaveholders. Some slaveholders also suspended slave labor for special occasions or celebrations. Every slaveholder organized his slaves differently, but most gave their slaves opportunities to hunt around Christmas. Some slaves also received free time on Saturdays and on more vaguely defined "off days." For Ransom Sidney Taylor, a North Carolinan who hunted rabbits and opossum, the best opportunities for hunting came during "layby time" (a lull in the agricultural cycle that varied with each staple crop), the Fourth of July, and Christmas.[54]

Ultimately, slaves' opportunities for hunting depended upon their owners' caprice. Some slaveholders banned hunting altogether. Suppression could spring from a variety of motives, including caution about allowing slaves any autonomy, fear of arming slaves, and unwillingness to limit their labor in the fields; but in many cases it came from slaveholders' personal idiosyncrasies. Slaveholders' power circumscribed slaves' lives in peculiar ways, as illustrated by the memories of Elias Thomas, a slave who grew up in Chatham County, North Carolina. In his description of the various methods by which the slaves on his plantation supplemented their incomes, he interjected, "Ole missus wouldn't allow us to eat rabbits but she let us catch and eat possums." His explanation for this apparently arbitrary restriction remains enigmatically brief: "Missus didn't have any use for a rabbit." Most slaveholders followed fairly logical and pragmatic criteria when they set restrictions upon their slaves, but white supremacy ensured that slaveholders could shape and circumscribe the lives of their slaves in whatever way they saw fit.[55]

Hunting promised so many potential benefits that in many cases slaves simply hunted on the sly, without their owners' consent or knowledge. Berry Clay, a free black employed by the president of the Central Georgia Railroad, put it quite forthrightly when he explained that in his neighborhood "hunting and fishing were recreations in which the slaves were not allowed to participate although they frequently went on secret excursions of this nature." Faced with evidence of these illicit hunting expeditions, most slaveholders adopted a policy of willful disinterest. James Bolton of Oglethorpe County, Georgia, explained that his owner, Whitfield Bolton, forbade hunting, but "jes' the same, we had plenny 'possums, an no buddy ax' how we cotch 'em."[56]

Whether their hunting was sanctioned or on the sly, in the field slave hunters faced a second major obstacle. Even if they found an opportunity for hunting, few possessed reliable means for killing or capturing game. Legally forbidden from owning any form of property (for they were property themselves), the vast majority of slaves lacked the instrument preferred by white hunters throughout the South: the gun. Ranged and relatively accurate in experienced hands, it provided a devastatingly effective mechanism for killing animals. This effectiveness, when combined with the talismanic resonance between guns and white manhood and the usefulness of firearms in slave rebellions, greatly encouraged the efforts of white individuals, communities, and governments to restrict the use of guns to white males.[57] By and large, these efforts remained successful throughout the antebellum era, but when statute law confronted the desires of individual slaveholders, the latter often prevailed. Most slaveholders, but particularly those with a paternalistic bent, delegated power without questioning the possibility that their most trusted slaves might pursue an aim other than the maximization of their sport. Patriarchy interposed the personal relationship of master and slave between huntsmen

and the law, which emphasized the power of the slaveholder. His ownership of land and slaves made his word law within his domain.[58]

Slave hunters often borrowed guns from their owners (who expected
their prompt return), but in some instances they apparently owned the
guns outright.[59] Especially trusted slaves even received guns as gifts from
their owners. After Charles Ball was sold and moved to a plantation near
Milledgeville, Georgia, his new owner presented him with "an old gun that
had seen much hard service, for the stock was quite shattered to pieces,
and the lock would not strike fire." Undeterred, Ball took the gun to a local
blacksmith who repaired the lock. He then, in contravention of several of
the most dearly held tenets of Georgia law, owned a gun. Despite his previous success as a trapper, Ball felt that the acquisition of a gun signified
his elevation into a more rarefied stratum of hunters. Equipped with a
functional gun, he declared, "I now, for the first time in my life, became
a hunter, in the proper sense of the word." By increasing his effectiveness
in the field, the gun meant that he "began to live well," which made him
"in some measure, an independent man."[60]

Only the most trusted slaves carried guns with their owners' consent,
but the ubiquity of bird minders, huntsmen, and other trusted slaves
meant that slaves did carry guns—and without much comment from
white observers. As historian Eugene Genovese has observed, "With or
without legal sanction, masters did as they pleased, and the sight of slaves
hunting with guns rarely raised eyebrows." This was because slaveholders took few chances when it came to slaves and guns. Slaves realized this
and prized guns so highly that those who acquired guns—whether from
their owners, through purchase, or by theft—monopolized their use
within their communities. When combined with white efforts at gun control, this reluctance to share ensured that no more than a handful of slaves
possessed more than a vague, secondhand familiarity with guns.[61]

Many slaves yearned for the guns they could never have, but restrictions
upon the use of firearms rarely dissuaded slave hunters. Pressed by their
hunger and a desire to improve their quality of life, they used whatever
means seemed most effective in securing game for themselves and their
families. To this end, slaves adopted a variety of methods that many white
hunters characterized as crass and artless. Living near Belton, South Carolina, Tom Hawkins and his companions "got 'possums and rabbits de
best ways us could"; they "cotch 'em in traps, hit 'em wid rocks, and trailed

'em wid dogs."[62] Amos Lincoln worked on the Elshay Guidry plantation in southern Louisiana where he and some of the other slaves employed a variety of methods to capture game. "Us had good food mos' time," he recalled. "Steel an' log traps fo' big game; dig pit traps in de woods 'bout so long an' se deep, an' kiver dem wid bresh an' leaves. Dat kotch 'possum, 'coon, an' uder t'ings w'at come 'long in d' night." "Den us lace willow twigs wid strings," he continued, "an' put a cross piece on d' top an' d' bottom, an' a little piece 'r' wood on d' top edge. D' trap was put 'bout two feet off d'groun' t' kotch d' birds. W'at birds? O, jus' birds fly 'round' d' house, doves, black birds, any kin' birds y' kin eat. . . . Us shoot plenty ducks wid a mustet (musket) too."[63]

Unlike most of their owners, who generally desired ostentatious display, most slaves adopted methods that evaded easy detection. Because some slaveholders forbade hunting and many customarily appropriated some of the game brought in by slaves, all slave hunters (even those with the sanction of their owners) profited from silence and discretion. These concerns ensured that slave hunters remained as innocuous as possible. The slave hunters who hunted in John Smith's area of Johnson County, North Carolina, could not "carry guns or hunt without some white man with him unless his marster give him a pass." Consequently they "caught rabbits in gums, birds in traps an' hunted possums wid dogs at night."[64] Hunting, when pared down to its barest essentials, required nothing more than opportunity, desire, and a reliable stick. Even slaves with guns resorted to these methods because of the expense of powder and shot. Recalling her days in Texas during slavery, Silvia King explained: "De young ones wuz purty handy trappin' quail, partridges, an' squirrel. Dey didn't shoot effen de could cotch eny thing some odder way caze de powder an' lead wuz sca'ce."[65]

In their quest for game, inventive slaves employed a variety of unorthodox methods, but most preferred two methods used to great effect by many whites — traps and dogs.[66] Because of their effectiveness, slaves using these methods often infuriated most white hunters. Traps attracted criticism from a wide variety of white hunters. When Daniel R. Hundley described how slaves snared rabbits, constructed turkey pens, and set traps for squirrel, quail, and ducks, he complained that these methods "destroy large quantities, owning to their great abundance all through the South."[67] Slaves built a dazzling array of traps, each of which varied in construction according to the skill and resources of the trapper. They covered the gamut from the rudimentary "drowning trap" (a hole halfway filled with water) to carefully constructed turkey traps, handmade "rabbit gums" (wooden boxes with spring-loaded doors), and even traps for wild hogs.[68] Some slaves even used commercially manufactured steel traps. Convenient, easy to maintain, and relatively quiet, traps proved impossible to suppress. Because of their effectiveness, both John Stuart Skinner and Johnson Jones Hooper encouraged the destruction of traps.[69] Because trapping lacked the drama, challenge, and selectivity of the chase, many whites did not even consider it a form of hunting. Most white writers maintained that although trapping provided white boys with good training and gave desperate frontiersmen a source of pelts, it remained a suspicious and underhanded activity, especially in areas with a noticeably declining supply of game. These concerns were irrelevant to the needs and lives of slaves. Mastered in childhood, such pothunter methods remained important skills for adult slave hunters, who rarely made a distinction between hunting and trapping; they were simply different means to the same end—meat.

Dogs taxed slaves' limited resources more heavily than traps, but they provided more than an effective instrument for hunting. They could also become loyal companions.[70] The narrative of James Smith, a Virginia runaway who escaped to the North in 1843, illustrated the depths of this devotion. Trained for hunting, his dog proved invaluable when Smith resolved to escape his slavery. He planned his escape attempt with the help of a friend who occasionally accompanied him on his hunting outings. In this attempt his dog proved that its loyalty exceeded that of Smith's presumed accomplice, who sold him out for "one dollar in money, and a half gallon of whiskey." Proceeding according to their plan, Smith stole away from his master and, accompanied by his dog, made for the woods. The treachery of Smith's "professed friend" became apparent when Smith reached their rendezvous in the woods. Instead of finding a traveling companion, he stumbled into a party of armed whites who seized him. In the ensuing scuffle Smith's dog bit two of the attackers, but the animal reluctantly fled when Smith was finally overcome.

After subduing and flogging Smith, they took him to the home of his erstwhile friend who repeated their plans for escape. The man received his payment, and the "whole crowd drank whiskey so freely, that night that they became stupid and careless about Smith, after they supposed that they had got him drunk, for they made him drink several times, after which he made them believe that he was almost dead drunk." Thinking "he was so drunk that he would not be able to stir before the next morning," they left him lying on the kitchen floor. About an hour after the party left, Smith lit out again. "He had not proceeded far from the house before he was again greeted by his devoted hunting dog, which seemed to be filled with joy at the release of his master." Even though Smith tried to drive him away, "the dog was determined to follow him." After the two traveled about fifteen miles, dawn began to break, so Smith sought a "place of concealment." As they crouched by the side of an old mossy log, "the dog seemed to be quite restless and to be filled with fearful apprehensions . . . so that Smith thought that he had better kill him, lest some one should be passing though the woods and the dog bark at them which would betray his whereabouts." Resolving to kill his devoted companion, Smith tied a rope around his dog's neck and "led him to a small tree where the poor fellow was to be executed. The dog looked up at his master while he was tying the rope, with all the intelligence of a human being and the devotion of an undaunted friend, making no resistance whatever but appeared to be willing to lay down his life for the liberation of his master."

Moved by the apparent devotion of his dog, the desperate slave asked himself "whether it would be right in the sight of God for him to take the life of that dog, which had proved as true to him in the hour of danger? Just as he was reflecting over the matter he heard the yelling of a pack of blood hounds coming on his trail, so he immediately released the dog and started on a run, but did not proceed far before they were overtaken by the dogs." Arming himself with a wooden club, Smith prepared for the arrival of the bloodhounds. At their approach his dog "seized one of them by the neck and held him fast." In the ensuing fight Smith killed two of the bloodhounds with his club. His dog held his own, and the other bloodhound "was glad to escape with his life, which was in great danger." His dog's conduct during this victorious struggle "endeared him to his master stronger than ever; for without his aid Smith must have been taken back into slavery."

Traveling by night and keeping concealed by day, they reached the Ohio River with no other aid than the North Star. After finding a skiff tied to a tree on the shore, Smith began rowing himself across, leaving his dog on the Virginia shore. Undaunted, the dog plunged into the water and "succeeded in crossing even before his master." The next morning Smith saw a man chopping poles and ventured to speak with him. Fortunately, the man was an abolitionist who took Smith and his dog to his home, fed them, and sent them on to another friend who hired Smith as a farm laborer. While Smith was employed in Ohio, his loyal dog died.[71]

Slaves who did not own dogs themselves often borrowed them from other slaves or their owners. Loans of dogs were apparently quite common. Agatha Babine explained that during slavery "we didn't have no dogs but dere was some in de neighborhood what hed 'em and dey lend 'em to other men what didn't have none."[72] The slaves on Judge Thompson Rector's plantation in Travis County, Texas, customarily borrowed his dog, Ring. Unlike guns, dogs lacked an attendant bundle of responsibility and power; they could be loaned out without a careful calculation of consequences.[73] Slaveholders loaned out their dogs fairly readily because although they made firm distinctions between their own dogs and the "curs" that lived in the quarters, all of the dogs on the plantation were usually cared for by slaves. Whites might take a special role in the training of their pack, but the daily labor of feeding and cleaning the dogs often fell to the slaves. If slaveholders withheld permission, their slaves might just borrow the dogs anyway.[74]

Although slaves exploited whatever opportunities presented themselves, the crushing demands of staple crop production ensured that many slaves simply lacked the time for hunting. Because slaves approached their free time with a pragmatic eye, they took up whatever activities seemed best suited to their situation. Opposition by slaveholders, paucity of game, or the attractiveness of other options could all squeeze hunting out of the picture. Andy Marion of South Carolina noted that his owner encouraged married slaves to keep up their own gardens, but this left them with "no time for fishin' or huntin'."[75] Forced labor could consume every ounce of available energy. Mississippian Mollie Edmonds asked, "Who dat, on us place, got time to go hunting and fishing?" She went on to explain that "them niggers worked in the day time and slept all night. They didn't squander their time with the like of that. We had plenty good of something to eat, but it sure warn't possum, rabbit, or fish."[76]

Even if slaves did decide to go hunting, their limited time and resources meant that they often lacked the skills and equipment necessary to be effective in the field. Smith Simmons of Mississippi never ate "game like possums and rabbits" because he and the slaves he knew "didn't have no way to kill them."[77] Becoming a capable hunter required time and opportunity. Effective hunters required both skills and knowledge, which only came through practice and experience. The length of this learning curve, the lack of guns, and the possibility of punishment for those who hunted without a pass meant that unless they lived in areas with especially bountiful game, slaves with owners who expressly forbade hunting and actively interdicted slave hunters probably dropped hunting from their list of activities.

Those slaves who persisted in hunting received many benefits from the activity. More than a crudely functional source of supplemental provisions, hunting improved slaves' lives in a number of ways. Hunting became a driving force in the development and maintenance of slave culture because although slave hunters participated in the internal economy, they also enjoyed hunting as a leisure activity. By reconceptualizing hunting as an activity that benefited the slave community, these hunters also found ways to create their own meanings for the labor they performed at the behest of their owners. If slave hunters played their roles with care, they denied the power of white hegemony; they could also gain a modicum of influence over their erstwhile masters. Slave hunters overcame numerous obstacles in their pursuit of these ends, including the appropriation of game by slave owners, a shortage of effective weapons, and a paucity of opportunity. In spite of these impediments, thousands of slave men (and a few slave women) took the field throughout the antebellum era.

Epilogue

God created man and He created the world for him to live in; I reckon He created the kind of a world He would have wanted to live in if He had been a man—the ground to walk on, the Big Woods, the trees and the water, and the game to live in it. And maybe He didn't put the desire to hunt and kill game in man, but I reckon He knew it was going to be there, that man was going to teach himself that, since he wasn't quite God yet. So I reckon He foreknew man would follow and kill the game. I believe He said, So be it. I reckon He even foresaw the end. But He said, I will give him a chance, I will give him warning and foreknowledge too, along with the desire to follow and the power to slay. The woods and the fields he ravages and the game he devastates will be the consequence and signature of his crime and guilt, and his punishment.

William Faulkner, *Big Woods*

O NCE THE Civil War began, southern hunters carried on as best they could. Whether as soldiers or noncombatants, they continued taking the field throughout the war. The promise of fresh meat, marketable hides, and momentary distraction from the war ensured that a few particularly determined hunters like David Golightly Harris, a farmer in the North Carolina piedmont, went hunting several times a month. Indeed, four days after hearing of Lee's surrender at Appomattox, he lit out in pursuit of wild turkey.[1]

In the wake of emancipation and the economic and social upheavals that followed the war, many southerners turned to hunting out of necessity. Hardship made everyone a pothunter.[2] Snares and traps remained popular because of their effectiveness, low cost, and relative ease. However, the wartime production of guns translated into a postwar boom in gun hunting. Although the initial increase came from veterans who kept their personal weapons when they were mustered out of service, refinements in marketing and manufacturing led to a postbellum proliferation of guns.[3]

The wrenching change brought by emancipation, the defeat of the Confederacy, and economic collapse also contributed to the sustained popularity of hunting. During Reconstruction many whites embraced the more dramatic aspects of the hunt with eager enthusiasm. For some white hunters the quest for opportunities to display their prowess and masculinity became so important that they stepped up their participation in the forms of the hunt that emphasized drama over utility.[4] Foxhunting was usually the favored form of hunting spectacle. Taking the field in groups of armed white men, these dramatic forms of the hunt dramatized the unvanquished power of white supremacy. During Reconstruction the spectacle of groups of armed and mounted whites taking the field with their dogs and guns remained a powerful and unambiguous symbol of white power. This was especially true after the formation of violent vigilante groups like the Ku Klux Klan.

These groups of armed white southerners, however, were anathema to the federal authorities during Reconstruction. In order to present a more benign image, some paramilitary groups disguised themselves as hunting fraternities. In his description of the Carolina Rifle Club, John B. Irving of South Carolina noted that "the organizers decided to evade the laws of the Military Government, then imposed on Charleston, and organized a Rifle Club with the innocuous constitution of a social group bent on sport." Given the long association between hunting and the military, such an organization was hardly "innocuous," especially considering "they got themselves up in grey hunting shirts like General Marion's of the Revolution, with green tabs to show rank, slouch hats and *sixteen shooter Winchesters* to use on the 'range.'" The pretense of sport, however, apparently proved effective camouflage.[5]

Even as they performed familiar dramas of masculinity that exhibited their determination to maintain white supremacy, white hunters used hunting as a vehicle to confirm the developing mythology of the Old South. This representation of antebellum southern culture was premised upon the fiction of a paternalistic master-slave relationship in which caring white masters and happy slaves lived harmoniously and happily together. In some white depictions of the South, the loyal black huntsman became the male counterpart to the devoted black mammy—an individual so bound up in the bonds of paternalism that independence became an impossible and unwanted betrayal of beloved white authority. This image became an important component of white nostalgia.[6]

The continuing interaction among black and white hunters meant that a relatively stable patron-client relationship developed, one that survived well into the twentieth century. For many black hunters this became the path of least resistance. Black hunters continued hunting alone, but white hostility to armed blacks, the closing of the open range, and requirements for hunting licenses made hunting an often difficult proposition for poor rural blacks. Some freedmen adapted to these new constraints, while others employed illicit techniques similar to those practiced by their enslaved predecessors. Still, many African Americans apparently gave up hunting altogether.[7]

As living memory of the antebellum world faded, nostalgic whites contrived a mythical lost world of contentment and plenty. This detailed and audacious creation had little to do with the social and economic forces transforming the South during the twentieth century, but it did influence white southerners' conceptions of themselves. In the process it shaped their understanding of the hunt, which remained an important bellwether of southern culture. During the twentieth century hunting retained its associations with the past, but it also reflected the development of new understandings of race, gender, class, and society.

Hunting remained culturally significant because it combined tradition and adaptability. Changes in hunting law, the sporting press, weapons technology, and the southern environment, economy, and social structure all affected the form and meaning of the hunt, and white hunters of every class adapted. The closing of the open range, the advent of game wardens, an often baffling system of hunting seasons, and the slow return of relatively plentiful game all modified the form and substance of the hunt. Despite these changes, many white hunters emphatically insisted on an intimate connection between themselves and an increasingly indistinct and idealized past. Even as they adapted to a modernizing South, white hunters often conceived of the hunt as a portal into an immutable (if substantially fictional) South.[8]

This commingling of constancy and change appeared in the transformation of the meaning of meat. Game remained an essential source of protein for many poor white and black hunters, but for most southerners (especially the growing ranks of urbanites and suburbanites), the advent of various modern conveniences like prepackaged food, refrigeration, and grocery stores made game economically insignificant. The affluence of these hunters further elevated sport and trophies, but meat remained an important aspect of the hunt because hunters endowed it with a new meaning. Meat became a trophy in and of itself. Because families no longer depended upon game as a source of food, hunters who provided their families with game no longer ran the risk of being labeled pot-hunters. By divorcing meat from the household economy, these hunters made it a symbol of masculine achievement suitable for display on back-yard grills and at office picnics. The kill remained of paramount importance, but by the end of the twentieth century, killing for pleasure alone had become unpardonably unfashionable. Southern hunters always consumed most of what they killed, but in the twentieth century they gloried in doing so.

The modernization of southern society also changed the ways in which southerners socialized. Most southerners still hunted with their friends and family, but as the population of the South became increasingly mobile and urban, more and more southern hunters turned to private hunting clubs and reserves. Throughout the twentieth century southern hunters continued taking the field in informal hunting fraternities, but an increasing number of hunters joined clubs that reorganized themselves as private resorts. These commercially oriented clubs supported themselves on the dues of their members and the expenses incurred by "dude" huntsmen. Many of these began catering to a northern clientele, which provided the financial wherewithal to purchase and manage extremely large plots of land.[9]

Despite changes in southern hunting and culture, the relationship between hunting and masculinity remained powerful; however, it was not unchanged. The qualities of prowess and self-control still defined the character of the ideal hunter, but as wilderness gave way to wildlife management areas, and as hierarchical relationships based upon personal dependency became increasingly rare, mastery became a shadow of its former self. As a product of slave society and an untamed environment, mastery became increasingly irrelevant. The erosion of mastery removed an important element of southern distinctiveness, and as the twentieth century progressed, southern conceptions of masculinity grew to resemble those of the North.[10]

By the end of the twentieth century, the relationship between hunting and southern culture rested upon hundreds of years of tradition and adaptation. Variables like the supply of game, the structure of hunting fraternities, the role of sport, the substance of the law, and the meaning of meat gradually altered hunters' behavior, but beneath this constantly shifting surface, many of the essentials remained the same. This continuity owed a great deal to southerners' interest in tradition, but in most cases hunting remained popular because it retained the elements that made it a favored pastime in the first place. It was fun, it was convenient, and most importantly it provided southerners with a familiar drama for the verification of their masculinity and an unrivaled venue for the display of their ideas about race, gender, community, and nature.

Notes

Abbreviations

AF   *American Farmer*
AS   Federal Writers' Project, *The American Slave: A Composite Autobiography*,
       41 vols. (Westport, Conn., 1972–77)
ATR   *American Turf Register*
Duke Manuscripts Department, William R. Perkins Library, Duke University,
       Durham, North Carolina
Emory Special Collections Department, Robert W. Woodruff Library, Emory
       University, Atlanta
HNO   Williams Research Center, Historic New Orleans, New Orleans
LOC   Library of Congress, Washington, D.C.
LSU   Department of Archives and Manuscripts, Hill Memorial Library,
       Louisiana State University, Baton Rouge
SCL   Manuscripts Division, South Caroliniana Library, University of South
       Carolina, Columbia
SHC   Southern Historical Collection, University of North Carolina at
       Chapel Hill
SLM   *Southern Literary Messenger*
SOT   *Spirit of the Times*
SQR   *Southern Quarterly Review*
Tulane Manuscripts, Rare Books, and University Archives, Howard-Tilton
       Memorial Library, Tulane University, New Orleans
UVA   Special Collections Department, University of Virginia Library,
       Charlottesville
W&M   Manuscripts and Rare Books, Earl Gregg Swem Memorial Library,
       College of William and Mary, Williamsburg, Virginia

1. Game, Landscape, and the Law

1. Waddell, *Indians,* 40–42, 377 n. 233; Hudson, *Southeastern Indians,* 275–76, 279–81, 340, 346; Rountree, *Powhatan Indians,* chap. 4; Usner, *Indians, Settlers, and Slaves,* 150–54, 165, 169–70; Cowdrey, *This Land, This South,* 11–14; Lawson, *Lawson's History of North Carolina,* 3, 5, 11, 18, 23, 30, 46, 50–51, 184, 219–20; Bartram, *Travels,* 73, 212, 242, 359–60; Boyd, *William Byrd's History,* 116.

2. Lawson, *Lawson's History of North Carolina,* 219; Boyd, *William Byrd's History,* 42–44, 105, 162–63, 189, 196, 211, 230–31, 248, 267, 279; Waddell, *Indians,* 40–41;

Usner, *Indians, Settlers, and Slaves,* 63, 120, 130, 149, 155, 160–61, 168; Bellesîles, *Arming America,* 103–5.

3. Doddridge, *Notes on the Settlement,* 148–49; Brickell, *Natural History,* 46, 260, 361; Waselkov and Braund, *William Bartram,* 15–16, 273 n. 45; Marks, *Southern Hunting in Black and White,* 29; Cowdrey, *This Land, This South,* 50–52; Silver, *A New Face,* 92–93; Usner, *Indians, Settlers, and Slaves,* 64, 126, 173, 254–56, 267–68.

4. Hardin, "Laws of Nature," 137–62; Fogleman, "American Attitudes towards Wolves," 63–94; Marks, *Southern Hunting in Black and White,* 30; Whitney, *Coastal Wilderness,* 302–3; Brickell, *Natural History,* 52, 264–65; Tober, *Who Owns Wildlife?* 23–24; Hening, *Statutes at Large* 1:199, 3:282–83.

5. Hening, *Statutes at Large* 1:199, 228, 248, 258, 437, quotations from 199, 228; Tober, *Who Owns Wildlife?* 19–20.

6. Catesby, *Natural History of Carolina* 2:xi–xii. See also Silver, *A New Face,* 89–94, 102; Hudson, "Why the Southeastern Indians Slaughtered Deer," 155–76; Braund, "Mutual Convenience."

7. Bartram, *Travels,* 212.

8. Doddridge, *Notes on the Settlement,* 138. On the image of the vanguard of settlement, see Slotkin, *Regeneration through Violence;* Smith, *Virgin Land;* Moore, *Frontier Mind;* Silver, *A New Face,* 96–97.

9. Crèvecoeur, *Letters,* 42–43, 47–49. On the frontier, see Crane, *Southern Frontier;* Cashin, *Family Venture;* Johnson, *Frontier in the Colonial South;* Usner, *Indians, Settlers, and Slaves.*

10. Klein, *Unification,* 52; Doddridge, *Notes on the Settlement,* 110; Baily, *Journal,* 103, 115–16; Usner, *Indians, Settlers, and Slaves,* 176; Slotkin, *Regeneration through Violence,* 219; Faragher, *Daniel Boone,* 20–22, 31, 60–61.

11. Crèvecoeur, *Letters,* 42–43, 47–49.

12. Boyd, *William Byrd's History,* 90, 92, 116, quotation from 304; Lockridge, *Diary, and Life, of William Byrd II,* 138.

13. Faragher, *Daniel Boone,* 35, 80, quotation from 123. Cf. Rafferty, *Rude Pursuits,* 79; Bartram, *Travels,* xvii–xviii, 68, 198, 218–19, 264; Woodmason, *Carolina Backcountry,* 245–46; Boyd, *William Byrd's History,* 69; Crockett, *Narrative of the Life,* 151, 153–54, 193; Ashe, *Travels in America* 1:100–102; Hening, *Statutes at Large* 5:60; Klein, *Unification,* 55–6.

14. Hardin, "Alterations They Have Made," 184–93; Hening, *Statutes at Large* 5:62, 431; Palmer, *Chronology,* 16, 20; Klein, *Unification,* 51, 55–6; Faragher, *Daniel Boone,* 80. On ring-firehunting, see Boyd, *William Byrd's History,* 66, 80, 284, 285; Doddridge, *Notes on the Settlement,* 26; Lawson, *Lawson's History of North Carolina,* 5, 219; Whitney, *Coastal Wilderness,* 300–301.

15. On night hunting by firelight, see Browning, *Forty-Four Years,* 210, 392–93; Gosse, *Letters from Alabama,* 268–69; Smith, *Sporting Family,* 128; Bernard, *Retrospections,* 206; G. M., "South Carolina," 246–50, 337–41; Lund, *American Wildlife Law,* 7.

16. Waddell, *Indians,* 40–42.

17. Hening, *Statutes at Large* 5:60–62; Palmer, *Chronology,* 15; Klein, *Unification,* 53; Marks, *Southern Hunting in Black and White,* 30; Tober, *Who Owns Wildlife?* 24–26; Cowdrey, *This Land, This South,* 55–57.

18. Hening, *Statutes at Large* 5:60–62.

19. Ibid., 3:328.

20. Klein, *Unification,* 51, 53; Marks, *Southern Hunting in Black and White,* 30–31; Cooper, *Statutes at Large* 4:310–12.

21. Lund, *American Wildlife Law,* 21–23, 104; Hening, *Statutes at Large* 5:450; Tober, *Who Owns Wildlife?* 27–28.

22. On "Black Laws," see Itzkowitz, *Peculiar Priviledge;* Thompson, *Whigs and Hunters;* Munsche, *Gentlemen and Poachers;* Hopkins, *Long Affray;* Carr, *English Fox Hunting.*

23. Palmer, *Chronology,* 16, 20–21; Lund, *American Wildlife Law,* 19–21, 23; Hening, *Statutes at Large* 5:531; Hall, *Africans in Colonial Louisiana,* 219–20.

24. Friedman, *History of American Law,* 165; Lund, *American Wildlife Law,* 59, 104.

25. Lund, *American Wildlife Law,* 122 n. 95; Palmer, *Chronology,* 21.

26. *Reports of Judicial Decisions* 2:244–46; Lund, *American Wildlife Law,* 121 n. 81; Nott and McCord, *Reports of Cases* 2:338–41.

27. On the English sporting press, see Welcome, *Sporting World;* Bovill, *England of Nimrod;* Itzkowitz, *Peculiar Priviledge,* 10, 13–15, 40, 59–60. On the early American sporting press, see Berryman, "Sport, Health, and the Rural-Urban Conflict," 43–61, and "The Tenuous Attempts," 33–61.

28. Skinner, *ATR* 1:1 (Sept. 1829): 1; Poore, *Biographical Sketch;* Pergram, "The *American Turf Register,*" 4–21.

29. "Prospectus," *SOT* 1:1 (Dec. 10, 1831): 1; Brinley, *Life of William T. Porter;* Current-Garcia, "York's Tall Son," 371–84; Yates, "The *Spirit of the Times,*" 117–48; Yates, *William T. Porter and the Spirit of the Times,* chaps. 3–6.

30. On the veracity of these narratives, see Bellesîles, *Arming America,* 325.

31. Ibid., 323–40, quotation from 323. There were a few southern critics: Vicksburg, "Trial of Two Fox Hunters for Assault," *SOT* 19:13 (May 19, 1849): 151; Henry, *Inquiry;* Browning, *Forty-Four Years,* 96, 118. Some criticism appears tongue-in-cheek: Juliana Rosebud, "Miseries of a Sportsman's Wife," *ATR* 2:7 (March 1831): 339–40.

32. Filson, *Discovery.*

33. Cooper, *Pioneers.* Cf. Simms, *Woodcraft;* Flint, *First White Man;* Bryan, *Mountain Muse.* On the rehabilitation of the frontiersman in literature, see Slotkin, *Regeneration through Violence,* 348–54; Faragher, *Daniel Boone,* 322–33; Moore, *Frontier Mind,* 146–64.

34. Audubon, *Ornithological Biography* 1:205–10, 232.

35. Lanman, *Adventures,* v, 151, 159–60, 191–92, 194, 197, 209; S. L. C., "A Hunting Article," *SLM* 17:1 (Jan. 1851): 44–49; L., "Traits of Backwoodsmen," *SOT* 16:28 (Oct. 5, 1846): 331; Bernard, *Retrospections,* 178; "Story of a Hunter," *SOT* 27:15 (May 23, 1857): 171; Moore, *Emergence of the Cotton Kingdom,* 155.

36. Olmsted, *Cotton Kingdom,* 390–91.

37. Beaty, *John Esten Cooke,* 18.

38. One of the Hunters, "A Deer Hunt in Pike and Covington Counties, Alabama," *SOT* 19:12 (May 12, 1849): 136–37.

39. Webber, *Hunter-Naturalist,* 142; Whitehead, *Wild Sports in the South,* 8–11, 45, 73–74; Ingraham, *South-West,* 133–34, 136, 170–72; Browning, *Forty-Four Years,* 256–57; Gaskins, *Life and Adventures,* 68; Natty Bumpo, "Deerhunting," *ATR* 3:7 (March 1832): 352–54.

40. Smith, *Sporting Family,* 114; New Orleans *Bee,* March 26, 1830, 2; Tracy, *In the Master's Eye,* 17. For backwoodsmen as paramilitaries, see Rafferty, *Rude Pursuits,* 62–63; Ramsay, *Ramsay's History* 2:225; Hall, *Letters,* 86; Leather Stockings, "Rifle Shooting," *ATR* 4:8 (April 1833): 410.

41. McCurry, *Masters of Small Worlds.*

42. Tober, *Who Owns Wildlife?* 43–49; Marks, *Southern Hunting in Black and White,* 44–45.

43. *ATR* 3:8 (April 1832): 399; Hooper, *Dog and Gun,* 9; Manton, "June Sport in Georgia," *SOT* 28:22 (July 10, 1858): 253.

44. The Turkey Runner, "The Chase in the South West," *SOT* 15:29 (July 12, 1845): 225–26; Keller, "'Th' Guv'ner Wuz a Writer," 394–411.

45. Smith, *Sporting Family,* 118.

46. Tober, *Who Owns Wildlife?* chap. 2. On depletion, see Calhoun, *Witness to Sorrow,* 43; Hunter, *Huntsman in the South* 1:83; Browning, *Forty-Four Years,* 198–99, 358–59; *AS,* supp., ser. 1, vol. 1, Ala., 260–61; ibid., vol. 6, Miss., pt. 1, 322–23; ibid., vol. 4, Ga., pt. 2, 364, 498.

47. On firearms technology, see Potowmac, "Theory of Projectiles," *ATR* 1:7 (March 1830): 341; Elliott, *Carolina Sports,* 253; R. L. R., "The Game Season—Field Sports: The Proper Season to Hunt Game," *SOT* 30:40 (Nov. 10, 1860): 479–80; "Reflections of a Life-Time and More," 30, Henry Beasley Ansell Papers, SHC; Trefethen, *American Crusade,* 59–60; Roberts, *Muzzle-Loading Cap Lock Rifle;* Garvaglia and Worman, *Firearms of the American West.*

48. Kennedy, *Blackwater Chronicle,* 7.

49. R. L. B., "Field Sports of South Carolina," *SOT* 29:50 (Jan. 21, 1860): 590; R. L. B., "Game in South Carolina," ibid., 28:11 (April 24, 1858): 128; Montesano, "Bear Steaks and Canebrakes," ibid., 28:50 (Jan. 22, 1859): 591; "A Sporting Adventure across the Lake," ibid., 17:47 (Jan. 15, 1848): 551; Ocoee, "A Hunting Excursion in East Tennessee," ibid., 27:50 (Jan. 23, 1858): 591; "A Trip to the Wilderness," ibid., 29:30 (Sept. 3, 1859): 350–51; Le J D Berry to "Ferdy" [Whitaker], Oct. 19, 1859, F. H. Whitaker Papers, Duke.

50. Henry William Herbert quoted in Trefethen, *American Crusade,* 62. On market hunters, see Tober, *Who Owns Wildlife?* 52–56; Browning, *Forty-Four Years,* 111–13, 117, 194, 198–99; Audubon, *Ornithological Biography* 3:540; Elliott, *Carolina Sports,* 253–54.

51. Hooper, *Dog and Gun,* 60; Number Eight, "Game in Alabama: Suggestions to Sportsmen," *SOT* 23:22 (July 16, 1853): 254; Boyd, *William Byrd's History,* 151, 252; Quail, "Game in Maryland," *SOT* 25:52 (Feb. 9, 1856): 618; Natty Bumpo, "A Deerhunt in North Carolina," *ATR* 4:6 (Feb. 1833): 305–6; Tober, *Who Owns Wildlife?* 46.

52. Elliott, *Carolina Sports,* 253–54.

53. *SQR* 12 (July 1847): 79; R. L. B., "Game in South Carolina," *SOT* 28:11 (April 24, 1858): 128.

54. Browning, *Forty-Four Years,* vi; Elliott, *Carolina Sports,* 169. Cf. "Reflections of a Life-Time and More," 30–31, Henry Beasley Ansell Papers, SHC.

55. Cor de Chasse, "Snipe Shooting in Florida," in Hooper, *Dog and Gun,* 100. On wanton killing, see Kennedy, *Blackwater Chronicle,* 133, 163–64; *SQR* 12 (July 1847): 79;

Boyd, *William Byrd's History,* 69, 151; Ranger, "Sporting at the South: Week on Cooper River," *SOT* 16:2 (March 7, 1846): 13–15; Lyell, *Second Visit* 2:88; Bennett Barrow Diary, LSU; Manton, "A Week's Shooting in Louisiana," *SOT* 18:13 (May 20, 1848): 145–47; One of the Hunters, "A Deer Hunt in Pike and Covington Counties, Alabama," ibid., 19:12 (May 12, 1849): 136–37; Dan, "Hunting Expedition," ibid., 20:44 (Dec. 21, 1850): 519; "Shooting in Louisiana," ibid., 21:46 (Jan. 3, 1852): 546; Adjutant Haile, "Sporting Trip to 'The Lakes,'" ibid., 13:41 (Dec. 9, 1843): 481; Bubble, "A Story of Duck Shooting," ibid., 22:45 (Dec. 25, 1852): 531; *ATR* 3:8 (April, 1832): 399; Hooper, *Dog and Gun,* 69–70; Bob Tail, "Snipe Shooting in Virginia," *SOT* 21:10 (April 24, 1852): 110.

56. Elliott, *Carolina Sports,* 252–53; G. T. N., "Field Sports: Their Utility—Modes of Hunting Deer and Turkeys in Virginia, Interspersed with Hunting Anecdotes," *ATR* 7:7 (March 1836): 317.

57. Hilliard, *Hog Meat and Hoecake,* 74; Evans, "Gerstaecker and the Konwells," 34–35; Bennett Barrow Diary, April 12, 1840, LSU; Browning, *Forty-Four Years,* 198–99; Old Dominion, "Sporting Epistle from 'Old Dominion,'" *SOT* 28:50 (Jan. 22, 1859): 590; Rosengarten, *Tombee,* 127; [Charles Ball], *Fifty Years in Chains,* 278–79; "A Sporting Letter from Mississippi," *SOT* 9:23 (Aug. 10, 1839): 271–72.

58. Whitney, *Coastal Wilderness,* 304–8, quotation from 307.

59. Ibid., 313.

60. Audubon and Bachman, *Quadrupeds of North America* 1:170, 2:110; Lyell, *A Second Visit* 2:17; Smith, *Sporting Family,* 212; Hardin, "Laws of Nature," 137–62; Usner, *Indians, Settlers, and Slaves,* 152 n. 5; Browning, *Forty-Four Years,* 102, 285, 310.

61. Rosengarten, *Tombee,* 127; Irving, *Day on the Cooper River,* 126–27.

62. Elliott, *Carolina Sports,* 255–60, quotation from 258–59; R. L. B., "Fishing and Shooting Excursion to the 'Island of Kia-Wah,'" *SOT* 30:31 (Sept. 8, 1860): 371–72; Wellman, *Giant in Gray,* 40, 43; Rosengarten, *Tombee,* 127; Diary of Samuel Catawba Lowry, Nov. 1, 1861, SCL; "Rules, Adopted by the Proprietors, and to Be Observed, for the Increase and Preservation of Game in Dogue's Neck," *ATR* 2:4 (Dec. 1830): 186–87; Hardin, "Laws of Nature," 146.

63. Faragher, *Daniel Boone,* 28–29, 53, 71, 76–79, 93, 281; Michaux, *Travels to the Westward,* 51, 53; Mackay, *Western World,* 3:36–37; "The Ring-Tail Panther," *SOT* 8:19 (June 23, 1838): 146; Usner, *Indians, Settlers, and Slaves,* 174–76.

64. Palmer, *Chronology,* 22; Trefethen, *American Crusade,* 106–7; Smith, *Sporting Family,* 129.

65. Palmer, *Chronology,* 22.

66. Trefethen, *American Crusade,* 72–73; John Smith Jr., "Duck Shooting on the Waters of the Chesapeake," *SOT* 22:39 (Nov. 13, 1852): 458, John Smith Jr., "Duck Shooting on the Waters of the Chesapeake, No. 2," ibid., 22:40 (Nov. 20, 1852): 472, John Smith Jr., "Duck Shooting on the Waters of the Chesapeake, No. 3," ibid., 22:51 (Feb. 5, 1853): 603; "Duck Shooting in Maryland," ibid., 26:44 (Dec. 13, 1856): 522.

67. "Duck Shooting in Maryland," *SOT* 26:44 (Dec. 13, 1856): 522.

68. Smith, *Sporting Family,* 129.

69. Elliott, *Carolina Sports,* 252, 254.

70. Ibid., 256–57.

71. Ibid., 256–59.

72. Ibid., 260.

73. Ibid., 252; *SQR* 12 (July 1847): 67–90.

74. Lund, *American Wildlife Law,* 30–33, 105; Trefethen, *American Crusade,* 73–74; "The New York Association for the Protection of Game," *Forest and Stream* 33:23 (Dec. 26, 1889): 450.

75. "Protection of Game in South Carolina," *SOT* 27:20 (June 27, 1857): 229. Cf. Quail, "Game Laws in Maryland," ibid., 26:10 (April 19, 1856): 114.

76. "Preservation of Game," ibid., 27:42 (Nov. 28, 1857): 500.

77. R. L. B., "Game in South Carolina," ibid., 28:11 (April 24, 1858): 128.

78. "Dogs — Rabies — Game in South Carolina," ibid., 28:32 (Sept. 18, 1858): 375–76; Diving Bell, "Hunting in Georgia, with a Game or Two of 'Poker,'" ibid., 24:22 (July 15, 1854): 259–60; Skinner, *Dog and Sportsman,* 79; Hunter, *Huntsman in the South* 1:157; C. of Philadelphia, "Season for Shooting Game" *ATR* 1:10 (June 1830): 500–503; Joe Manton, "June Sport in Georgia," *SOT* 28:22 (July 10, 1858): 253; East Mississippi, "Sport in Mississippi, etc.," ibid., 24:22 (July 15, 1854): 254.

79. Lewis quoted in Lund, *American Wildlife Law,* 60; Hunter, *Huntsman in the South* 1:314.

2. Hunters at Home and in the Field

1. R. L. R., "The Game Season — Field Sports: The Proper Season to Hunt Game," *SOT* 30:40 (Nov. 10, 1860): 479–80; "Partridge Shooting — *Commenced,*" *AF* 6:34 (Nov. 12, 1824): 271; "The Road to Health — or, A Physician's Opinion of Hunting," ibid., 7:26 (Sept. 16, 1825): 207; "The Baltimore Hunt," ibid., 7:34 (Nov. 11, 1825): 271; Struna, *People of Prowess,* 107–10, 166.

2. G. T. N., "Field Sports, Their Utility — Modes of Hunting Deer and Turkeys in Virginia, Interspersed with Hunting Anecdotes," *ATR* 7:7 (March, 1836): 314–23; Elliott, *Carolina Sports,* 174, 192; M. Gourman to George L. F. Birdsong, March 2, [1864?], Birdsong Correspondence, box 1, folder 5, Emory; Audubon and Bachman, *Quadrupeds of North America* 1:169; S. L. C., "A Hunting Article," *SLM* 17:1 (Jan. 1851): 44–49.

3. Elliott, *Carolina Sports,* 247; Aceton, "Deer Hunting," *ATR* 1:8 (April 1830): 404–6; "Hunting," *SOT* 1:16 (March 31, 1832): 3; Terra, "The Philosophy of Field Sports," ibid., 11:7 (April 17, 1841): 76.

4. *SQR* 12 (July 1847): 86–87.

5. Gorn, "Gouge and Bite," 39; Wyatt-Brown, *Southern Honor,* 74; Peristiany and Pitt-Rivers, *Honor and Grace.*

6. For historical analysis of display in the antebellum South, see Stowe, *Intimacy and Power,* 12–13, 22, 49; Gorn, "Gouge and Bite," 21–22, 39; Isaac, *Transformation of Virginia,* chaps. 5–6; Breen, "Horses and Gentlemen," 239–57; Wyatt-Brown, *Southern Honor,* passim; Mayfield, "The Soul of a Man!" 477–500.

7. Lyell, *Second Visit* 2:247.

8. Caroline De Clouet Benoist to cousin Josephine Favrot, Feb. 6, 1818, Favrot Papers, Tulane. On mothers and boys, see Wyatt-Brown, *Southern Honor,* 159; Fox-Genovese, *Within the Plantation Household,* 16.

9. Faragher, *Daniel Boone,* 271; Malone, *Thomas Jefferson,* 46–47. On fathers, see G. T. N., "Field Sports: Their Utility—Modes of Hunting Deer and Turkeys in Virginia, Interspersed with Hunting Anecdotes," *ATR* 7:7 (March 1836): 314–23. On mentors, see Joe Manton, "Coons and Coon-Hunting," *SOT* 28:45 (Dec. 18, 1858): 532–33; Smith, *Sporting Family,* chaps. 4–5. On autodidacts, see Mark, "A Deer Hunt in Georgia," *SOT* 19:21 (July 14, 1849): 246.

10. Locksley, "An Old Sportsman: Outmanoevered by His Pupil," *ATR* 5:2 (Oct. 1833): 93–94.

11. Smith, "A Plantation Boyhood," 85.

12. George A. Mercer Diary, SHC.

13. Smith, *Sporting Family,* 121.

14. Ibid., 93, 127.

15. P. I., "Country Notes," *SLM* 18:10 (Oct. 1852): 611; Gosse, *Letters from Alabama,* 44.

16. Webber, *Hunter-Naturalist,* 47.

17. Ibid., 48–49.

18. Ibid.

19. On guns and white men, see Gay, "The Tangled Skein," 88; Bellesîles, *Arming America,* 329, 336–37, 340; "Instructions to Young Sportsmen," *AF* 9:37 (Nov. 30, 1827): 295. Ordinarily only white men carried guns, but on occasion slaves and free blacks also carried them; see *AS,* ser. 2, vol. 12, Ga., pt. 1, 82; Smith, "A Plantation Boyhood," 67; Riley, "Diary of a Mississippi Planter," 434; Olmsted, *Journey,* 447; Olmsted, *Cotton Kingdom,* 200; Stewart, *What Nature Suffers to Groe,* 175, 318 nn. 47–50.

20. Bellesîles, "The Origins of Gun Culture," 425–55; Bellesîles, *Arming America,* 445.

21. George A. Mercer Diary, SHC; Faragher, *Daniel Boone,* 15; Smith, "A Plantation Boyhood," 85; Keefe and Morrow, *White River Chronicles,* 87; "Reflections of a Life-Time and More," 42, Henry Beasley Ansell Papers, SHC.

22. Webber, *Hunter-Naturalist,* 58–59.

23. Ibid., 59; Gosse, *Letters from Alabama,* 130.

24. Wyche-Otey Papers, ser. 1.2, folder 3, SHC. For women using guns, see Keefe and Morrow, *White River Chronicles,* 108; Ludwell, "Boundary Line Proceedings," 10; Faragher, *Daniel Boone,* 50.

25. George A. Mercer Diary, April 1850, SHC.

26. Armand DeRossett Young Diary, vol. 2, Jan. 27, 1860, Langdon, Young, and Meares Family Papers, ser. 3.2, SHC; "Reflections of a Life-Time and More," 10–12, Henry Beasley Ansell Papers, ibid.; Old Dominion, "Sporting Epistle from 'Old Dominion,'" *SOT* 28:50 (Jan. 22, 1859): 590; Latrobe, *Impressions,* 130.

27. Gosse, *Letters from Alabama,* 44, 57, 96; Doddridge, *Notes on the Settlement,* 74; Faragher, *Daniel Boone,* 16. For a description of "rabbit twisting," see *AS,* ser. 2, vol. 12, Ga., pt. 2, 223.

28. Gosse, *Letters from Alabama,* 108.

29. Ibid., 130.

30. Stowe, *Intimacy and Power,* chap. 3; Wyatt-Brown, *Southern Honor,* chap. 6. On the maintenance of friendship, see T. Hunter, "The Turkey-Hunter in His Closet," *SLM* 17:10 (Oct.–Nov. 1851): 660; George B. Conway to Reubin T. Thornton, Jan. 15, 1841, Pi Kappa Alpha Letters, UVA; W. G., "Bear-Hunting in Louisiana," *SOT* 21:23 (July 26, 1851): 271; C. A. P., "My First and Last Turkey Hunt," ibid., 17:43 (Dec. 18, 1847): 507.

31. Falconer, "A Day at 'Rookwood,'" *SOT* 26:7 (March 29, 1856): 79; W. G., "Bear-Hunting in Louisiana," ibid., 21:23 (July 26, 1851): 271; Tucker, *George Balcombe* 2:261; Hundley, *Social Relations,* 168.

32. The Old "Squire," "The Louisiana Swamp in a Blaze," *SOT* 29:10 (April 16, 1859): 115–16.

33. Crèvecoeur, *Letters,* 47–49; Kennedy, *Swallow Barn,* xii, 253, 255–57, 258; Tracy, *In the Master's Eye,* 57; Ralph Ranger, "Sporting at the South: or A Week on Cooper River," *SOT* 15:52 (Feb. 21, 1846): 609–10; Hentz Family Papers, subseries 6.1, Diaries, SHC; "Fragments of Hunting and Fishing Record of W. Russell Robinson," UVA; Keefe and Morrow, *White River Chronicles,* 84, 94, 118; Gaskins, *Life and Adventures,* 63, 72, 75.

34. Whitehead, *Wild Sports,* 56; Ralph Ranger, "Sporting at the South: Week on Cooper River," *SOT* 16:1 (Feb. 28, 1846): 1–2; An Old North Carolina Correspondent, "The Pastur Buck," ibid., 19:38 (Nov. 10, 1849): 451; *AS,* supp., ser. 1, vol. 3, Ga., pt. 1, 172; Mark, "Hunting and Fishing on the Sea-Coast of Georgia," *SOT* 18:12 (May 13, 1848): 135.

35. Gorn, "Gouge and Bite," 22; Henry William Harrington Papers, Dec. 4, 1856, SHC,; Benjamin Brown French MSS, Oct. 29, 1841, LOC; R. L. B., "Fishing and Shooting Excursion to the 'Island of Kia-Wah,'" *SOT* 30:31 (Sept. 8, 1860): 371–72; G. C., "Stag Hunting in Virginia," *ATR* 1:3 (Nov. 1829): 130; C. A. Hentz Diary, Hentz Family Papers, subseries 6.1, SHC; Bennett Barrow Diary, LSU; Gilman, *Recollections,* 209–10.

36. John Ball and Keating Simons Ball Books, folder 5a, Plantation Daybook, vol. 5, 1849–71, SHC; Kennedy, *Blackwater Chronicle,* 15, 18; Gaskins, *Life and Adventures,* 33.

37. Keefe and Morrow, *White River Chronicles,* 96–97, 84; Rafferty, *Rude Pursuits,* 56; Evans, "Gerstaecker and the Konwells," 10; Racine, *Piedmont Farmer,* 61, 63, 154; Gilman, *Recollections,* 208–9.

38. C. A. Hentz Diary, Dec. 26, 1848, Hentz Family Papers, subseries 6.1, SHC; Stowe, *Hentz Diary.*

39. Kirk, *History,* 3–5, 12; *Rules and History of the Hot and Hot Fish Club;* Bill Beans, "Deer-Hunting in Mississippi," *SOT* 27:3 (Feb. 28, 1857): 27–29; Wilson, *Address,* 8, 21; Irving, *Day on the Cooper,* 80; T. W. Peyre to Robert Marion Deveaux, Jan. 6, 1837, July 17, 1841, Singleton Family Papers, LOC; Easterby, "St. Thomas Hunting Club," 123–24; Stoney, "Memoirs of Frederick Augustus Porcher," 37; John Ball and Keating Simons Ball Books, folder 5a, Plantation Daybook, Nov. 20, 1849, vol. 5, 1849–71, SHC; Ramsay, *Ramsay's History,* 226.

40. Rosengarten, *Tombee,* 128.

41. Seebright, "A Panther Hunt on the Blue Ridge," *SOT* 7:46 (Dec. 30, 1837): 364–65, 7:49 (Jan. 20, 1838): 389–90. For comparisons of women to game, see Cooke, *Virginia Comedians* 2:268–69; Tucker, *Valley of Shenandoah,* 76–79.

42. Gilman, *Recollections,* viii, 208, 213–14; Pholo-therus, "Foxhunting in Washington," *ATR* 6:6 (Feb. 1835): 292; Tally-Ho, "The Chase and Its Votaries," ibid., 5:7 (March 1834): 371–73; Smith, *Sporting Family,* 269–70.

43. Hunter, *Huntsman in the South,* 1:89–100; Easterby, "St. Thomas Hunting Club," 123–31, 209–13. For women as advocates for game, see Gilman, *Recollections,* 208–14; Whitehead, *Wild Sports,* 120; Porte Crayon, *Virginia Illustrated,* 124–25.

44. Whitehead, *Wild Sports,* 37, 39, 55–56, 59, 66, 120, 140–41, 143. See also Wyatt-Brown, *Southern Honor,* 231–32; Clinkscales, *On the Old Plantation,* 102.

45. Cousin Olivia to "Cousin Reel" [Octavia Wyche], Nov. 17, 1847, Wyche-Otey Papers, ser. 1.2, folder 3, SHC.

46. H. C. Wyche to Octavia Wyche, Nov. 28, 1847, and Sept. 4, 1848, ibid.

47. Octavia Wyche Diary, ibid., ser. 3.1, folder 40.

48. Davis, "The Ball Papers," 1–15; Scafidel, "Letters of William Elliott," 2:425.

49. John T. Barraud to Ann Barraud, Jan. 3, 1820, Barraud Papers, W&M.

50. C. R. Cochran to Ella Noland, March 22, 1849, Noland Family Papers, UVA; David Draffin to Joseph Bieller, Aug. 9, 1833, Alonzo Snyder Papers, box 1, folder 7, LSU; W. F. Weeks to Mary C. Weeks Moore, Sept. 1, 1845, David Weeks and Family Papers, box 13, folder 90, LSU; Gilman, *Recollections,* 213.

51. One of the Hunters, "A Deer Hunt in Pike and Covington Counties, Alabama," *SOT* 19:12 (May 12, 1849): 136–37; Zenas C. Preston Account Book, Oct. 30, 1836, LOC; Keefe and Morrow, *White River Chronicles,* 99; Gaskins, *Life and Adventures,* 49. Despite this general disinterest, a handful of women writers recorded hunting episodes; see Hentz, *Planter's Northern Bride,* 215, 131; Gilman, *Recollections,* 24–25; Louisa Maria DeLoach, "A Sketch of My Travels through Sabine While Looking at the Country," MS 370, HNO; The Old "Squire," "The Louisiana Swamp in a Blaze," *SOT* 29:10 (April 16, 1859): 115–16; Mary Dickinson to "Lodo," June 6, 1862, folder 1, Andrew Haynes Gay and Family Papers, LSU.

52. Rosengarten, *Tombee,* 128; Scafidel, "Letters of William Elliott," 2:450–52, 674, 698–99; Browning, *Forty-Four Years,* 122; Mary Bateman Diary, Aug. 16, 1856, SHC; Everard Green Baker Diaries, April 24, 1849, ser. J, pt. 6, reel 16, SHC; D. M., "Grassee Hunting in Louisiana," *ATR* 3:3 (Nov. 1831): 117–18.

53. A notable exception: Cor de Chasse, "Snipe Shooting in Florida," 98. Cf. Mary Bateman Diary, Aug. 16, 1856, SHC.

54. Tucker, *Valley of Shenandoah,* 159–60.

55. Ringwood, "Deer Hunting," *ATR* 1:1 (Sept. 1829): 194–96; Elliott, *Carolina Sports,* 171; Hilliard, *Hog Meat and Hoecake.* On gift giving: Greenberg, *Honor and Slavery,* 52–53; Boyd, *William Byrd's History,* 45; T. W. Peyre to Robert Marion Deveaux, Oct. 1, 1837, Singleton Family Papers, LOC; Ralph Ranger, "Sporting at the South: Week on Cooper River," *SOT* 16:2 (March 7, 1846): 13–15; R. L. B., "Fishing and Shooting Excursion to the 'Island of Kia-Wah,'" ibid., 30:31 (Sept. 8, 1860): 371–72.

56. Browning, *Forty-Four Years,* 57, 106–7, 133; S. L., "Camp Hunting in Mississippi," *SOT* 17:47 (Jan. 15, 1848): 555; Boyd, *William Byrd's History,* 43–44, 161, 162; Keefe and Morrow, *White River Chronicles,* 96–97; Louisa Maria DeLoach, "A Sketch of My Travels through Sabine While Looking at the Country," MS 370, HNO; Gaskins, *Life and Adventures,* 98, 113; Kirk, *History,* 13; Arcumsaw, "Isaac Harris's Last 'Bar' Hunt," *SOT* 19:3 (March 10, 1849): 30–31; "The 'Ten Mile Tree' Fox," *SOT* 24:46 (Dec. 30, 1854): 544.

57. Smith, *Sporting Family,* 171, 125.

58. H., "The Game Sportsman, or Genuine Love of the Chase Exemplified," *ATR* 5:6 (Feb. 1834): 298–307.

59. Everard Green Baker Diaries, 1833–76, ser. J, pt. 6, reel 16, SHC; Roswell Elmer Diary, SHC; Gilman, *Recollections,* 75; C. A. Hentz Diary, Hentz Family Papers, subseries 6.1, SHC; Thorpe and Patterson, "Stoke Stout of Louisiana," *Big Bear,* 147–49; Faragher, *Daniel Boone,* 45; Browning, *Forty-Four Years,* 76, 87; Gaskins, *Life and Adventures,* 51.

60. Armand DeRossett Young Diary, vol. 2, Langdon, Young, and Meares Family Papers, ser. 3.2, SHC; C. A. Hentz Diary, Oct. 17, 1860, Hentz Family Papers, subseries 6.1, SHC.

61. Wyatt-Brown, *Southern Honor,* 74, 114, 357.

62. Calhoun, *Witness to Sorrow,* 64–65; Rafferty, *Rude Pursuits,* 52–53, Heyward, *Seed from Madagascar,* 117–18.

63. "A Sporting Letter from Mississippi," *SOT* 9:23 (Aug. 10, 1839): 271–72. Small game still excited inexperienced hunters; see Escott, *North Carolina Yeoman,* 62–63; Clifton, *Life and Labor,* 358; Benjamin Brown French MSS, Oct. 29, 1841, LOC.

64. Mathew, *Agriculture, Geology, and Society,* 177.

65. "Bears and Bear Hunting," *SOT* 25:39 (Nov. 10, 1855): 459–61.

66. Smith, *Sporting Family,* 121, 130; "Deer Hunt in Louisiana," *SOT* 9:8 (April 27, 1839): 87.

67. Evans, "Gerstaecker and the Konwells," 22.

68. S. L., "Camp Hunting in Mississippi" *SOT* 17:47 (Jan. 15, 1848): 555.

69. W., "The Chase in Louisiana," ibid., 10:51 (Feb. 20, 1841): 607; Elliott, *Carolina Sports,* 151.

3. Hunting and the Masculine Ideal

1. "The Big Buck," *SOT* 24:21 (July 8, 1854): 244. See also Ralph Ranger, "Sporting at the South: or A Week on Cooper River," ibid., 15:52 (Feb. 21, 1846): 609–10; "A Panther-Hunt in Kentucky," *Knickerbocker Magazine,* rept., ibid., 25:4 (March 10, 1855): 39; J. B. Keatts, "An Arkansas Bear Hunt," ibid., 16:3 (March 14, 1846): 28.

2. Catesby, *Natural History of Carolina* 1:vii–xii; Oriard, *Sporting with the Gods,* 10; "The Chase," *ATR* 1:6 (Feb. 1830): 309; Lyell, *Travels* 1:144; Skinner, *Dog and Sportsman,* 42, 44.

3. Breen, "Horses and Gentlemen," 239–57; Struna, *People of Prowess,* 112, 116–17; Isaac, *Transformation of Virginia,* 120; Ownby, *Subduing Satan,* 12–16.

4. J. S. Skinner, *ATR* 1:1 (Sept. 1829): 2.

5. Everard Green Baker Diaries, June 30, 1861, ser. J, pt. 6, reel 16, SHC.

6. Mathews, *Religion in the Old South,* 113; Heyrman, *Southern Cross;* Gay, "Tangled Skein," 78–81.

7. Gay, "Tangled Skein," 78–80.

8. Stowe, *Intimacy and Power,* chap. 1; Bruce, *Violence and Culture,* 8–10, 44; Bruce, "Play, Work, and Ethics," 33–51; Gay, "Tangled Skein," 74–84; Isaac, *Transformation of Virginia,* 169–70; Struna, *People of Prowess,* 106; Mathews, *Religion in the Old South,* chap. 3; Gorn, *Manly Art,* 140–41, 252; Scafidel, "Letters of William Elliott," 2:551–52, 573, 580; Bryan, *Mountain Muse,* 45–46, 52; Webber, *Hunter-Naturalist,* 66–69, 76–86; Hundley, *Social Relations,* 31–32, 34; W. J. G., "The Character of the Gentleman," *SQR* 23 (Jan. 1853): 54–63.

9. Smith, *Sporting Family,* 118–19, 149–51; S. L. C., "A Hunting Article," *SLM* 17:1 (Jan. 1851): 44–49; Bruce, *Violence and Culture,* 8–12, 200–209.

10. Gaskins, *Life and Adventures,* xiv; Ringwood, "Deer Hunting," *ATR* 1:1 (Sept. 1829): 194–96; J. B., "A Deer Hunt in South Carolina," *SOT* 11:27 (Oct. 4, 1841): 318; Hundley, *Social Relations,* 39–40; J. B. Keatts, "An Arkansas Bear Hunt," ibid., 16:3 (March 14, 1846): 28; Locksley, "An Old Sportsman: Outmanoevered By His Pupil," *ATR* 5:2 (Oct. 1833): 93–94; Gorn, "Gouge," 22–23, 37.

11. S. L. C., "A Hunting Article," *SLM* 17:1 (Jan. 1851): 44–49.

12. Rosengarten, *Tombee,* 128; Ingraham, *South-West* 2:98; *AS,* vol. 7, Okla., 238.

13. Skinner, *Dog and Sportsman,* 73.

14. Hooper, *Dog and Gun,* 34, 44–45.

15. "Field Sports in Virginia," *ATR* 9:11 (Nov. 1838): 508–11.

16. "The Big Buck," *SOT* 24:21 (July 8, 1854): 244. See also Webber, *Hunter-Naturalist,* 55; Hentz, *Planter's Northern Bride,* 331; "A Panther-Hunt in Kentucky," *SOT* 25:4 (March 10, 1855): 39; Dusinberre, *Them Dark Days,* 230, 251; *AS,* vol. 7, Okla., 301; ibid., ser. 2, vol. 12, Ga., pt. 2, 117; ibid., supp., ser. 2, vol. 6, Tex., pt. 9, 4099.

17. M., "Field Sports of Mississippi," *SOT* 10:9 (May 2, 1840): 97; *AS,* supp., ser. 2, vol. 6, Tex., pt. 9, 4327.

18. Smith, *Sporting Family,* 263; Webber, *Hunter-Naturalist,* chaps. 2–4; Rosengarten, *Tombee,* 129; Greenberg, *Honor and Slavery,* 125–26, 133.

19. Montesano, "Game Steaks and Cane Brakes," *SOT* 29:2 (Jan. 19, 1859): 13–14.

20. Cor de Chasse, "Deer Hunting in Florida," ibid., 18:5 (March 25, 1848): 54–55.See also Ingraham, *Sunny South,* 160; McCall, *Letters from the Frontiers,* 31–32; Elliott, *Carolina Sports,* 162; Hundley, *Social Relations,* 28–29, 35.

21. Elliott, *Carolina Sports,* 163–65.

22. M., "Field Sports of Mississippi," *SOT* 10:9 (May 2, 1840): 97.

23. Ibid., 97.

24. Keefe and Morrow, *White River Chronicles,* 119.

25. Smith, *Sporting Family,* 125.

26. Jefferson, *Notes,* 162–63.

27. Cunliffe, *Soldiers and Civilians;* Wyatt-Brown, *Southern Honor,* 191; Doddridge, *Notes on the Settlement,* 174–75; Elliott, *Carolina Sports,* 240; "Fox Hunting," *AF* 9:42

(Jan. 4, 1828): 335–36; X. Y. Z., "Shooting Extraordinary," *ATR* 1:10 (June 1830): 495–97; Gosse, *Letters from Alabama,* 130; Ramsay, *Ramsay's History,* 225–26.

28. Myrtle, "Foxhunting in Baltimore County," *ATR* 5:12 (Aug. 1834): 613; "Mr. Catchpenny's First Camp Hunt in Arkansas," *SOT* 19:5 (March 24, 1849): 56; The Old "Squire," "The Louisiana Swamp in a Blaze," ibid., 29:11 (April 23, 1859): 121–22.

29. "A Trip to the Wilderness," *SOT* 29:30 (Sept. 3, 1859): 350–51.

30. A South Carolinan, "A Day in the Woods," ibid., 11:30 (Oct. 25, 1841): 355, 349.

31. Smith, *Sporting Family,* 150.

32. Seebright, "A Panther Hunt on the Blue Ridge," *SOT* 7:46 (Dec. 30, 1837): 364–65, 7:49 (Jan. 20, 1838): 390.

33. Ibid.

4. Finding Peers: The Criteria of Exclusion

1. Ralph Ranger, "Sporting at the South: or A Week on Cooper River," *SOT* 15:52 (Feb. 21, 1846): 609–10; Bernard, *Retrospections,* 151–52; W., "The Chase in Louisiana," *SOT* 10:51 (Feb. 20, 1841): 607; Spurs, "Rabbit Chasing in Kentucky," ibid., 25:45 (Dec. 22, 1855): 534; A. F. Holt to George L. F. Birdsong, Jan. 23, 1843, Birdsong Correspondence, box 1, folder 1, Emory.

2. A. B., "A Deer Hunt in North Carolina," *SOT* 13:7 (Oct. 2, 1843): 319.

3. Hundley, *Social Relations,* 32–34; M. P. S., "Billy Scott's Bear Hunt," *SOT* 12:17 (June 25, 1842): 202.

4. Smith, *Sporting Family,* 146; "A Trip to the Wilderness," *SOT* 29:30 (Sept. 3, 1859): 350–51; St. John Richardson Liddell Notebook, 1851–52, Moses Liddell, St. John R. Liddell, and Family Papers, LSU.

5. Smith, *Sporting Family,* 146–47. See also G. W. Bradbury, "Two Days at Jeffries' Springs," *SOT* 15:29 (Sept. 13, 1845): 334; Bubble, "A Story of Duck Shooting," ibid., 22:45 (Dec. 25, 1852): 531; Falconer, "A Day at 'Rookwood,'" ibid., 26:7 (March 29, 1856): 79.

6. A Gentleman, *Sportsman's Companion.*

7. Ralph Ranger, "Sporting at the South: or A Week on Cooper River," *SOT* 15:52 (Feb. 21, 1846): 609–10; Huron, "Weston's First Deer Hunt at Broughton Island," ibid., 23:1 (Feb. 19, 1853): 3.

8. Seebright, "A Panther Hunt on the Blue Ridge," ibid., 7:46 (Dec. 30 1837): 364–65, 7:49 (Jan. 20, 1838): 389–90.

9. Ibid., 389–90.

10. Ibid., 389.

11. Ransom-Hogan and Davis, *William Johnson's Natchez,* 41, 43, 54–55.

12. A South Carolinan, "A Day in the Woods," *SOT* 11:30 (Oct. 25, 1841): 355, 349. See also Smith, *Sporting Family,* 360, 362; H., "The Game Sportsman, or Genuine Love of the Chase Exemplified," *ATR* 5:6 (Feb. 1834): 298–307.

13. Unsigned letter to George L. F. Birdsong, March 14, 1860, Birdsong Correspondence, box 1, folder 4, Emory.

14. Alhatma, "Deer Hunting on the Seaboard of Georgia," *ATR* 3:1 (Sept. 1831): 28–30. It is difficult to gauge the net impact of dogs on the household economy, but many observers considered them a drain; see Douglass, *My Bondage,* 110; Ingraham, *Sunny South,* 102–3.

15. Hooper, *Dog and Gun,* 13–16; Marcus Gaines to Thomas Gaines, April 30, 1850, Gaines Family Papers, UVA; Bellesîles, *Arming America,* 333–34, 379.

16. Benjamin Mills to St. John Liddell, April 15, 1851, Moses Liddell, St. John R. Liddell, and Family Papers, box 7, folder 44, LSU; Escott, *North Carolina Yeoman,* 56; Bellesîles, *Arming America,* 333–34, 379.

17. Aversa, "Foxhunting, a Patrician Sport," 83–100; Breen, "Horses and Gentlemen," 239–57; Struna, *People of Prowess.*

18. Alhatma, "Deer Hunting on the Seaboard of Georgia," *ATR* 3:1 (Sept. 1831): 28–30. See also Kennedy, *Blackwater Chronicle;* "A Trip to the Wilderness," *SOT* 29:30 (Sept. 3, 1859): 350–51.

19. Kirk, *History of the St. John's Hunting Club,* 7, 12; Easterby, "The St. Thomas Hunting Club," 123–31, 209–13; Harwell, "The Hot and Hot Fish Club," 40–47; Wilson, *An Address,* 21.

20. *SQR,* new ser., 4:7 (July 1851): 250; Greenburg, *Honor and Slavery,* 130.

21. Scissors, "Three Day's Goose-Hunting at 'Walnut Bend,'" *SOT* 21:50 (Jan. 31, 1852): 595; T., "Deer Hunting in Arkansas, My First Fire Hunt," ibid., 15:28 (Oct. 6, 1845): 321; Louisa Maria DeLoach, "A Sketch of My Travels through Sabine While Looking at the Country," HNO; William Henry Harrington Papers, Dec. 1833, SHC.

22. P. Z., "Wild Turkey Hunting," *SOT* 17:7 (April 10, 1847): 78.

23. Audubon, *Audubon and His Journals* 2:469–70.

24. Cor de Chasse, "Deer Hunting in Florida," *SOT* 12:41 (Dec. 10, 1842): 489; Elliott, *Carolina Sports,* 218–31; Whitehead, *Wild Sports,* 30, 41–44; H. P. L., "Pigwidgeon's First Fire-Hunt," *SOT* 25:34 (Oct. 6, 1855): 399; [Thompson], "My First and Last Fire Hunt," ibid., 15:1 (March 1, 1845): 13.

25. On turkey trapping, see G. T. N., "Field Sports: Their Utility—Modes of Hunting Deer and Turkeys in Virginia, Interspersed with Hunting Anecdotes," *ATR* 7:7 (March 1836): 314–23. On battery shooting, see "Ducks and Duck Shooting on the Chesapeake," *SOT* 24:44 (Dec. 16, 1854): 524–25; "Reflections of a Life-Time and More," 39–40, Henry Beasley Ansell Papers, SHC. On shooting hibernating bears, see Evans, "Gerstaecker and the Konwells," 9–10. On salt licks, see Smith, *Sporting Family,* 118, 127. On trapping deer, see Audubon and Bachman, *Quadrupeds of North America* 2:233.

26. Ownby, *Subduing Satan,* 28–37.

27. Cor de Chasse, "Snipe Shooting in Florida," in Hooper, *Dog and Gun,* 100. Cor de Chasse was the pseudonym of William Stockton (ibid., 95).

28. Ibid., 101.

29. Cor de Chasse, "Deer Hunting in Florida," *SOT* 12:41 (Dec. 10, 1842): 489.

30. Hooper, *Adventures of Captain Simon Suggs,* 12, 31; Somers, *Johnson J. Hooper,* 40; Hoole, *Alias Simon Suggs;* Current-Garcia, "Alabama Writers in the *Spirit,*" 243–69.

31. Hooper, *Dog and Gun,* 16, 19.

32. Ibid.

33. Elliott, *Carolina Sports*, 219–20.

34. Ibid., 220.

35. Ibid., 222, 224.

36. Ibid., 226–30.

37. Cf. response to D. Owens, n.d., Singleton Family Papers, LOC; Tensas, "Dave Trigger's Panther," *SOT* 18:28 (Oct. 2, 1848): 326.

38. [Thompson], "My First and Last Fire Hunt," *SOT* 15:1 (March 1, 1845): 13.

39. Ibid.

40. Doc, "Interesting Letter from 'Doc,'" ibid., 28:34 (Oct. 2, 1858): 403.

5. The Community of the Hunt

1. On recreation and class identity, see Lewis, "Ladies and Gentlemen on Display"; Ownby, *Subduing Satan*, 2; Click, *Spirit of the Times*, 98–99, 104; Isaac, *Transformation of Virginia*, 118–20.

2. G. T. N., "Field Sports, Their Utility — Modes of Hunting Deer and Turkeys in Virginia, Interspersed with Hunting Anecdotes," *ATR* 7:7 (March 1836): 317–19.

3. Greenberg, *Honor and Slavery*, 37–43; One of the Hunters, "A Deer Hunt in Pike and Covington Counties, Alabama," *SOT* 19:12 (May 12, 1849): 136–37; The Bee Hunter, "Enemy in Front and Rear, or A Bear and Snake Story," ibid., 17:35 (Oct. 23, 1847): 4; Va. Subscriber, "Bagging a Friend's Birds," ibid., 27:4 (March 7, 1857): 38; Cor de Chasse, "Deer Hunting in Florida," ibid., 19:27 (Aug. 25, 1849): 319–20.

4. Forty-Two Snipe, "Duck Shooting in Georgia," *SOT* 25:4 (March 10, 1855): 37.

5. X. Y. Z., "Shooting Extraordinary," *ATR* 1:10 (June 1830): 495–97.

6. H. S. D., "Hunting Extraordinary," *SOT* 12:47 (Jan. 21, 1843): 555.

7. Beagle, "Field Sports in Mississippi," ibid., 20:50 (Feb. 1, 1851): 595; Autauga, "Deer-Hunting in Alabama; or A Camp in Coosa," ibid., 11:37 (Nov. 13, 1841): 439. Cf. Heyrman, *Southern Cross*, 19–22, 39; Isaac, *Transformation of Virginia*, 165–71, 259–60; Lewis, "Ladies and Gentlemen on Display."

8. Zenas C. Preston Account Book, June 4, 1844, LOC.

9. M., "Mr. Catchpenny's First Camp Hunt in Arkansas," *SOT* 19:1 (Feb. 2, 1849): 8.

10. Ibid., 56.

11. Elliott, *Carolina Sports*, 153–55. See also Audubon and Bachman, *Quadrupeds of North America* 2:237; Rosengarten, *Tombee*, 129; Smith, *A Sporting Family*, 351; Greenberg, *Honor and Slavery*, 40.

12. Elliott, *Carolina Sports*, 155.

13. Ibid., 156.

14. Ibid., 169.

15. Bill Beans, "Deer-Hunting in Mississippi," *SOT* 27:3 (Feb. 28, 1857): 27–29.

16. John Ball and Keating Simons Ball Books, folder 5a, Plantation Daybook, April 25, 1850, vol. 5, SHC; Mary Dickinson to "Lodo," June 6, 1862, Andrew Haynes Gay and Family Papers, folder 1, LSU; Bennett Barrow Diary, July 27, 1844, LSU; S. T. W., "Deer Hunting and Fly-Fishing in Florida," *SOT* 12:22 (July 30, 1842): 253.

17. Everard Green Baker Diaries, ser. J, pt. 6, reel 16, SHC. See also Roswell Elmer Diary, SHC; Gilman, *Recollections,* 75; C. A. Hentz Diary, Hentz Family Papers, subseries 6.1, SHC; Faragher, *Daniel Boone,* 45; Browning, *Forty-Four Years,* 76, 87.

18. "Mr. Catchpenny's First Camp Hunt in Arkansas," *SOT* 19:5 (March 24, 1849): 56; Beagle, "Field Sports in Mississippi," ibid., 20:50 (Feb. 1, 1851): 595; C. A. Hentz Diary, Hentz Family Papers, subseries 6.1, SHC.

19. One of the Hunters, "A Deer Hunt in Pike and Covington Counties, Alabama," *SOT* 19:12 (May 12, 1849): 136–37; Bill Beans, "Deer-Hunting in Mississippi," ibid., 27:3 (Feb. 28, 1857): 27–29.

20. Smith, *A Sporting Family,* 118, 127.

21. "Field Sports in Virginia," *SOT* 8:36 (Oct. 20, 1838): 282.

22. "The Usefulness of Sporting," ibid., 7:2 (Feb. 25, 1837): 1.

23. Smith, *A Sporting Family,* 120; Skinner, *Dog and Sportsman;* Elliott, *Carolina Sports,* 147.

24. Ralph Ranger, "Sporting at the South, Week on Cooper River," *SOT* 16:2 (March 7, 1846): 13–15; Greenwood, "Deer Hunt," *ATR* 9:3 (March 1838): 98–100; M., "Mr. Catchpenny's First Camp Hunt in Arkansas," *SOT* 19:1 (Feb. 24, 1849): 8; Gain Twist, "Wildcat Shooting," ibid., 25:27 (Aug. 18, 1855): 314.

25. Scissors, "Another Day at 'Walnut Bend,' or 'Pestle' in 'a Drive,'" *SOT* 22:9 (April 17, 1852): 100.

26. W., "The Chase in Louisiana," ibid., 10:51 (Feb. 20, 1841): 607.

27. Mark, "A Deer Hunt in Georgia," ibid., 19:21 (July 14, 1849): 246. "Mark" is identified as Randolph Spalding in Keller, "Reputable Writers, Phony Names," 208.

28. Nimrod, "The Enthusiastic Hunter," *ATR* 5:3 (Nov. 1833): 134–35; Alhatma, "Deer Hunting on the Seaboard of Georgia," ibid., 3:1 (Sept. 1831): 28–30; "Field Sports in Virginia," *SOT* 8:36 (Oct. 20, 1838): 282.

29. S. H., "Bull Hunt in Washitaw," *ATR* 4:8 (April 1833): 400–402.

30. S. L. C., "A Hunting Article," *SLM* 17:1 (Jan. 1851): 44–49. See also Autauga, "Deer-Hunting in Alabama; or A Camp in Coosa," *SOT* 11:37 (Nov. 13, 1841): 439; Natt. Phillips, "Wedding and Deer Hunt in Kentucky," ibid., 9:49 (Feb. 8, 1840): 583; Smith, *A Sporting Family,* 120, 150.

31. "Field Sports in Virginia," *SOT* 8:36 (Oct. 20, 1838): 282.

32. S. L. C., "A Hunting Article," *SLM* 17:1 (Jan. 1851): 44–49.

33. Hunter, *Huntsman in the South* 1: 213.

34. A South Carolinan, "A Day in the Woods," *SOT* 11:30 (Oct. 25, 1841): 355, 349. See also Vale, "Mems. of a Visit to South Carolina—No. 2," ibid., 23:22 (July 16, 1853): 255; "Field Sports in Virginia," ibid., 8:36 (Oct. 20, 1838): 282; Athos, "Shooting near the 'Crescent City,'" ibid., 29:37 (Oct. 22, 1859): 433; The Bee Hunter, "Enemy in Front and Rear, or A Bear and Snake Story," ibid., 17:35 (Oct. 23, 1847): 4.

35. Wilson, *An Address,* 8.

36. Cor de Chasse, "Deer Hunting in Florida," *SOT* 19:27 (Aug. 25, 1849): 319–20.

37. Greenwood, "Deer Hunt," *ATR* 9:3 (March 1838): 98–100.

38. A Subscriber, "Doe and Fawn Chase in Georgia," ibid., 2:1 (Sept. 1830): 38–40; T. B. Thorpe, "Sporting in Louisiana," *SOT* 10:48 (Jan. 30, 1841): 571; "A Sporting Letter from Mississippi," ibid., 9:23 (Aug. 10, 1839): 271–72.

39. W. L., "A Wolf Chase in West Florida," *ATR* 6:2 (Oct. 1834): 82–87.

40. Tarkill, "A Deer Hunt in North Carolina," ibid., 12:2 (Feb. 1841): 61–3; Tarkill, "Deerhunt Continued," ibid., 12:4 (April, 1841): 185.

6. Slavery, Paternalism, and the Hunt

1. Greenberg, *Honor and Slavery,* 134. On rare occasions white hunters insisted that the pleasures of camp life erased racial distinctions; see Bill Beans, "Deer-Hunting in Mississippi," *SOT* 27:3 (Feb. 28, 1857): 27–29; Rackensack, "Coon Hunting in Kentucky," ibid., 17:48 (Jan. 22, 1848): 567.

2. Notable exceptions: Mark, "Hunting and Fishing on the Sea-Coast of Georgia," *SOT* 18:21 (May 13, 1848): 135; "A Trip to the Wilderness," ibid., 29:30 (Sept. 3, 1859): 350–51; Whitehead, *Wild Sports,* 140.

3. Ingraham, *Sunny South,* 97; One of the Hunters, "A Deer Hunt in Pike and Covington Counties, Alabama," *SOT* 19:12 (May 12, 1849): 136–37; Gosse, *Letters from Alabama,* 227; Lambda, "Duck Shooting on the Potomac," *SOT* 22:13 (May 15, 1852): 146; Audubon and Bachman, *Quadrupeds of North America* 3:191; W., "The Chase in Louisiana," *SOT* 10:51 (Feb. 20, 1841): 607; "Black Island against Dogue Neck," *ATR* 1:9 (May 1830): 443–45.

4. Cor de Chasse, "Deer Hunting in Florida," *SOT* 19:27 (Aug. 25, 1849): 319–20; H., "Deerhunting in South Carolina," *ATR* 4:5, 236–38; Tarkill, "Deerhunt Continued," ibid., 12:4 (April 1841): 185; Ingraham, *Sunny South,* 483; Whitehead, *Wild Sports,* 154–64; Mark, "Hunting and Fishing on the Sea-Coast of Georgia," *SOT* 18:21 (May 13, 1848): 135; R. L. B., "Fishing and Shooting Excursion to the 'Island of Kia-Wah,'" ibid., 30:31 (Sept. 8, 1860): 371–72.

5. Whitehead, *Wild Sports,* 56, 59; H., "Deerhunting in South Carolina," *ATR* 4:5, 236–38; J. B., "A Deer Hunt in South Carolina," *SOT* 11:27 (Oct. 4, 1841): 318; Audubon, *Audubon and His Journals* 2:496; One of the Hunters, "A Deer Hunt in Pike and Covington Counties, Alabama," *SOT* 19:12 (May 12, 1849): 136–37; A South Carolinan, "A Day in the Woods," ibid., 11:30 (Oct. 25, 1841): 355, 349; The Old 'Squire,' "The Louisiana Swamp in a Blaze," ibid., 29:10 (April 16, 1859): 115–16.

6. Thompson, *Major Jones's Courtship,* 51, 53. Compare a description by a slave: *AS,* supp., ser. 1, vol. 8, Miss., pt. 3, 1293.

7. Flack, *A Hunter's Experiences,* 112–13.

8. *AS,* supp., ser. 2, vol. 4, Tex., pt. 3, 1343–44.

9. Jenkins, *Pro-Slavery Thought;* Faust, *Ideology of Slavery;* Tise, *Proslavery.*

10. Genovese, *Roll, Jordan, Roll.*

11. *AS,* ser. 2, vol. 12, Ga., pt. 1, 199–200; ibid., supp., ser. 1, vol. 7, Miss., pt. 2, 570–71; Harwell, "The Hot and Hot Fish Club," 40–47; Ralph Ranger, "Sporting in the South: or A Week on Cooper River," *SOT* 15:52 (Feb. 21, 1846): 609–10; Calhoun, *Witness to Sorrow,* 43.

12. Elliott, *Carolina Sports,* 157–58, 187.

13. The Old "Squire," "The Louisiana Swamp in a Blaze," *SOT* 29:10 (April 16, 1859): 115–16.

14. Audubon and Bachman, *Quadrupeds of North America* 1:8–9.

15. Gibbs et al., "Nutrition in a Slave Population," 175–262; Berlin and Morgan, *Cultivation and Culture,* 22–24; Schlotterbeck, "The Internal Economy of Slavery," 170–82; *AS,* supp., ser. 2, vol. 4, Tex., pt. 3, 1022; ibid., ser. 1, vol. 4, Ga., pt. 2, 507.

16. G. T. N., "Field Sports," *ATR* 7:7 (March 1836): 320; *AS,* supp., ser. 2, vol. 4, Tex., pt. 3, 970.

17. *AS,* supp., ser. 1, vol. 10, Miss., pt. 5, 2048; ibid., ser. 2, vol. 4, Tex., pt. 3, 1098; ibid., vol. 6, Tex., pt. 5, 2136.

18. Heyward, *Seed from Madagascar,* 123–27.

19. Mark, "A Deer Hunt in Georgia," *SOT* 19:21 (July 14, 1849): 246; Keller, "Reputable Writers, Phony Names," 208.

20. Whitehead, *Wild Sports,* 139.

21. W. G., "Bear-Hunting in Louisiana," *SOT* 21:23 (July 26, 1851): 271.

22. Brickell, *Natural History of North-Carolina,* 107–37; Boyd, *William Byrd's History,* 44, 50, 166, 197, 209, 224, 230, 248, 250, 278, 296, 297; Bartram, *Travels,* 61, 277; Latrobe, *Impressions,* 14.

23. Elliott, *Carolina Sports,* 232, 241; Lambda, "Duck Shooting on the Potomac," *SOT* 22:13 (May 15, 1852): 146.

24. Reiger, *American Sportsmen,* 26.

25. Keefe and Morrow, *White River Chronicles,* 84, 87; Joseph Bieller to Jacob Bieller, Aug. 27, 1827, June 1, 1828, Oct. 1, 1830, Alonzo Snyder Papers, box 1, folders 6–7, LSU; M. "Death of the Big Buck," *ATR* 6:7 (March 1835): 353–54; Gosse, *Letters from Alabama,* 128–29, 221; Smith, *A Sporting Family,* 127, 131, 160; Beagle, "Coon Hunting in Mississippi," *SOT* 21:11 (May 3, 1851): 121; Bennett Barrow Diary, April 13, 1838, LSU.

26. Northup, *Twelve Years a Slave,* 334–35.

27. Hunter, *Huntsman in the South* 1:82; Lyell, *A Second Visit,* 17; Hundley, *Social Relations,* 343; Joe Manton, "Opening of the Hunting Season," *SOT* 28:35 (Oct. 9, 1858): 413.

28. G. M., "South Carolina," *New England Magazine* 1 (Sept.–Oct. 1831): 246–50, 337–41.

29. Audubon and Bachman, *Quadrupeds of North America* 2:113; Audubon, *Audubon and His Journals* 2:496. For dissent see Joe Manton, "Coons and Coon-Hunting," *SOT* 28:45 (Dec. 18, 1858): 532–33.

30. Jordan, *White over Black,* 24–8; Whitehead, *Wild Sports,* 17.

31. Manton, "Opening of the Hunting Season," *SOT* 28:35 (Oct. 9, 1858): 413; Webber, *Hunter-Naturalist,* 48–49; Montesano, "Game Steaks and Cane Brakes," *SOT* 29:2 (Jan. 19, 1859): 13–14; Whitehead, *Wild Sports,* 118; G. M., "South Carolina," *New England Magazine* 1 (Sept.–Oct. 1831): 246–50, 337–41; Elliott, *Carolina Sports,* 220, 222.

32. Ralph Ranger, "Sporting at the South: Week on Cooper River," *SOT* 16:2 (March 7, 1846): 13–15.

33. Tracy, *In the Master's Eye,* 60.

34. Seebright, "A Panther Hunt on the Blue Ridge," *SOT* 7:46 (Dec. 30, 1837): 364–65, 7:49 (Jan. 20, 1838): 389–90.

35. Ibid.

36. Ibid.

37. Rosengarten, *Tombee,* 128; Schaefer, *Slavery, the Civil Law, and the Supreme Court,* 110; Smith, *A Sporting Family,* 230, 321.

38. Kennedy, *Swallow Barn,* 396–97.

39. Ibid., 399–400, 405–6.

40. Ibid., 401–4.

41. Ibid., 407–8.

42. Ibid., 410–11.

43. The Old "Squire," "The Louisiana Swamp in a Blaze," *SOT* 29:11 (April 23, 1859): 121–22; Mark, "Hunting and Fishing on the Sea-Coast of Georgia," ibid., 18:12 (May 13, 1848): 135; Webber, *Hunter-Naturalist,* 76–86.

44. The notable exception: Kemble, *Journal.*

45. Heyward, *Seed from Madagascar,* 123–27.

46. Nassau, "Funeral of a Negro Huntsman," *SOT* 27:19 (June 20, 1857): 219.

7. Slave Perceptions of the Hunt

1. Perdue et al., *Weevils in the Wheat,* 281; *AS,* vol. 7, Okla., 238.

2. *AS,* ser. 1, vol. 2, S.C., pt. 2, 75–76.

3. ibid., supp., ser. 2, vol. 6, Tex., pt. 5, 2229; King, *Stolen Childhood,* chap. 3.

4. *AS,* supp., ser. 1, vol. 9, Miss., pt. 4, 1409.

5. Ibid., ser. 2, vol. 12, Ga., pt. 1, 266–70.

6. Ibid., supp., ser. 2, vol. 2, Tex., pt. 1, 398; Wyatt-Brown, *Southern Honor,* 152–53.

7. *AS,* supp., ser. 1, vol. 9, Miss., pt. 4, 1659–61.

8. King, *Stolen Childhood,* 21–41; Dusinberre, *Them Dark Days,* 188–89; Blassingame, *Slave Community,* 184; Escott, *Slavery Remembered,* 16.

9. *AS,* vol. 17, Fla., 328.

10. Bruce, *New Man,* 17–18.

11. *AS,* supp., ser. 2, vol. 3, Tex., pt. 2, 515; ibid., ser. 1, vol. 10, Miss., pt. 5, 2389.

12. Ibid., ser. 2, vol. 6, Tex., pt. 9, 4208.

13. King, *Stolen Childhood,* 21–41, 44; Berlin and Morgan, *Cultivation and Culture,* 19.

14. On slave culture, see Blassingame, *Slave Community;* Joyner, *Down by the Riverside;* Levine, *Black Culture and Black Consciousness;* Wood, *Black Majority.*

15. On the internal economy, see Berlin and Morgan, *Cultivation and Culture;* Hudson, *To Have and To Hold;* Betty Wood, "'White Society' and 'Informal' Slave Economies."

16. *AS,* supp., ser. 2, vol. 4, Tex., pt. 3, 1022; ibid., ser. 1, vol. 3, Ga., pt. 1, 77–78; Dusinberre, *Them Dark Days,* 233; Genovese, *Roll, Jordan, Roll,* 486; Hall, *Africans in Colonial Louisiana,* 196–98; Berlin and Morgan, *Cultivation and Culture,* 22–24; Schlotterbeck, "The Internal Economy of Slavery," 170–82; Gibbs et al., "Nutrition in a Slave Population," 175–262; Trinkey, *History and Archaeology,* 351–52; Ferguson, *Uncommon Ground,* 96; Trinkey, *Archaeological Investigations,* 254; Otto, "Status Differences."

17. *AS,* ser. 2, vol. 16, Md., 30.

18. Whitehead, *Wild Sports,* 120; *AS,* supp., ser. 2, vol. 3, Tex., pt. 2, 586, 945; M., "Field Sports of Miss.," *SOT* 10:9 (May 2, 1840): 97; Your Friend in the Swamp, "The

Way *We* Do It," ibid., 20:19 (June 26, 1852): 222; Audubon and Bachman, *Quadrupeds of North America* 2:230; Trinkey, *Archaeological Investigations,* 253.

19. *AS,* supp. ser. 2, vol. 3, Tex., pt. 2, 786.

20. Ibid., vol. 4, Tex., pt. 3, 1239; ibid., ser. 1, vol. 10, Miss., pt. 5, 2048.

21. Webber, *Hunter-Naturalist,* 69, 76–86; Gosse, *Letters from Alabama,* 234; G. M., "South Carolina," *New England Magazine* 1 (Sept.–Oct. 1831): 246–50, 337, 341; Thompson, *Major Jones' Courtship,* 51, 53; Audubon and Bachman, *Quadrupeds of North America* 2:80; Audubon, *Audubon and His Journals* 2:495–96.

22. *AS,* ser. 2, vol. 12, Ga., pt. 1, 302; ibid., supp., ser. 1, vol. 8, Miss., pt. 3, 1288; ibid., ser. 1, vol. 6, Miss., pt. 1, 20; G. M., "South Carolina," *New England Magazine* 1 (Sept.–Oct. 1831): 246–50, 337–41.

23. *AS,* ser. 2, vol. 12, Ga., pt. 1, 3–4; Northup, *Twelve Years a Slave,* 334–35.

24. *AS,* supp., ser. 2, vol. 3, Tex., pt. 2, 602; ibid., vol. 2, Tex., pt. 1, 169, 187–88, 325–26; ibid., vol. 6, Tex., pt. 5, 2371–72; ibid., ser. 2, vol. 16, Ohio, 44; ibid., vol. 7, Okla., 193–94; ibid., Miss., 85; ibid., supp., ser. 1, vol. 10, Miss., pt. 5, 1971, 2186; ibid., vol. 3, S.C., pt. 4, 128.

25. Ibid., ser. 2, vol. 12, Ga., pt. 1, 347.

26. Ibid., ser. 1, vol. 2, S.C., pt. 2, 81.

27. Ibid., supp., ser. 2, vol. 2, Tex., pt. 1, 199.

28. Audubon and Bachman, *Quadrupeds of North America* 2:115; *AS,* ser. 2, vol. 12, Ga., pt. 1, 41, 308; ibid., supp., ser. 2, vol. 2, Tex., pt. 1, 6, 176.

29. Betty Wood, "'White Society' and 'Informal' Slave Economies," 313–31; [Ball], *Fifty Years in Chains,* 195–96; Berlin and Morgan, *Cultivation and Culture,* 33; Reidy, "Obligation and Right," 140, 152–53; Genovese, *Roll, Jordan, Roll,* 539; *AS,* supp., ser. 1, vol. 1, Ala., 166; ibid., vol. 7, Miss., pt. 2, 770; ibid., ser. 2, vol. 12, Ga., pt. 2, 3; Henry, *Police Control of the Slave,* 91–95. In isolated cases, slave owners took an active role in the promotion of slaves' entrance into the cash economy; see *AS,* ser. 2, vol. 15, N.C., pt. 2, 318–19.

30. *AS,* ser. 1, vol. 2, S.C., pt. 2, 44.

31. Ibid., ser. 2, vol. 12, Ga., pt. 1, 126.

32. Blassingame, *Slave Community,* chap. 3, 105–6.

33. *AS,* supp., ser. 1, vol. 7, Miss., pt. 2, 770.

34. Dixon, *Ride Out the Wilderness;* Georgia Writers' Project, *Drums and Shadows,* 79, 110–11, 160–61, 171; Jones-Jackson, *When Roots Die;* Joyner, *Down by the Riverside,* 172–95; Levine, *Black Culture and Black Consciousness,* 81–135; Blassingame, *Slave Community,* 57; Stuckey, *Slave Culture,* 17–18; Higginson, *Army Life in a Black Regiment,* 36–38.

35. [Ball], *Fifty Years in Chains,* 346, 358, quotation from 163.

36. *AS,* supp., ser. 1, vol. 3, Ga., pt. 1, 169–70, 82; ibid., ser. 2, vol. 12, Ga., pt. 1, 24; ibid., pt. 2, 14–15, 324; ibid., vol. 8, Ark., pts. 1 and 2, 50, 276; ibid., supp., ser. 2, vol. 3, Tex., pt. 2, 861; ibid., ser. 1, vol. 3, Ga., pt. 1, 101; Mackay, *Life and Liberty* 1:273, 276; Olmsted, *Cotton Kingdom,* 121; Audubon, *Audubon and His Journals* 2:267–73.

37. *AS,* supp., ser. 2, vol. 3, Tex., pt. 2, 861, 808; Lyell, *A Second Visit,* 38–40; Olmsted, *Cotton Kingdom,* 114–15, 121; Hall, *Africans in Colonial Louisiana,* 142.

38. Mark, "Hunting and Fishing on the Sea-Coast of Georgia," *SOT* 18:12 (May 13, 1848): 135.

39. Ibid.

40. Blassingame, *Slave Community,* 172–73, 178–79.

41. *Games against Nature,* 118. In Africa, as elsewhere, the connection between men and hunting was not a hard and fast rule; see Kelly, *Foraging Spectrum,* chap. 7.

42. Reidy, "Obligation and Right," 142, 149; Berlin and Morgan, *Cultivation and Culture,* 36; *AS,* vol. 2, S.C., pt. 1, 62, 152, 241, 215; ibid., vol. 3, S.C., pt. 4, 10, 57, 89; ibid., vol. 6, Miss., pt. 1, 217, 259; ibid., vol. 7, Miss., pt. 2, 570, 616; ibid., vol. 12, Ga., pt. 1, 41; ibid., 40; ibid., vol. 13, Ga., pt. 3, 156; ibid., pt. 4, 120, 154; ibid., vol. 14, pt. 1, N.C., 3, 46; ibid., supp., ser. 1, vol. 1, Ala., 117, 137, 174, 226, 266; ibid., vol. 6, Ala., 22, 166, 365; ibid., supp., ser. 1, vol. 11, N.C. and S.C., 132–33; ibid., ser. 2, vol. 6, Tex., pt. 5, 2124; ibid., ser. 2, vol. 16, Ohio, 22. There are two notable exceptions: ibid., Ark., pt. 2, 6; ibid., ser. 1, vol. 2, S.C., pt. 2, 8.

43. [Ball], *Fifty Years in Chains,* 195–96, 202.

44. *AS,* supp., ser. 1, vol. 6, Miss., pt. 1, 217.

45. Ibid., ser. 2, vol. 12, Ga., pt. 1, 308.

46. [Ball], *Fifty Years in Chains,* 195–96.

47. *AS,* supp., ser. 1., vol. 8, Miss., pt. 3, 1197; ibid., ser. 2, vol. 6, Tex., pt. 9, 4280; Joyner, *Down by the Riverside,* 132.

48. *AS,* supp., ser. 1, vol. 1, Ala., pt. 1, 41.

49. Ibid., 113.

50. Genovese, *Roll, Jordan, Roll,* 487; King, *Stolen Childhood,* 58–59; Blassingame, *Slave Community,* 106–8; *AS,* supp., ser. 1, vol. 3, Ga., pt. 1, 226.

51. Morgan, *Slave Counterpoint,* 185–86; Hudson, *To Have and To Hold,* 2–10; Washington, *A Peculiar People.*

52. *AS,* ser. 2, vol. 12, Ga., pt. 1, 240.

53. Ibid., vol. 3, S.C., pt. 3, 172, 219, 221; ibid., ser. 1, vol. 2, S.C., pt. 2, 138; ibid., supp., ser. 1, vol. 8, Miss., pt. 3, 1197; ibid., ser. 2, vol. 4, Tex., pt. 3, 1022, 1064; Joyner, *Down by the Riverside,* 101, 133.

54. King, *Stolen Childhood,* 59; Genovese, *Roll, Jordan, Roll,* 234; Joyner, *Down by the Riverside,* 135–37; Northrup, *Twelve Years a Slave,* 213; [Ball], *Fifty Years in Chains,* 278–79; *AS,* ser. 2, vol. 15, N.C., pt. 2, 339; ibid., vol. 12, Ga., pt. 2, 132; ibid., supp., ser. 1, vol. 8, Miss., pt. 3, 1218; ibid., ser. 2, vol. 3, Tex., pt. 2, 632.

55. *AS,* ser. 2, vol. 15, N.C., pt. 2, 344.

56. Ibid., vol. 12, Ga., pt. 1, 189; ibid., supp., ser. 1, vol. 3, Ga., pt. 1, 77–78.

57. Morris, *Southern Slavery and the Law,* 349; Marks, *Southern Hunting in Black and White,* 290–91 n. 52.

58. Beagle, "Coon Hunting in Miss.," *SOT* 21:11 (May 3, 1851): 121; McCurry, *Masters of Small Worlds.*

59. Dusinberre, *Them Dark Days,* 161, 249, 372; "Mr. Catchpenny's First Camp Hunt in Arkansas," *SOT* 19:5 (March 24, 1849): 56; Whitehead, *Wild Sports,* 113–39; *AS,* supp., ser. 2, vol. 4, Tex., pt. 3, 1310; Hoffmann and Hoffmann, "The Limits of Paternalism," 329; H., "The Game Sportsman, or Genuine Love of the Chase Exem-

plified," *ATR* 5:6 (Feb. 1834): 298–307; Olmsted, *Cotton Kingdom,* 200, Olmsted, *Journey,* 447; Usner, *Indians, Settlers, and Slaves,* 164–65, 168; Wood, *Slavery in Colonial Georgia,* 45; Taylor, *Negro Slavery in Louisiana,* 126; Stewart, *What Nature Suffers to Groe,* 175–76, 319 n. 49.

60. [Ball], *Fifty Years in Chains,* 278–79.

61. Genovese, *Roll, Jordan, Roll,* 488. See also The Old "Squire," "The Louisiana Swamp in a Blaze," *SOT* 29:10 (April 16, 1859): 115–16; Mark, "Hunting and Fishing on the Sea-Coast of Georgia," ibid., 18:12 (May 13, 1848): 135; J. B. I., "Extraordinary Sporting Incident," ibid., 12:37 (Nov. 12, 1842): 433; J. A. J., "Beaufort and the Sea Islands: Their History and Traditions," ninth in a series, *Beaufort Republican* 3:23 (March 13, 1873): 4–5; Thompson, *Major Jones' Courtship,* 51, 53; [Daniel Dennett], "A Bear Hunt on Bayou Sale," *Planter's Banner* 15:51 (Dec. 26, 1850): 2; Hundley, *Social Relations,* 361.

62. *AS,* ser. 2, vol. 12, Ga., pt. 2, 128.

63. Ibid., supp., ser. 2, vol. 6, Tex., pt. 5, 2371–72.

64. Ibid., ser. 2, vol. 15, N.C., pt. 2, 277–78.

65. Ibid., supp., ser. 2, vol. 6, Tex., pt. 5, 2232.

66. On traps, see ibid., 2371–72, 2335; ibid., ser. 1, vol. 1, Ala., pt. 1, 174; ibid., ser. 2, vol. 12, Ga., pt. 2, 3; ibid., supp., ser. 1, vol. 10, Miss., pt. 5, 2209; ibid., vol. 3, Ga., pt. 1, 77–78. On dogs, see Campbell, "My Constant Companion."

67. Hundley, *Social Relations,* 343.

68. *AS,* ser. 1, vol. 2, S.C., pt. 1, 191; Audubon and Bachman, *Quadrupeds of North America* 1:12; *AS,* supp., ser. 2, vol. 3, Tex., pt. 2, 548; ibid., ser. 1, vol. 1, Ala., pt. 1, 43; ibid., ser. 1, vol. 2, S.C., pt. 2, 215; ibid., vol. 3, S.C., pt. 4, 71; ibid., ser. 2, vol. 12, Ga., pt. 1, 199–200.

69. Smith, *A Sporting Family,* 177; Hooper, *Dog and Gun,* 60–61.

70. Campbell, "My Constant Companion," 53–76; [Ball], *Fifty Years in Chains,* 309.

71. Blassingame, *Slave Testimony,* 276–84.

72. *AS,* supp., ser. 2, vol. 2, Tex., pt. 1, 139.

73. Ibid., vol. 4, Tex., pt. 3, 998; ibid., ser. 2, vol. 12, Ga., pt. 2, 246; ibid., supp., ser. 1, vol. 3, Ga., pt. 1, 77–8; ibid., ser. 2, vol. 3, Tex., pt. 2, 740; ibid., ser. 1, vol. 2, S.C., pt. 2, 75; Hundley, *Social Relations,* 343.

74. Hundley, *Social Relations,* 343; G. M., "South Carolina," *New England Magazine* 1 (Sept.–Oct. 1831): 246–50, 337–41; Ingraham, *Sunny South,* 32, 103; *AS,* ser. 1, vol. 2, S.C., pt. 1, 231; ibid., pt. 2, 194.

75. *AS,* vol. 3, S.C., pt. 3, 168.

76. Ibid., supp., ser. 1, vol. 7, Miss., pt. 2, 670.

77. Ibid., vol. 10, Miss., pt. 5, 1936.

Epilogue

1. Racine, *Piedmont Farmer,* 372 and passim.

2. *AS,* supp., ser. 2, vol. 6, Tex., pt. 9, 4143.

3. Bellesîles, "The Origins of Gun Culture," 452; Trudeau, *Out of the Storm,* 379.

4. Racine, *Piedmont Farmer,* 424, 449, 474; George L. F. Birdsong Correspondence, box 1, folders 7 and 9, Emory.

5. Irving, *A Day on Cooper River,* 89–90.

6. J. A. J., "Beaufort and the Sea Islands: Their History and Traditions," *Beaufort Republican* 3:23 (March 13, 1873): 4–5; *AS,* supp., ser. 2, vol. 3, Tex., pt. 2, 905.

7. Marks, *Southern Hunting in Black and White,* 68 and passim; Lewis, "The World around Hampton," 468–69.

8. Mike Allen, "Hunting the Antebellum Way, Sort of," *New York Times,* Nov. 25, 1995, 7.

9. Dunlap, *Saving America's Wildlife,* 10; Hallock, *Hallock's American Club List,* 60–68; Reiger, *American Sportsmen,* 23, 39–40, 118–22, and passim; Hunter, *Huntsman in the South* 1:145–51, 251–86; Marks, *Southern Hunting in Black and White,* 165–67.

10. Ownby, *Subduing Satan;* Marks, *Southern Hunting in Black and White,* chaps. 2–10; Bergman, *Orion's Legacy,* chap. 7; Oriard, *Sporting with the Gods;* Kerasote, *Bloodties;* Marks, *Southern Hunting in Black and White,* 160–61, 168.

Selected Bibliography

Manuscripts

Alabama Department of Archives and History, Montgomery
    John Witherspoon DuBose, "Recollections of the Plantation"
Manuscripts Department, William R. Perkins Library, Duke University, Durham,
    North Carolina
        George T. Nichols Papers
        F. H. Whitaker Papers
Special Collections Department, Robert W. Woodruff Library, Emory University,
    Atlanta
        George Lawrence Forsythe Birdsong Papers
        William Harmon Harden Papers
        Tracy Mattewson Papers
Williams Research Center, Historic New Orleans, New Orleans
        Louisa Maria DeLoach, "A Sketch of My Travels through Sabine While
            Looking at the Country"
        Edward Lewis Sturtevant Letters
Library of Congress, Washington, D.C.
        Benjamin Brown French Manuscripts
        Zeras Preston Account Book
        Singleton Family Papers
Department of Archives and Manuscripts, Hill Memorial Library, Louisiana State
    University, Baton Rouge
        Bennett H. Barrow Diary
        Lemuel P. Conner and Family Papers
        Joseph Embree and Family Papers
        Andrew Hynes Gay and Family Papers
        Moses Liddell, St. John R. Liddell, and Family Papers
        Max Nuebling Letter-Book
        Alonzo Snyder Papers
        David Weeks and Family Papers
Manuscripts, Rare Books, and University Archives, Howard-Tilton Memorial Library,
    Tulane University, New Orleans
        Favrot Papers
        Charles Colcock Jones Papers
        Armand Soubie Papers

Hargrett Rare Book and Manuscript Library, University of Georgia, Athens
    William Dickey Collection
    Stephen Elliott Scrapbook
Southern Historical Collection, University of North Carolina at Chapel Hill
    William S. Alexander Papers
    Henry Beasley Ansell Papers
    Everard Green Baker Papers
    John Ball and Keating Simons Ball Books
    Mary Bateman Diary
    Bayside Plantation Records
    Thomas C. Bowie Diary
    Fred M. Burnett Papers
    Henry L. Cathell Diary
    Elliott-Gonzales Papers
    Roswell Elmer Diary
    John Edwin Fripp Papers
    Henry William Harrington Papers
    Heiskell, McCambell, Wilkes, and Steel Family Materials
    Hentz Family Papers
    Walter John Hoxie Papers
    Langdon, Young, and Meares Family Papers
    George Anderson Mercer Papers
    Frank F. Steel Letters
    David Franklin Thorpe Papers
    John L. Trone Letter
    Wyche and Otey Family Papers

Manuscripts Division, South Caroliniana Library, University of South Carolina, Columbia
    Henry Edwards Davis, "'Old Betsy': Stories of Hunting with the Old Percussion Muzzle Loader and Its Successors"
    Samuel Catawba Lowry Journal

Special Collections Department, University of Virginia Library, Charlottesville
    Gaines Family Papers
    Noland Family Papers
    Pi Kappa Alpha Letters
Manuscripts and Rare Books, Earl Gregg Swem Memorial Library, College of William and Mary, Williamsburg, Virginia
    Austin-Twyman Papers
    Barraud Family Papers
    Skipwith Papers

Periodicals

American Farmer
American Monthly Magazine
American Sportsman
American Turf Register and Sporting Magazine
Beaufort Republican
[Burton's] Gentleman's Magazine
Countryman
Harper's Weekly
Knickerbocker Magazine
Porter's Spirit of the Times
Southern Cultivator
Southern Literary Journal
Southern Literary Messenger
Southern Quarterly Review
Spirit of the Times
Wilkes' Spirit of the Times

Published Primary Sources

Anderson, Ephraim McD. *Memoirs: Historical and Personal; Including the Campaigns of of the First Missouri Confederate Brigade*. St. Louis, 1868.
Arfwedson, Carl David. *The United States and Canada, in 1832, 1833, and 1834*. London, 1834.
Ashe, Thomas. *Travels in America, Performed in 1806, for the Purpose of Exploring the Rivers Alleghany, Monogahela, Ohio, and Mississippi, and Ascertaining the Produce and Condition of Their Banks and Vicinity*. 3 vols. London, 1808.
Audubon, John James. *Ornithological Biography, or An Account of the Habits of the Birds of the United States of America*. Edinburgh, 1831.
Audubon, John James, and John Bachman. *The Quadrupeds of North America*. 3 vols. New York, 1849.
Audubon, Maria, ed. *Audubon and His Journals*. Vol. 2. Rept. Gloucester, Mass., 1972.
Baily, Francis. *Journal of a Tour in Unsettled Parts of North America, in 1796 and 1797*. Ed. Jack D. L. Holmes. Carbondale, Ill., 1969.
Ball, Charles. *Fifty Years in Chains; or, The Life of an American Slave*. New York, 1858.
Bartram, William. *Travels through North and South Carolina, Georgia, East and West Florida, the Cherokee Country, the Extensive Territories of the Muscogulges, or Creek Confederacy, and the Country of the Chactaws*. Philadelphia, 1791.
Benwell, J. *An Englishman's Travels in America: His Observations of Life and Manner in the Free and Slave States*. London, [1853?].
Bernard, John. *Retrospections of America, 1797–1811*. New York, 1887.
Birdsong, George Lawrence Forsyth. *Sporting Sketches from the* Countryman, *1863–1864*. Atlanta, 1955.

Bodichon, Barbara Leigh Smith. *An American Diary, 1857–8.* Ed. Joseph W. Reed Jr. London, 1972.

Boney, F. N., ed. *Slave Life in Georgia: A Narrative of the Life, Sufferings, and Escape of John Brown, a Fugitive Slave.* Savannah, 1972.

Boyd, William K., ed. *William Byrd's History of the Dividing Line betwixt Virginia and North Carolina.* New York, 1967.

Brickell, John. *The Natural History of North-Carolina.* Murfreesboro, N.C., 1968.

Browning, Meshach. *Forty-Four Years of the Life of a Hunter; Being Reminiscences of Meshach Browning, a Maryland Hunter.* Rev. and illustrated by E[dward] Stabler. Philadelphia, 1859.

Bruce, H. C. *The New Man: Twenty-Nine Years a Slave, Twenty-Nine Years a Free Man.* 1895; rept. New York, 1969.

Bryan, Daniel. *The Mountain Muse: Comprising the Adventures of Daniel Boone; and the Power of Virtuous and Refined Beauty.* Harrisonburg, Va., 1813.

Byrd, William. *The Westover Manuscripts: Containing The History of the Dividing Line betwixt Virginia and North Carolina; A Journey to the Land of Eden, A.D. 1733; and A Progress to the Mines.* Petersburg, Va., 1841.

Calhoun, Richard J., ed. *Witness to Sorrow: The Antebellum Autobiography of William J. Grayson.* Columbia, S.C., 1990.

Caruthers, William Alexander. *The Cavaliers of Virginia, or The Recluse of Jamestown: An Historical Romance of the Old Dominion.* 1834–35; rept. Ridgewood, N.J., 1968.

——. *The Knights of the Golden Horse-Shoe: A Traditionary Tale of the Cocked Hat Gentry in the Old Dominion.* Rept. Chapel Hill, N.C., 1970.

Catesby, Mark. *The Natural History of Carolina, Florida, and the Bahama Islands.* 3d ed., 2 vols., London, 1771.

Clifton, James. *Life and Labor on Argyle Island: Letters and Documents of a Savannah River Rice Plantation, 1833–1867.* Savannah, 1978.

Clinkscales, J. G. *On the Old Plantation: Reminiscences of His Childhood.* Spartanburg, S.C., 1916.

Clinton, Charles A. *A Winter from Home.* New York, 1852.

Cooper, James Fenimore. *The Pioneers.* Rept. New York, 1991.

Crèvecoeur, J. Hector St. John de. *Letters from an American Farmer.* Rept. New York, 1957.

Crockett, David. *A Narrative of the Life of David Crockett of the State of Tennessee.* Rept. Lincoln, Nebr., 1987.

Cunynghame, Arthur [Augustus Thurlow]. *A Glimpse of the Great Western Republic.* London, 1851.

Dabbs, Edith M. *Sea Island Diary: A History of St. Helena Island.* Spartanburg, S.C., 1983.

Davis, Edwin Adams. *Plantation Life in the Florida Parishes of Louisiana, 1836–1846, as Reflected in the Diary of Bennet H. Barrow.* New York, 1943.

Davy Crockett's Almanack, 1837. Rept. San Marino, Calif., 1971.

Davy Crockett's Almanack of Wild Sports in the West, Life in the Backwoods, and Sketches of Texas. San Marino, Calif., 1971.

Doddridge, Joseph. *Notes on the Settlement and Indian Wars, of the Western Parts of Virginia and Pennsylvania, from 1763 to 1783, Inclusive, Together with a View of the State of Society, and Manners of the First Settlers of the Western Country.* Rept. New York, 1972.

Drysdale, Isabel. *Scenes in Georgia.* Philadelphia, 1827.

Dunbar, William. *Life, Letters, and Papers of William Dunbar: of Elgin, Morayshire, Scotland, and Natchez, Mississippi: Pioneer Scientist of the Southern United States.* Ed. Eron Rowland. Jackson, Miss., 1930.

Elliott, William. *Carolina Sports by Land and Water, Including Incidents of Devil-Fishing, Wild-Cat, Deer, and Bear Hunting, etc.* 1846; rept., Columbia, S.C., 1994.

Escott, Paul D., ed. *North Carolina Yeoman: The Diary of Basil Armstrong Thomasson, 1853–1862.* Athens, Ga., 1996.

——. *Slavery Remembered: A Record of Twentieth-Century Slave Narratives.* Chapel Hill, N.C., 1979.

Everest, Robert. *A Journey through the United States and Part of Canada.* London, 1855.

Faulkner, William. *Big Woods: The Hunting Stories.* Rept. New York, 1994.

Federal Writers' Project. *The American Slave: A Composite Autobiography.* 41 vols. Westport, Conn., 1972.

Filson, John. *The Discovery, Settlement, and Present State of Kentucke.* New York, 1966.

Flack, Captain. *A Hunter's Experiences in the Southern States of America.* London, 1866.

Flint, Timothy. *The First White Man of the West; or The Life and Exploits of Col. Dan'l Boone, the First Settler of Kentucky, Interspersed with Incidents in the Early Annals of the Country.* Cincinnati, 1856.

——. *Recollections of the Last Ten Years.* Boston, 1826.

Forester, Frank [Henry William Herbert]. *American Game in its Seasons.* New York, 1853.

——. *The Complete Manual for Young Sportsmen.* New York, 1856.

——. *Frank Forester's Field Sports of the United States, and British Provinces of North America* .... New York, 1849.

——. *Frank Forester's Fugitive Sporting Sketches.* Westfield, Wis., 1879.

G. M. "South Carolina." *New England Magazine* 1 (Sept.–Oct. 1831): 246–50, 337–41.

G. S. S. "Sketches of the South Santee." *American Monthly Magazine* 8 (Oct.–Nov. 1836): 313–19, 431–42.

Gadsen, Sam. *An Oral History of Edisto Island: Sam Gadsen Tells the Story.* Trans. Nick Lindsay. Goshen, Ind., 1974.

Gaskins, John. *Life and Adventures of John Gaskins, in the Early History of Northwest Arkansas.* Rept. Eureka Springs, Ark., 1893.

A Gentleman .... *The Sportsman's Companion; or, An Essay on Shooting, Illustriously Shewing in What Manner to Fire at Birds of Game, in Various Directions and Situations; and, Directions to Gentlemen for the Treatment and Breaking Their Own Pointers and Spaniels, and the Necessary Precautions to Guard against Many Accidents That Attend This Pleasant Diversion, with Several Other Useful and Interesting Particulars Relative Thereto.* New York, 1783.

Georgia Writers' Project. *Drums and Shadows: Survival Studies among the Georgia Coastal Negroes.* Athens, Ga., 1940.

Gerstäcker, Frederick. *Western Lands and Western Waters.* London, 1864.

Gilman, Caroline. *Recollections of a Southern Matron.* New York, 1838.

Gonzales, Ambrose Elliott. *The Black Border.* Columbia, S.C., 1922.

——— *Two Gullah Tales: The Turkey Hunter at the Cross Roads Store.* New York, 1926.

Gosse, Philip Henry. *Letters from Alabama, (U.S.) Chiefly Relating to Natural History.* 1859; annotated ed., Tuscaloosa, Ala., 1993.

Greene, Jack P., ed. *The Diary of Colonel Landon Carter of Sabine Hall, 1752–1778.* Vol. 2. Charlottesville, Va., 1965.

Hall, James. *Letters from the West; Containing Sketches of Scenery, Manners, and Customs; and Anecdotes Connected with the First Settlements of the Western Sections of the United States.* Gainesville, Fla., 1967.

Henry, T. Charlton. *An Inquiry into the Consistency of Popular Amusements with a Profession of Christianity.* Charleston, S.C., 1825.

Hentz, Caroline Lee. *Marcus Warland; or, The Long Moss Spring: A Tale of the South.* Philadelphia, 1852.

———. *The Planter's Northern Bride.* Chapel Hill, N.C., 1970.

Higginson, Thomas Wentworth. *Army Life in a Black Regiment.* Boston, 1962.

Holland, Rupert Sargent, ed. *Letters and Diary of Laura M. Towne: Written from the Sea Islands of South Carolina, 1862–1884.* New York, 1969.

Hooper, Johnson J[ones]. *Adventures of Captain Simon Suggs.* Nashville, 1993.

———. *Dog and Gun: A Few Loose Chapters on Shooting.* Tuscaloosa, Ala., 1992.

Hundley, Daniel R. *Social Relations in Our Southern States.* New York, 1860.

Hungerford, James. *The Old Plantation, and What I Gathered There in an Autumn Month.* New York, 1859.

Hunter, Alexander. *The Huntsman in the South.* New York, 1908.

Ingraham, Joseph Holt. *The South-West. By a Yankee.* Vol. 1. New York, 1835.

———, ed. *The Sunny South; or, The Southerner at Home, Embracing Five Years' Experience of a Northern Governess in the Land of the Sugar and the Cotton.* Philadelphia, 1860.

Irving, John B. *A Day on the Cooper River.* 3d ed. Ed. Louisa Cheves Stoney. Columbia, S.C., 1969.

———. *Local Events and Incidents at Home.* Charleston, S.C., 1850.

James, George P. R. "Virginia Country Life." *Knickerbocker Magazine* 52 (Sept. 1858): 269–82.

Jefferson, Thomas. *Notes on the State of Virginia.* Ed. William Peden. Rept. New York, 1982.

Johnson, John Archibald. "Beaufort and the Sea Islands: Their History and Traditions." *Beaufort, S.C., Republican* 17:7 Jan. 16–July 3, 1873.

Jones, Charles Colcock. *Negro Myths from the Georgia Coast, Told in the Vernacular.* Boston, 1888.

Keefe, James F., and Lynn Morrow, eds. *The White River Chronicles of S. C. Turnbo: Man and Wildlife on the Ozarks Frontier.* Fayetteville, Ark., 1994.

Kemble, Frances Anne. *Journal of a Residence on a Georgian Plantation in 1838–1839.* 1852; ed. John A. Scott, Athens, Ga., 1984.

Kennedy, John Pendleton. *The Blackwater Chronicle, a Narrative of an Expedition into the Land of Canaan, in Randolph County, Virginia, a County Flowing with Wild Animals, Such As Panthers, Bears, Wolves, Elk, Deer, Otter, Badger, &c., &c., with Innumerable Trout—By Five Adventurous Gentlemen, without Aid of Any Government, and Solely by Their Own Resources, in the Summer of 1851 by the "Clerke of Oxenforde."* New York, 1853.

———. *Horse-Shoe Robinson.* Rept. New York, 1937.

———. *Swallow Barn; or, A Sojourn in the Old Dominion.* 1832; rept. Baton Rouge, La., 1986.

Kester, Jesse Y. *The American Shooters Manual.* Philadelphia, 1827.

Lanman, Charles. *Adventures in the Wilds of North America.* Ed. Charles Richard Weld. London, 1854.

Latrobe, Benjamin Henry Boneval. *Impressions respecting New Orleans.* Rept. New York, 1951.

Laussat, Pierre Clément de. *Memoirs of My Life, to My Son during the Years 1803 and After, Which I Spent in Public Service in Louisiana as Commissioner of the French Government for the Retrocession to France of That Colony and for Its Transfer to the United States.* Trans. Agnes-Josephine Pastwa. Baton Rouge, La., 1978.

Lawson, John. *Lawson's History of North Carolina: Containing the Exact Description and Natural History of That Country, Together with the Present State Thereof and a Journal of a Thousand Miles Traveled through Several Nations of Indians, Giving a Particular Account of Their Customs, Manners, etc., etc.* Richmond, 1937.

Lewis, Elisha J[arrett]. *The American Sportsman: Containing Hints to Sportsmen, Notes on Shooting, and the Habits of Game Birds, and Wild Fowl of America.* Philadelphia, 1855.

Lockridge, Kenneth A. *The Diary, and Life, of William Byrd II of Virginia, 1674–1744.* Chapel Hill, N.C., 1987.

Longstreet, Augustus Baldwin. *Georgia Scenes, Characters, Incidents, etc., in the First Half Century of the Republic.* 2d ed., New York, 1840.

Ludwell, Philip. "Boundary Line Proceedings, 1710." *Virginia Magazine of History and Biography* 5 (July 1897): 1–21.

Lyell, Charles. *A Second Visit to the United States of North America.* 2 vols. New York, 1849.

McCall, George Archibald. *Letters from the Frontiers: Written during a Period of Thirty Years' Service in the Army of the United States.* Philadelphia, 1868.

Mackay, Alexander. *The Western World; or Travels in the United States in 1846–47: Exhibiting Them in Their Latest Development, Social, Political, and Industrial.* 3 vols. London, 1849.

Mackay, Charles. *Life and Liberty in America; or, Sketches of a Tour in the United States and Canada, in 1857–8.* Vol. 1. London, 1859.

Mather, Fred. *In the Louisiana Lowlands: A Sketch of Plantation Life, Fishing, and Camping Just after the Civil War, and Other Tales.* New York, 1900.

Michaux, F. A. *Travels to the Westward of the Allegheny Mountains, in the States of Ohio, Kentucky, and Tennessee, in the Year 1802.* London, 1805.

Norman, B. M. "Rambles in the Swamps of Louisiana." *Arthur's Magazine* 1 (Jan. 1844): 9–12.

Northup, Solomon. *Twelve Years a Slave.* Rept. in *Puttin' On Ole Massa,* ed. Gilbert Osofsky. New York, 1969.

Olmsted, Frederick Law. *The Cotton Kingdom.* Ed. Arthur M. Schlesinger Sr. Rept. New York, 1984.

———. *A Journey in the Seaboard Slave States with Remarks on Their Economy.* New York, 1968.

Pearson, Elizabeth Ware. *Letters from Port Royal.* Cambridge, Mass., n.d.

Perdue, Thomas E., Jr., Thomas E. Barden, and Robert K. Phillips, eds. *Weevils in the Wheat: Interviews with Virginia Ex-Slaves.* Charlottesville, Va., 1976.

Pickney, Elise, ed. "The Journal of John Pierpont, Tutor on a Waccamaw River Plantation." *South Carolina Historical Magazine* 87:3 (July 1986): 148–61.

Porte Crayon [David Hunter Strother]. *The Old South Illustrated.* Ed. Cecil D. Eby Jr. Chapel Hill, N.C., 1959.

———. *Virginia Illustrated: Containing a Visit to the Virginian Canaan, and the Adventures of Porte Crayon and His Cousins.* New York, 1871.

Porter, William Trotter. *The Big Bear of Arkansas, and Other Sketches.* Philadelphia, 1845.

———. *Instructions to Young Sportsmen, in All That Relates to Guns and Shooting, by Lieut. Col. Hawker. To Which Is Added the Hunting and Shooting of North America.* Philadelphia, 1846.

Porter, William Trotter, and Felix Octavious Carr Darley. *Big Bear's Adventures and Travels.* Philadelphia, 1858.

Racine, Philip N., ed. *Piedmont Farmer: The Journals of David Golightly Harris, 1855–1870.* Knoxville, Tenn., 1990.

Rafferty, Milton D., ed. *Rude Pursuits and Rugged Peaks: Schoolcraft's Ozark Journal, 1818–1819.* Fayetteville, Ark., 1996.

Ramsay, David. *Ramsay's History of South Carolina from Its First Settlement in 1670 to the Year 1808.* Newberry, S.C., 1858.

Ransom-Hogan, William, and Edwin Adams Davis. *William Johnson's Natchez: The Ante-Bellum Diary of a Free Negro.* Baton Rouge, La., 1951.

[Rembert, W. R.] *The Georgia Bequest—Manolia; or The Vale of Tallulah.* Augusta, Ga., 1854.

Riley, Franklin L., ed. "Diary of a Mississippi Planter." *Publications of the Mississippi Historical Society* 10 (1909): 305–481.

Robin, C. C. *Voyage to Louisiana.* Trans. Stuart O. Landry Jr. New Orleans, 1966.

Rules and History of the Hot and Hot Fish Club of All Saints Parish, South Carolina. Charleston, S.C., 1860.

Russell, Theodore Pease. *A Connecticut Yankee in the Frontier Ozarks: The Writings of Theodore Pease Russell.* Ed. James F. Keefe and Lynn Morrow. Columbia, Mo., 1988.

Simms, William Gilmore. *Border Beagles: A Tale of Mississippi.* Ed. John Caldwell Guilds. Fayetteville, Ark., 1996.

———. *Woodcraft or, Hawks about the Dovecote.* Rept. New York, 1961.

Skinner, John Stuart. *The Dog and the Sportsman.* Philadelphia, 1845.

Smith, D. E. Huger. "A Plantation Boyhood." In Alice R. Huger Smith. *A Carolina Rice Plantation of the Fifties,* pp. 57–97. New York, 1936.

Some Early American Hunters: Being Stories from the Cabinet of Natural History and American Rural Sports First Published in 1830 at Philadelphia. New York, 1928.

The Sportsman's Portfolio of American Field Sports. 1855. Rept., New York, n.d.

Stephens, Henry. *The Book of the Farm.* Ed. John S. Skinner. New York, 1857.

Stoney, Samuel Gaillard, ed. "The Memoirs of Frederick Augustus Porcher." *South Carolina Historical and Genealogical Magazine* 44 (1944): 30–40.

Stowe, Steven M., ed. *The Diary and Autobiography of Charles A. Hentz, M.D.* Charlottesville, Va., 2000.

Thompson, William Tappan. *Chronicles of Pineville: Embracing Sketches of Georgia, Scenes, Incidents, and Characters.* Philadelphia, 1845.

———. *Major Jones's Courtship: Detailed, with Other Scenes, Incidents, and Adventures, in a Series of Letters by Himself.* Rev. ed., Atlanta, 1973.

Thorpe, Thomas Bangs. "The American Deer: Its Habits and Associations." *Harper's New Monthly Magazine* 17 (1858): 606–21.

———. *The Big Bear of Arkansas.* Ed. William T. Porter. Philadelphia, 1843.

———. *Colonel Thorpe's Scenes in Arkansaw.* Philadelphia, 1858.

———. "Deer and Deer Hunting in Louisiana." *De Bow's Review* 5 (1848): 220–29.

———. *The Hive of "The Bee-Hunter."* New York, 1854.

———. *The Mysteries of the Backwoods.* Philadelphia, 1846.

Tucker, George. *Valley of Shenandoah; or, Memoirs of the Graysons.* 1824; rept. Chapel Hill, N.C., 1970.

Tucker, Nathaniel Beverley. *George Balcombe.* 2 vols. New York, 1836.

Webber, Charles Wilkins. *The Hunter-Naturalist: Romance of Sporting; or, Wild Scenes and Wild Hunters.* Philadelphia, 1851.

———. "The Viviparous Quadrupeds of North America." *Southern Quarterly Review* 12 (1847): 273–306.

Whitehead, Charles Edward. *Wild Sports in the South; or, The Camp-Fires of the Everglades.* 1860; rept. Gainesville, Fla., 1991.

Woodmason, Charles. *The Carolina Backcountry on the Eve of the Revolution: The Journal and Other Writings of Charles Woodmason, Anglican Itinerant.* Ed. Richard J. Hooker. Chapel Hill, N.C., 1953.

Secondary Sources

Books

Arthur, John Preston. *Western North Carolina.* Raleigh, N.C., 1914.

Ayers, Edward L. *Vengeance and Justice: Crime and Punishment in the Nineteenth-Century American South.* New York, 1984.

Bean, Michael J., and Melanie J. Rowland. *The Evolution of National Wildlife Law.* 3d ed., Westport, Conn., 1997.

Beaty, John O. *John Esten Cooke, Virginian.* New York, 1922.

Bellesîles, Michael A. *Arming America: The Origins of a National Gun Culture.* New York, 2000.

Bergman, Charles. *Orion's Legacy: A Cultural History of Man as Hunter.* New York, 1996.

Berkhofer, Robert F., Jr. *The White Man's Indian: Images of the American Indian from Columbus to the Present.* New York, 1978.

Berlin, Ira, and Philip Morgan, eds. *Cultivation and Culture: Labor and the Shaping of Slave Life in the Americas.* Charlottesville, Va., 1993.

———. *The Slaves' Economy: Independent Production by Slaves in the Americas.* London, 1991.

Blassingame, John W. *The Slave Community: Plantation Life in the Ante-Bellum South.* New York, 1972.

———, ed. *Slave Testimony: Two Centuries of Letters, Speeches, Interviews, and Autobiographies.* Baton Rouge, La., 1977.

Bovill, E. W. *The England of Nimrod and Surtees, 1815–1854.* New York, 1959.

Brinley, Francis. *Life of William T. Porter.* New York, 1860.

Bruce, Dickson D., Jr. *Violence and Culture in the Antebellum South.* Austin, Tex., 1979.

Carnes, Mark C. *Secret Ritual and Manhood in Victorian America.* New Haven, 1989.

Carson, Jane. *Colonial Virginians at Play.* Charlottesville, Va., 1965.

Cartmill, Matt. *A View to a Death in the Morning: The Nature of Hunting through History.* Cambridge, Mass., 1993.

Cashin, Joan E. *A Family Venture: Men and Women on the Southern Frontier.* New York, 1991.

Clark, Thomas D., ed. *Travels in the Old South: A Bibliography.* Vol. 3. *The Ante Bellum South, 1825–1860: Cotton, Slavery, and Conflict.* Norman, Okla., 1959.

Click, Patricia, *Spirit of the Times: Amusements in Nineteenth-Century Baltimore, Norfolk, and Richmond.* Charlottesville, Va., 1989.

Cohen, Hennig, and William B. Dillingham, eds. *Humor of the Old Southwest.* 3d ed., Athens, Ga., 1994.

Cott, Nancy F. *The Bonds of Womanhood: "Woman's Sphere" in New England, 1780–1835.* New Haven, 1977.

Cowdrey, Albert E. *This Land, This South: An Environmental History.* Lexington, Ky., 1983.

Crane, Werner. *The Southern Frontier, 1670–1732.* Durham, N.C., 1928.

Creel, Margaret Washington. *A Peculiar People: Slave Religion and Community-Culture among the Gullahs.* New York, 1988.

Crum, Mason. *Gullah: Negro Life in the Carolina Sea Islands.* Durham, N.C., 1940.

Cunliffe, Marcus. *Soldiers and Civilians: The Martial Spirit in America, 1775–1865.* Boston, 1968.

Deas, Anne Simons. *Recollections of the Ball Family of South Carolina and the Comingtee Plantation.* Charleston, S.C., 1978.

Dixon, Melvin. *Ride Out the Wilderness: Geography and Identity in Afro-American Literature.* Urbana, Ill., 1987.

Dunlap, Thomas R. *Saving America's Wildlife.* Princeton, N.J., 1991.

Dusinberre, William. *Them Dark Days: Slavery in the American Rice Swamps.* New York, 1996.

Faragher, John Mack. *Daniel Boone: The Life and Legend of an American Pioneer.* New York, 1992.

Faust, Drew Gilpin, ed. *The Ideology of Slavery: Proslavery Thought in the Antebellum South, 1830–1860.* Baton Rouge, La., 1981.

Fox-Genovese, Elizabeth. *Within the Plantation Household: Black and White Women of the Old South.* Chapel Hill, N.C., 1988.

Friedman, Lawrence Meir. *A History of American Law.* New York, 1973.

Garvaglia, Louis A., and Charles G. Worman. *Firearms of the American West, 1803–1865.* Albuquerque, N.M., 1984.

Gee, Ernest. *Early American Sporting Books, 1734 to 1844.* New York, 1928.

Genovese, Eugene D. *Roll, Jordan, Roll: The World the Slaves Made.* New York, 1976.

Ghodes, Clarence Louis Frank. *Hunting in the Old South: Original Narratives of the Hunters.* Baton Rouge, La., 1967.

Gorn, Elliott. *The Manly Art: Bare-Knuckle Prize Fighting in America.* Ithaca, N.Y., 1986.

Greenberg, Kenneth S. *Honor and Slavery: Lies, Duels, Noses, Masks, Dressing as a Woman, Gifts, Strangers, Humanitarianism, Death, Slave Rebellions, the Pro-Slavery Argument, Baseball, Hunting, and Gambling in the Old South.* Princeton, N.J., 1996.

Hall, Gwendolyn Midlo. *Africans in Colonial Louisiana: The Development of Afro-Creole Culture in the Eighteenth Century.* Baton Rouge, La., 1992.

Hallock, Charles. *Hallock's American Club List and Sportsman's Glossary.* New York, 1878.

Halls, Lowell K., and John J Stransky. *Atlas of Southern Forest Game.* Washington, D.C., 1971.

Harms, Robert. *Games against Nature: An Eco-Cultural History of the Nunu of Equatorial Africa.* Cambridge, 1987.

Hatley, Tom. *The Dividing Paths: Cherokees and South Carolinians through the Era of Revolution.* New York, 1995.

Henry, H. M. *The Police Control of the Slave in South Carolina.* Emory, Va., 1914.

Heyrman, Christine Leigh. *Southern Cross: The Beginnings of the Bible Belt.* New York, 1997.

Heyward, Duncan Clinch. *Seed from Madagascar.* Chapel Hill, N.C., 1937.

Hilliard, Sam Bowers. *Hog Meat and Hoecake: Food Supply in the Old South, 1840–1860.* Carbondale, Ill., 1972.

Hoole, W. S. *Alias Simon Suggs: The Life and Times of Johnson Jones Hooper.* University, Ala., 1952.

Hopkins, Harry. *The Long Affray: The Poaching Wars, 1760–1914.* London, 1985.

Hudson, Charles. *The Southeastern Indians.* Knoxville, Tenn., 1976.

Hudson, Larry E., Jr. *To Have and to Hold: Slave Work and Family Life in Antebellum South Carolina.* Athens, Ga., 1997.

Hunt, William Southworth. *Frank Forester (Henry William Herbert): A Tragedy in Exile.* Newark, N.J., 1933.

Isaac, Rhys. *The Transformation of Virginia, 1740–1790.* New York, 1982.

Itzkowitz, David C. *Peculiar Priviledge: A Social History of English Foxhunting, 1753–1885.* Hassocks, Eng., 1977.

Jenkins, William Sumner. *Pro-Slavery Thought in the Old South.* Gloucester, Mass., 1960.

Johnson, George Lloyd, Jr. *The Frontier in the Colonial South: South Carolina Backcountry, 1736–1800.* Westport, Conn., 1997.

Johnson, Guy B. *Folk Culture on St. Helena Island, South Carolina.* Chapel Hill, N.C., 1930.

Jones, Norrence T., Jr., *Born a Child of Freedom Yet a Slave: Mechanisms of Control and Strategies of Resistance in Antebellum South Carolina.* Middletown, Conn., 1990.

Jones-Jackson, Patricia. *When Roots Die: Endangered Traditions of the Sea Islands.* Athens, Ga., 1987.

Jordan, Winthrop D. *White over Black: American Attitudes toward the Negro, 1550–1812.* 1968; rept. New York, 1977.

Joyner, Charles. *Down by the Riverside: A South Carolina Slave Community.* Urbana, Ill., 1984.

Kelly, Robert L. *The Foraging Spectrum: Diversity in Hunter-Gatherer Lifeways.* Washington, D.C., 1995.

Kenzer, Robert C. *Kinship and Neighborhood in a Southern Community: Orange County, North Carolina, 1849–1881.* Knoxville, Tenn., 1987.

Kerasote, Ted. *Bloodties: Nature, Culture, and the Hunt.* New York, 1993.

King, Wilma. *Stolen Childhood: Slave Youth in Nineteenth-Century America.* Bloomington, Ind., 1995.

Kirk, Francis Marion. *A History of the St. John's Hunting Club.* N.p., 1950.

Klein, Rachel N. *Unification of a Slave State: The Rise of the Planter Class in the South Carolina Backcountry, 1760–1808.* Chapel Hill, N.C., 1990.

Kreyling, Michael. *Figures of the Hero in Southern Narrative.* Baton Rouge, La., 1987.

Levine, Lawrence W. *Black Culture and Black Consciousness: Afro-American Folk Thought from Slavery to Freedom.* New York, 1977.

Lofaro, Michael A., ed. *The Tall Tales of Davy Crockett: The Second Nashville Series of Crockett Almanacs, 1839–1841.* Knoxville, Tenn., 1987.

Lowery, I. E. *Life on the Old Plantation in Ante-Bellum Days, or A Story Based on Facts,* Columbia, S.C., 1911.

Lund, Thomas A. *American Wildlife Law.* Berkeley, Calif., 1980.

McCurry, Stephanie. *Masters of Small Worlds: Yeoman Households, Gender Relations, and the Political Culture of the Antebellum South Carolina Low Country.* New York, 1995.

McCusker, John J., and Russell R. Menard. *The Economy of British North America, 1607–1789.* Chapel Hill, N.C., 1985.

Mackay-Smith, Alexander. *American Foxhunting; An Anthology.* Millwood, Va., 1970.

——. *Blue Ridge Hunt: The First Hundred Years.* Berryville, Va., 1988.

Malone, Dumas. *Thomas Jefferson, the Virginian.* Boston, 1948.

Manning, Roger B. *Hunters and Poachers: A Social and Cultural History of Unlawful Hunting in England, 1485–1640.* Oxford, 1993.

Marks, Stuart A. *Southern Hunting in Black and White: Nature, History, and Ritual in a Carolina Community.* Princeton, N.J., 1991.

Martin, Scott C. *Killing Time: Leisure and Culture in Southwestern Pennsylvania, 1800–1850.* Pittsburgh, 1995.

Mathew, William M., ed. *Agriculture, Geology, and Society in Antebellum South Carolina: The Private Diary of Edmund Ruffin, 1843.* Athens, Ga., 1992.

Merrell, James H. *The Indians' New World: Catawbas and Their Neighbors from European Contact through the Era of Removal.* Chapel Hill, N.C., 1989.

Miller, William Ian. *Humiliation: And Other Essays on Honor, Social Discomfort, and Violence.* Ithaca, N.Y., 1993.

Moore, Arthur K. *The Frontier Mind: A Cultural Analysis of the Kentucky Frontiersman.* Lexington, Ky., 1957.

Moore, John Hebron. *The Emergence of the Cotton Kingdom in the Old Southwest: Mississippi, 1770–1860.* Baton Rouge, La., 1988.

Morgan, Philip D. *Slave Counterpoint: Black Culture in the Eighteenth-Century Chesapeake and Lowcountry.* Chapel Hill, N.C., 1998.

Morris, Christopher. *Becoming Southern: The Evolution of a Way of Life, Warren County and Vicksburg, Mississippi, 1770–1860.* New York, 1995.

Morris, Thomas D. *Southern Slavery and the Law, 1619–1860.* Chapel Hill, N.C., 1996.

Munsche, P. B. *Gentlemen and Poachers: The English Game Laws, 1671–1831.* Cambridge, 1981.

Nash, Roderick. *Wilderness and the American Mind.* New Haven, 1967.

Nobles, Gregory H. *American Frontiers: Cultural Encounters and Continental Conquest.* New York, 1997.

Oakes, James. *The Ruling Race: A History of American Slaveholders.* New York, 1982.

Oriard, Michael. *Sporting with the Gods: The Rhetoric of Play and Game in American Culture.* Cambridge, 1991.

Ownby, Ted. *Subduing Satan: Religion, Recreation, and Manhood in the Rural South, 1865–1920.* Chapel Hill, N.C., 1990.

Owsley, Frank L. *Plain Folk of the Old South.* Baton Rouge, La., 1949.

Peristiany, J. G., and Julian Pitt-Rivers, eds. *Honor and Grace in Anthropology.* Cambridge, 1992.

Phillips, John C. *A Bibliography of American Sporting Books.* Boston, 1930.

Reidy, Joseph P. *From Slavery to Agrarian Capitalism in the Cotton Plantation South: Central Georgia, 1800–1880.* Chapel Hill, N.C., 1992.

Reiger, John F. *American Sportsmen and the Origins of Conservation.* Norman, Okla., 1986.

Remini, Robert V. *The Legacy of Andrew Jackson: Essays on Democracy, Indian Removal, and Slavery.* Baton Rouge, La., 1988.

Roberts, Ned H. *The Muzzle-Loading Cap Lock Rifle.* Harrisburg, Pa., 1952.

Rosengarten, Theodore. *Tombee: Portrait of a Cotton Planter.* New York, 1986.

Rountree, Helen C. *The Powhatan Indians of Virginia: Their Traditional Culture.* Norman, Okla., 1989.

———. *Pocahontas's People: The Powhatan Indians of Virginia through Four Centuries.* Norman, Okla., 1990.

Rubin, Louis D., Jr. *The Edge of the Swamp: A Study in the Literature and Society of the Old South.* Baton Rouge, La., 1989.

———. *William Elliott Shoots a Bear: Essays on the Southern Literary Imagination.* Baton Rouge, La., 1975.

Scarborough, William Kauffman. *The Overseer: Plantation Management in the Old South.* Baton Rouge, La., 1966.

Schafer, Judith Kelleher. *Slavery, the Civil Law, and the Supreme Court of Louisiana.* Baton Rouge, La., 1994.

Schwab, Eugene L., ed. *Travels in the Old South, Selected from Periodicals of the Times.* 2 vols. Lexington, Ky., 1973.

Silver, Timothy. *A New Face on the Countryside: Indians, Colonists, and Slaves in South Atlantic Forests, 1500–1800.* Cambridge, 1990.

Singleton, Theresa Ann, ed. *The Archaeology of Slavery and Plantation Life,* New York, 1985.

Slotkin, Richard. *Regeneration through Violence: The Mythology of the American Frontier, 1600–1860.* New York, 1996.

Smith, Harry Worcester. *A Sporting Family of the Old South.* Albany, 1936.

Smith, Henry Nash. *Virgin Land: The American West as Symbol and Myth.* Cambridge, Mass., 1950.

Smith, Julia Floyd. *Slavery and Rice Culture in Lowcountry Georgia, 1750–1860.* Knoxville, Tenn., 1985.

Sobel, Mechal. *The World They Made Together: Black and White Values in Eighteenth-Century Virginia.* Princeton, N.J., 1987.

Somers, Dale A. *The Rise of Sports in New Orleans, 1850–1900.* Baton Rouge, La., 1972.

Somers, Paul, Jr. *Johnson J. Hooper.* Boston, 1984.

Stewart, Mart Allen. *"What Nature Suffers to Groe": Life, Labor, and Landscape on the Georgia Coast, 1680–1920.* Athens, Ga., 1996.

Stowe, Steven M. *Intimacy and Power in the Old South: Ritual in the Lives of the Planters.* Baltimore, 1987.

Struna, Nancy L. *People of Prowess: Sport, Leisure, and Labor in Early Anglo-America.* Urbana, Ill., 1996.

Stuckey, Sterling. *Slave Culture: Nationalist Theory and the Foundations of Black America.* New York, 1987.

Taylor, J. G. *Negro Slavery in Louisiana.* Baton Rouge, La., 1963.

Thompson, Edward P. *Whigs and Hunters: The Origin of the Black Act.* London, 1975.

Tober, James A. *Who Owns Wildlife? The Political Economy of Conservation in Nineteenth-Century America.* Westport, Conn., 1981.

Tracy, Susan J. *In the Master's Eye: Representations of Women, Blacks, and Poor Whites in Antebellum Southern Literature.* Amherst, Mass., 1995.

Trefethen, James B. *An American Crusade for Wildlife.* New York, 1975.

Trinkey, Michael, ed. *Archaeological Investigations at Haig Point, Webb, and Oak Ridge, Daufuskie Island, Beaufort County, South Carolina.* Columbia, S.C., 1989.

———. *The History and Archaeology of Kiawah Island, Charleston County, South Carolina.* Research Series 30. Columbia, S.C., 1993.

Trudeau, Noah Andre. *Out of the Storm: The End of the Civil War, April–June, 1865.* Boston, 1994.

Tushnet, Mark. *The American Law of Slavery, 1810–1860: Considerations of Humanity and Interest.* Princeton, N.J., 1981.

Usner, Daniel M. *Indians, Settlers, and Slaves in a Frontier Exchange Economy: The Lower Mississippi Valley before 1783.* Chapel Hill, N.C., 1992.

Van Deburg, William L. *The Slave Drivers: Black Agricultural Labor Supervisors in the Antebellum South.* Westport, Conn., 1979.

Veblen, Thorstein. *The Theory of the Leisure Class: An Economic Study of Institutions.* New York, 1899.

Waddell, Gene. *Indians of the South Carolina Lowcountry, 1562–1751.* Spartanburg, S.C., 1980.

Waselkov, Gregory A., and Kathryn E. Holland Braund, eds. *William Bartram on the Southeastern Indians.* Lincoln, Nebr., 1995.

Welcome, John. *The Sporting World of R. S. Surtees.* Oxford, 1982.

Wellman, Manly Wade. *Giant in Gray: A Biography of Wade Hampton of South Carolina.* New York, 1949.

West, James L. W., III, ed. *Gyascutus: Studies in Antebellum Southern Humorous and Sporting Writing.* Atlantic Highlands, N.J., 1978.

White, Deborah G. *Ar'n't I a Woman?: Female Slaves in the Plantation South.* New York, 1985.

Whitney, Gordon G. *From Coastal Wilderness to Fruited Plain: A History of Environmental Change in Temperate North America 1500 to the Present.* Cambridge, 1994.

Wilson, Robert. *An Address Delivered before the St. John's Hunting Club at Indian Field Plantation, St. John's, Berkeley, July 4, 1907.* Charleston, S.C., 1907.

———. *Half Forgotten By-Ways of of the Old South.* Columbia, S.C., 1928.

Wood, Betty. *Slavery in Colonial Georgia, 1730–1775.* Athens, Ga., 1984.

Wood, Forrest, Jr. *The Delights and Dilemmas of Hunting: The Hunting versus Anti-Hunting Debate.* Lanham, Md., 1997.

Wood, Peter H. *Black Majority: Negroes in Colonial South Carolina from 1670 through the Stono Rebellion.* New York, 1975.

Wyatt-Brown, Bertram. *Southern Honor: Ethics and Behavior in the Old South.* New York, 1982.

Yates, Norris. *William T. Porter and the* Spirit of the Times: *A Study of the Big Bear School of Humor.* Baton Rouge, La., 1957.

Articles

Altherr, Thomas L. "The American Hunter-Naturalist and the Development of the Code of Sportsmanship." *Journal of Sport History* 5:1 (Spring 1978): 7–22.

Ascher, Robert, and Charles H. Fairbanks. "Excavation of a Slave Cabin: Georgia, U.S.A." *Historical Archeology* 5 (1971):3–17.

Aversa, Alfred, Jr. "Foxhunting: A Patrician Sport." *Review of Sport and Leisure* 6:2 (1981): 83–100.

Bellesîles, Michael A. "The Origins of Gun Culture in the United States, 1760–1865." *Journal of American History* 83:2 (Sept. 1996): 425–55.

Berryman, Jack W. "Sport, Health, and the Rural-Urban Conflict: Baltimore and John Stuart Skinner's *American Farmer,* 1819–1829." *Conspectus of History* 1:8 (1982): 43–61.

——. "The Tenuous Attempts of Americans to 'Catch-Up with John Bull': Specialty Magazines and Sporting Journalism, 1800–1835." *Canadian Journal of Sport and Physical Education* 10 (May 1974): 33–61.

Blassingame, John W. "Status and Social Structure in the Slave Community: Evidence from New Sources." In *Perspectives and Irony in American Slavery,* ed. Harry P. Owens, pp. 137–51. Jackson, Miss., 1976.

Breen, T. H. "Horses and Gentlemen: The Cultural Significance of Gambling among the Gentry of Virginia." *William and Mary Quarterly,* 3d ser., 34:2 (April 1977): 239–57.

Bruce, Dickson D., Jr. "Hunting: Dimensions of Antebellum Southern Culture." *Mississippi Quarterly* 30:2 (Spring 1977): 259–81.

——. "Play, Work, and Ethics in the Old South." *Southern Folklore Quarterly* 41 (1977): 33–51.

Bukey, Even Burr. "Frederick Gerstaecker in Arkansas." *Arkansas Historical Quarterly* 31 (Spring 1972): 3–14.

Campbell, John. "'My Constant Companion': Slaves and Their Dogs in the Antebellum South." In *Working toward Freedom: Slave Society and Domestic Economy in the American South,* ed. Larry E. Hudson Jr., pp. 53–76. Rochester, N.Y., 1994.

Current-Garcia, Eugene. "'York's Tall Son' and His Southern Correspondents." *American Quarterly* 7 (Winter 1955): 371–84.

Davis, Richard Beale. "The Ball Papers: A Pattern of Life in the Low Country, 1800–1825." *South Carolina Historical Magazine* 65 (Jan. 1964): 1–15.

Dean, David M. "Meshach Browning: Bear Hunter of Allegany County, 1781–1859." *Maryland Historical Magazine* 91:1 (Spring 1996): 73–83.

Dunlap, Thomas R. "Sport Hunting and Conservation, 1880–1920." *Environmental Review* 12:1 (Spring 1988): 51–60.

Easterby, J. H., ed. "The St. Thomas Hunting Club, 1785–1801." *South Carolina Historical and Genealogical Magazine* 46 (1945): 123–31, 209–13.

Evans, Clarence. "Gerstaecker and the Konwells of White River Valley." *Arkansas Historical Quarterly* 10:1 (Spring 1951): 1–36.

Fogleman, Valerie M. "American Attitudes towards Wolves: A History of Misconception." *Environmental Review* 10:4 (Winter 1988): 63–94.

Geertz, Clifford. "Deep Play: Notes on the Balinese Cockfight." *Daedalus* 101:1 (1972): 1–37.

Gibbs, Tyson, et al. "Nutrition in a Slave Population: An Anthropological Examination." *Medical Anthropology: Cross-Cultural Studies in Health and Illness* 4:2 (Spring 1980): 175–262.

Giddens, Anthony. "Notes on the Concepts of Play and Leisure." *Sociological Review* 12:1 (March 1964): 73–89.

Gorn, Elliott. "'Gouge and Bite, Pull Hair and Scratch': The Social Significance of Fighting in the Southern Backcountry." *American Historical Review* 90:1 (1985): 18–43.

Greenberg, Kenneth S. "The Nose, the Lie, and the Duel in the Antebellum South." *American Historical Review* 95:1 (Feb. 1990): 57–74.

Johnson, Pegram, III. "The *American Turf Register and Sporting Magazine:* 'A Quaint and Curious Volume of Forgotten Lore,'" *Maryland Historical Magazine* 89:1 (Spring 1994): 4–21.

Jones, Lewis P. "William Elliott, South Carolina Nonconformist." *Journal of Southern History* 17 (1951): 361–81.

Hahn, Steven. "Hunting, Fishing, and Foraging: Common Rights and Class Relations in the Postbellum South." *Radical History Review* 26 (1982): 37–64.

Hamilton, Phillip. "Education in the St. George Tucker Household: Change and Continuity in Jeffersonian Virginia." *Virginia Magazine of History and Biography* 102:2 (April 1994): 167–92.

Hardin, David. "Laws of Nature: Wildlife Management Legislation in Colonial Virginia." In *The American Environment: Interpretations of Past Geographies,* ed. Larry Dilsaver and Craig Colten, pp. 137–62. Lanham, Md., 1992.

Harrison, Fairfax. "Genesis of Foxhunting in Virginia." *Virginia Magazine of History and Biography* 37:2 (April 1929): 155–57.

Harwell, Richard B., ed. "The Hot and Hot Fish Club of All Saints Parish." *South Carolina Historical and Genealogical Magazine* 48 (1947): 40–47.

Higgs, Robert J. "The Sublime and the Beautiful: The Meaning of Sport in Collected Sketches of Thomas B. Thorpe." *Southern Studies* 25:3 (1986): 235–56.

Hoffmann, Charles, and Tess Hoffmann."The Limits of Paternalism: Driver-Master Relations on a Bryan County Plantation." *Georgia Historical Quarterly* 67:3 (Fall 1983): 321–35.

Hudson, Charles H., Jr. "Why the Southeastern Indians Slaughtered Deer." In *Indians, Animals, and the Fur Trade,* ed. Shephard Krech III, pp. 155–76. Athens, Ga., 1981.

Keller, Mark A. "'Th' Guv'ner Wuz a Writer'—Alexander G. McNutt of Mississippi." *Southern Studies* 20 (1981): 394–411.

——. "Reputable Writers, Phony Names: Identifying Pseudonyms in the *Spirit of the Times." Papers of the Bibliographical Society of America* 75:2 (1981): 198–209.

Kierner, Cynthia A. "Hospitality, Sociability, and Gender in the Southern Colonies." *Journal of Southern History* 42:3 (Aug. 1996): 449–80.

Lewis, Carolyn Baker. "The World around Hampton: Post-Bellum Life on a South Carolina Plantation." *Agricultural History* 58:3 (1984): 456–76.

Lofaro, Michael A., ed. "Riproarious Shemales: Legendary Women in the Tall Tale World of Davy Crockett." In *Crockett at Two Hundred: New Perspectives on the Man and the Myth,* ed. Michael A. Lofaro and Joe Cummings, pp. 114–52. Knoxville, Tenn., 1989.

Mayfield, John. "'The Soul of a Man!': William Gilmore Simms and the Myths of Southern Manhood." *Journal of the Early Republic* 15 (Fall 1995): 477–500.

Palmer, T. S. "Chronology and Index of the More Important Events in American Game Protection, 1776–1911." *U.S. Biological Survey Bulletin* 41 (1912).

Prewitt, Wiley C. "Going Inside: Transformation of Fox Hunting in Mississippi." *Mississippi Folklife* 28:1 (1995): 26–33.

Reidy, Joseph P. "Obligation and Right: Patterns of Labor, Subsistence, and Exchange in the Cotton Belt of Georgia, 1790–1860." In *Cultivation and Culture: Labor and the Shaping of Slave Life in the Americas,* ed. Ira Berlin and Philip Morgan, pp. 138–54. Charlottesville, Va., 1993.

Reiger, John F. "Commentary on Thomas R. Dunlap's Article." *Environmental Review* 12:3 (Fall 1988): 94–6.

Schlotterbeck, John T. "The Internal Economy of Slavery in Rural Piedmont Virginia." In *The Slaves' Economy: Independent Production by Slaves in the Americas,* ed. Ira Berlin and Philip D. Morgan. London, 1991.

Shingleton, Royce Gordon. "The Utility of Leisure: Game as a Source of Food in the Old South." *Mississippi Quarterly* 25 (Fall 1972): 429–45.

Thompson, Edgar E. "The Porter-Hooper Correspondence." In *Gyascutus: Studies in Antebellum Southern Humorous and Sporting Writing,* ed. James L. W. West III, pp. 219–34. Atlantic Highlands, N.J., 1978.

Watson, Harry L. "'The Common Rights of Mankind': Subsistence, Shad, and Commerce in the Early Republican South." *Journal of American History* 83:1 (June 1996): 13–43.

Wood, Betty. "'White Society' and 'Informal' Slave Economies of Lowcountry Georgia, c. 1763–1830." *Slavery and Abolition* 11:3 (1990): 313–31.

Worley, Ted R. "An Early Arkansas Sportsman: C. F. M. Noland." *Arkansas Historical Quarterly* 11 (Spring 1952): 25–39.

Yates, Norris. "The *Spirit of the Times*: Its Early History and Some of Its Contributors." *Papers of the Bibliographical Society of America* 48 (1954): 117–48.

Dissertations

Braund, Kathryn E. Holland. "Mutual Convenience — Mutual Dependence: The Creeks, Augusta, and the Deerskin Trade, 1733–1783." Ph.D. diss., Florida State University, 1986.

Brown, R. Ben. "The Southern Range: A Study in Nineteenth-Century Law and Society." Ph.D. diss., University of Michigan, 1993.

Gay, Dorothy Ann. "The Tangled Skein of Romanticism and Violence in the Old South: The Southern Response to Abolitionism and Feminism, 1830–1861." Ph.D. diss., University of North Carolina at Chapel Hill, 1975.

Hardin, David. "'Alterations They Have Made at This Day': Environment, Agriculture, and Landscape Change in Essex County, Virginia, 1600–1782." Ph.D. diss., University of Maryland-College Park, 1995.

Herron, Virginia. "Thomas Bangs Thorpe and the *Spirit of the Times*." M.A. thesis, Alabama Polytechnic Institute, 1953.

Klinko, Donald W. "Antebellum American Sporting Magazines and the Development of a Sportsmen's Ethic." Ph.D. diss., Washington State University, 1986.

Lewis, Charlene Marie. "Ladies and Gentlemen on Display: Planter Society at the Virginia Springs, 1790–1860." Ph.D. diss., University of Virginia, 1997.

Moore, Sue Mullins. "The Antebellum Barrier Island Plantation: In Search of an Archeological Pattern." Ph.D. diss., University of Florida, 1981.

Otto, John Solomon. "Status Differences and the Archaeological Record: A Comparison of Planter, Overseer, and Slave Sites from Cannon's Point Plantation (1794–1861, St. Simons Island, Georgia)." Ph.D. diss., University of Florida, 1975.

Prewitt, Wiley C. "The Best of All Breathing: Hunting and Environmental Change in Mississippi, 1900–1980." M.A. thesis, University of Mississippi, 1991.

Reeves, John Henry, Jr. "The History and Development of Wild Life Conservation in Virginia: A Critical Review." Ph.D. diss., Virginia Polytechnic Institute, 1960.

Scafidel, Beverly. "The Letters of William Elliott." 2 vols. Ph.D. diss., University of South Carolina, 1978.

Singleton, Theresa Ann. "The Archaeology of Afro-American Slavery in Coastal Georgia: A Regional Perception of Slave Household and Community Patterns." Ph.D. diss., University of Florida, 1980.

Stewart, Mart Allen. "Land Use and Landscapes: Environment and Social Change in Coastal Georgia, 1680–1880." Ph.D. diss., Emory University, 1988.

Ward, George Baxter, III. "Bloodbrothers in the Wilderness: The Sport Hunter and the Buckskin Hunter in the Preservation of the American Wilderness Experience." Ph.D. diss., University of Texas at Austin, 1980.

Index